SEE THE STRANGE
the gospel according to revelation

SEE THE STRANGE
the gospel according to revelation

BRETT DAVIS

for Joy Marie,
my bride, my pride, my clarity

I see with you

(CONTENTS)

FOREWORD

I have read many books about the Book of Revelation and I have written two myself. The worst books about Revelation treat it as a coded history of the future, predictions that we can tick off as they get fulfilled—except that those ticks have so far always turned out to be mistaken. Some of the worst books about Revelation read it as a nightmare to be inflicted on the world by a God who gloats over human suffering. But some of the best books, written by scholars who do see what the book is really about, unfortunately make it seem so complex and difficult one would need several years of study to unravel it. Revelation is indeed a masterpiece of intricate composition, packed with meaning, that actually will repay lengthy study. But the ordinary reader need not be deterred by the complexity. With a good guide, it is possible to steer a course through Revelation that takes in both the imaginative force of its often strange imagery and the core of its hopeful and challenging message.

As one of those good guides, Brett Davis has written a book about Revelation that is quite unique. When I am asked by someone who is baffled by Revelation how to approach it, this is now one of a handful of books I would recommend. Davis is an excellent guide because he has not only studied the text, but has also been deeply inspired by it and is eager to help others see what it is really about. He realises that the strangeness of Revelation is its way of enabling us see better by looking from a different perspective. He knows that what we see better through our immersion in its visionary world is nothing less than God himself, as he has made himself known in Jesus, and the way God is at work in the world, even when that is far from obvious. He sees that the nightmarish parts of Revelation are there to be superseded by the beautiful dream of the whole creation made new by God's love.

What makes the book unique is that all this is communicated to readers in ways that are both accessible and creative. He writes with verve and with an easy command of appealing illustrations from our contemporary world. He guides readers through the movement of Revelation's dramatic story, helping us feel its dynamic and keeping the plot in view all the time.

As Davis says, the purpose of the book of Revelation is not information so much as transformation. It tells a story that it asks us to join, becoming faithful witnesses to the truth amid the delusions of power and prosperity, following Jesus the faithful witness. Revelation is also a book that is constantly turning its message into prayer and worship. Davis does the same, turning each chapter's themes into a concluding prayer. That says a lot about the kind of book this is.

// Richard Bauckham
Emeritus Professor of New Testament
St. Andrews University, Scotland

First Words

This book grew from soil worth mentioning. *It began to germinate at a young age, and the seed was fear.* Since my childhood I have ruminated over the Bible's last book—its dragons and beasts, plagues and fire, horses and wrath. The mystery of it terrified me as a child. But since mystery pervades most of childhood, I assumed grown-ups must understand it all.

But as I entered adulthood, I realized that only a small number of people think about Revelation, and they obsess over it. But most don't think about it at all.

Those who obsess over Revelation often seemed like conspiracy theorists, gazing at a cork board webbed with yarn and pushpins. They can trace clippings of verses to clippings of daily headlines. They crack codes and analyze numbers. Their insights were truly extraordinary... and always being revised. Those insights were never able to deliver what they promised, namely predictions of the future. The wild web of their efforts looked impressive, and usually claimed the end of the world to be imminent. But the end still hasn't come. And, frustratingly, none of their work ever helped me *read* or *understand* Revelation.

The other group, those who don't think about Revelation, also couldn't help me. I don't share their apathy. I mean, it's the end of the Bible... does it really not matter? Does scripture really end with incomprehensibility? By guiding us into a fog?

So fear planted the seed, but beauty has since watered it. As I have continued to follow Jesus, I'm increasingly captured by his grace and captivated by his beauty. And Jesus has convinced me that his Scripture ends in breathtaking fashion. *I have come to see Revelation as a beautiful book—an ingenious, inspired masterpiece of literature, calling us into beautiful lives worthy of the beautiful future prepared for this world by our beautiful God.[1]*

As an adult I have become a pastor, and I meet people who have experienced similar fear regarding Revelation and who long to see some kind of beauty in it. But, frustratingly, I could not find an accessible book to gently hold people's hands and lead them into this masterwork. There are lots of verse-by-verse commentaries out there, but where's the guiding hand? The overview? People need a framework for reading Revelation. A starting place.

So I have written a book. That's an enormous task at any time, but it's doubly overwhelming when the subject is a book of the Bible. And it has been mind-boggling to write a book about Revelation. But beauty frequently drives us to the mind-boggling.

My goal in the pages that follow is modest. *I want to give readers a starting place for Revelation that centers around Jesus.* My hope is that this "reading" will put John's vision back in the hands of intimidated Christians... and maybe local churches. For it is to the local church that Revelation is addressed.

Allow me to confess something: *my goal is not to offer "the correct way" to read Revelation.* Obviously, I *do* think this reading finds support from saints and scholars. (I wouldn't do the laborious work of crafting a book if I thought it offered "the wrong way" to read Revelation.) To paraphrase one biblical scholar: "I'm confident that 80% of this is right... I just don't know which 80%."[2] We have no margin notes scribbled by God on the surviving copies of papyrus to tell us what the book means. Beyond a *correct* reading, we're looking for a *faithful*

---

[1] In theological language we could say, "the Spirit-inspired Word of God conforming us through sanctification to the *imago dei* for the sake of the eschatological hope stored up in the heavenly realms by the Triune God." We *could* say it that way... but we're not going to talk like that in this book. Ever. I'm utterly unconvinced that language is helpful to anyone... whether beginners or seasoned saints.

[2] N.T. Wright frequently makes this confession, paraphrasing, I believe, another scholar.

reading. How do we read Revelation in a way *faithful to* the good news about God and the world as revealed in Jesus? Our best strategy is to find a "North Star" that will give us direction as we explore this unruly text. And, as we'll see, Revelation gives us that North Star, and I will try to keep that star in our sights.[3]

I aim to offer a guiding hand into the book of Revelation. Like a friend who takes you hiking on a mountain too intimidating, this volume aims to escort you into unfamiliar terrain. By the end of our journey, you'll have some basic footing for navigating Revelation's structure, movements, and imagery. You'll have firm footing for exploring. And one day—if you keep exploring—you may even cheerfully disagree with me about the best way to navigate the mountain!

As we're getting a shape for the forest of Revelation, I've provided plenty of footnotes that should help illuminate certain details.[4] These notes are pauses to consider the trees without getting lost in them. And for those still itching to explore, the world is awash with books and commentaries that explore every crevice, canyon, and detail of the trail.[5]

As will become clear, *I'm convinced that John's strange vision is aimed at transformation more than information.* To that end, I've included small prayers at the end of each chapter. If we're not praying our way through Revelation, we're certainly missing its point.

The goal of Revelation is that we would faithfully follow the Lamb through suffering into the sunrise of his new world. My prayer is that this book will gently guide you into the nail-scarred hands of the One who holds the past, the present, and (yes) the future... for he is the One revealed by Revelation.

---

[3] Skip to page 102 if you need that North Star now.

[4] **Notes like this. Look at you... reading a footnote. Well done.**

[5] Among the best resources are G.K. Beale's massive commentary (New International Greek Testament Commentary) which provides massive analysis of cultural/historic details, Richard Bauckham's *The Climax of Prophecy* for in-depth study of Revelation's structure/movements, Michael Gorman's *Reading Revelation Responsibly* for an introduction, as well as George Caird's amazing and accessible commentary for pastors or teachers (Black's New Testament Commentary).

(Revelation 1v1-8)

The revelation from Jesus Christ, which God gave him to show his servants what must soon take place. He made it known by sending his angel to his servant John, who testifies to everything he saw—that is, the word of God and the testimony of Jesus Christ. Blessed is the one who reads aloud the words of this prophecy, and blessed are those who hear it and take to heart what is written in it, because the time is near.

John,

To the seven churches in the province of Asia:

Grace and peace to you from him who is, and who was, and who is to come, and from the seven spirits before his throne, and from Jesus Christ, who is the faithful witness, the firstborn from the dead, and the ruler of the kings of the earth.

To him who loves us and has freed us from our sins by his blood, and has made us to be a kingdom and priests to serve his God and Father—to him be glory and power for ever and ever! Amen.

"Look, he is coming with the clouds,"
    and "every eye will see him,
even those who pierced him";
    and all peoples on earth "will mourn because of him."
So shall it be! Amen.

"I am the Alpha and the Omega," says the Lord God, "who is, and who was, and who is to come, the Almighty."

01. Divine Peekaboo

A poet once said, "Anything can make us look, only art makes us see."[1] Some might think that's just the silly sort of thing that artists say, but it's true. The best art aims to open the eyes of the blind. Indeed, the best art aims to open *our* eyes. For it is we—not someone else somewhere else—who are the blind.

Our lives drift toward blindness. Whether it is autumn leaves or Christmas lights, or spring flowers, or our favorite scenic view, or our beautiful significant other. Give us enough time and we'll drift into blindness. Tourists may still stop and stare at the view. Strangers may still double-take our partner. Children may still dance in delight at twinkling houses.
We yawn.

Familiarity breeds blindness.

We've seen it all before. We've become blind to our little worlds and blind to the details of our lives. Should our eyes refuse to open—if we insist on slumbering and sleepwalking—then we're in danger of becoming blind to the entire world... blind to all life.

The darkness spreads from lights and leaves and lilies to eventually hide love itself. The cold cloud of blindness—lifeless, loveless, sightless—threatens to

---

[1] Archibald MacLeish.

block the sun in all our lives. We easily lose sight of everything that is important. It's almost like an Enemy is at work in these blinding billows.

Enter our protagonist, "The Apocalypse," from stage right.

That's the name of the Bible's last book. It's the very first word of the book in its original language. And even though the word "Apocalypse" frequently conjures images of *Mad Max* or *The Walking Dead,* that's not really what the word means. The word "Apocalypse" simply means "a revealing."

It's the kind of thing that happens when we flip over a rock, or swish open a curtain, or turn on floodlights, or open blind eyes.

My young daughters enjoy variations of the game of "Peek-a-boo." I veil my face with something (my hands, a small towel, whatever is handy) and then I ask (in an oddly involuntarily high voice), "Where's Daphne?... Peekaboo! Where's Daisy?... Apocalypse!"

Peek-a-boo is a game of tiny apocalypses.

The word "Apocalypse" is frequently translated "Revelation." The book's aim is in the book's title: *Apocalypse.* Reveal. Flip the rock. Swish the curtain. Let loose the light. Unblind us.

Despite its intimidating reputation, if there's anything "The Revelation" aims to do, it aims to help us see. That's literally the first word of the book.

Well, if that's the case, how exactly does the book work? I mean, it's a STRANGE book. What exactly is this book trying to help us see with its army of exotic images? It's chock full of exaggerated, larger-than-life characters; surreal scenarios; wild pictures; nightmarish worldwide disasters; strange patterns; and more than a few colors and numbers. Much of the book feels like a trippy kind of cartoon. If Revelation is a Peekaboo, what exactly are we playing peekaboo with?

What exactly does Revelation want us to see?

Ask almost anyone on the street about Revelation, and you'll probably get a variety of similar answers: "The future. The last days. Closing time. The end of the world. The final judgment."

Popular consensus tells us that Revelation wants us to see the future.

We should address the elephant in the room. Anywhere Revelation is discussed *Left Behind* will come up. This series of novels—which you can find in the fiction section—has sold 65 million copies worldwide and reinforces the idea of Revelation as a cryptic spyglass for seeing the future.[2] The plot of this series focuses on the sudden vanishing of all Christians from the planet ("the rapture"[3]), a seven-year period full of terrifying catastrophes to rival any Hollywood disaster movie ("the Great Tribulation"), the rise of the Antichrist as the head of something akin to the United Nations, and then the appearance of a Jesus who makes people explode with his voice. And the authors of this grand fiction utilize Revelation for much of their plot structure.

Naming this elephant simply helps us recognize that there are loud, influential, best-selling voices who say that Revelation primarily wants us to see the future. Revelation functions, they say, as a super long-range forecast providing us all the thrills of *Mad Max* or *The Walking Dead* christened for evangelical sensibility and marketability.

Their reading of Revelation latches onto the end of verse 3 ("the time is near") or verse 19 ("what will take place later") and never lets go. They see this book as an Almanac meant to provide us with a weather forecast of the future. This

---

[2] This "Left Behind" interpretation is a part of relatively recent tradition within Protestant Christianity called **Dispensationalism**. This movement was spear-headed by a fellow named **John Darby** in the mid-19th century and popularized by the **Scofield Reference Bible** in the early 20th century. If you've never heard of any of those names or terms before, don't worry—you're in good company. Most Christians across the world throughout church history have never heard of them either.

[3] **The rapture of the church** is noticeably absent from Revelation. The primary scripture used to support "the rapture" is found in 1 Thessalonians 4.16-18, with this pivotal event getting read into Revelation somewhere between the end of chapter 3 and the beginning of chapter 4.

perspective essentially believes God gave the church a document to function like a monkish meteorologist:

"Looking ahead a few thousand years, the extended forecast calls for a 100% chance of hail and fire mixed with blood.[4] Plan your weekend accordingly, because there will be a vast locust army emerging from the Abyss shortly afterwards.[5] Now, don't panic too much or cancel your travel plans. Once again, this is a VERY EXTENDED forecast that likely has nothing to do with anyone ever hearing it. It's extremely unlikely that it's coming THIS weekend... but it will come eventually."

Given its history in the last few decades of North America, most assume Revelation is primarily interested in helping us see the future.

I remember sitting on the floor as a kid with an open Bible on my lap thinking exactly that. Passages about dragons and monsters caught my attention, and I thought: "Man, it's all here. Beneath the surface. Under of all this strangeness. If I could just crack the code—if only I could un-strange all of this strangeness—THEN I would finally be able to see."

We assume that Revelation's strangeness stops us from seeing.

I assumed that God gave us a book about the future but coded it like a puzzle worthy of Indiana Jones... only the truly "worthy" would see it. Growing up, the strangeness of Revelation was ultimately a puzzle to solve so that we could get to its really important stuff. Given this assumption—that Revelation exists to show the future to a few lucky code-breakers—we often get frustrated with the book. Perhaps even with God. After all, a strange and scary future lies just beneath the surface for those willing and worthy to crack the code. But there's only one small problem: it's a code no one can crack.

---

[4] Rev. 8.7.
[5] Rev. 9.1-11.

No one in church history has agreed on exactly how to read the letter of Revelation. That is absolutely obvious; there is no consensus. But our obsessive decoding of the future is really recent. Consider how young the United States is in light of world history. But the United States has bells and buildings older than the Left-Behind-view of Revelation. The White House was built before this way of reading of Revelation. The Declaration of Independence was written before anyone thought of "the Rapture." The vast majority of the church throughout the centuries simply has not seen (and could not possibly see) the future so critically important to Left Behind. If seeing the future was God's primary reason for inspiring John to put quill to parchment, then Revelation has been a big fat failure for the church historic.

Obsessively decoding the future is demonstrably not the best way to read Revelation. To be sure, Revelation does indeed have some important things to say about the future. But, at a more basic level, *Revelation wants us to see something far more important than the future.*

John's opening words tell us what this Revelation reveals: This is the revelation (1v1)—the revealing, apocalypse, peekaboo—of Jesus, the Christ. The Greek word "Christ" and its Hebrew equivalent "Messiah" simply mean "Anointed One" or "King." This is the revealing *of* Jesus the King.

The NIV does a disservice when it flattens the Greek into *"from* Jesus Christ." Many translations rightly choose to keep the Greek's ambiguity. It literally reads "The revelation *of* Jesus Christ." Our English word "of" preserves the Greek's ambiguous meaning. It can simultaneously mean a revealing *from* Jesus and a revealing *about* Jesus. That's the point:

Revelation is a revealing
ABOUT Jesus
FROM Jesus.

Revelation reveals Jesus.

What Revelation reveals is a *Who*. Revelation wants us to see Jesus. We are meant to see the man who has shed his own blood (1v5) to set us free from our darkness and to include us in something big and beautiful and forever (1v6). To make us royalty, a kingdom. To give us the healing hands of priests. That's the language used. In all our discussion of Revelation, if we lose sight of Jesus—this King and his kingdom—then, whatever else we might be doing, we're not seeing what the book claims to reveal with its opening words.

Revelation is simultaneously a message *about* Jesus and *from* Jesus.

Lock that away.

And make note: "from Jesus" implies that Jesus is still... well, alive. That's the wild claim of the early church. That Jesus (a really real human being) is forever alive, pointing us toward what true humanity can, and should, and will be. Jesus is the faithful "witness," the center of history, the first back from the dead, and the King over the kings of the earth (1v5).

The early church relentlessly
claimed the man Jesus was alive,
but their claim gets even more scandalous than that.

John calls this man, Jesus, the faithful "witness" or "martyr" (1v5).[6] So what exactly is Jesus pointing us toward? Toward what does Jesus's life witness? Well, this becomes clear as Revelation opens. A shocking turn takes place in verses 4-6, and the disorienting language provides an excellent example of the way Revelation works: *Jesus gets included in the definition of God himself.* Jesus shows us what God is like. He shows more faithfully than anything or anyone else what "the Great Mystery behind the universe" is like.

---

[6] It's the same word in Greek... what we think of as a **"martyr"** is someone who "witnesses" to something to the point of death.

The early church also claimed this scandal—this foolishness—this idolatrous insanity should they be wrong. They claimed that this crucified first-century Jewish peasant is the Center of all reality. Jesus is God. In the wording of the first century: "Jesus is Lord." This is the consistent claim written all over the New Testament.[7] And this is exactly how Revelation begins.

John could have just written "grace and peace from God" or perhaps "grace and peace from Father, Son, and Spirit" for those early Christians already recognizing the Trinitarian nature of God.[8] "But no," thinks John, "most people will just sleep through that. We're blind to almost everything. Let's make sure God looks strange so that maybe we'll finally see the scandalous good news."

So in verses 4-6, John announces "grace and peace" from:

- "him who is and who was and who is to come,"
- and "from the seven spirits who are before his throne,"
- and "from Jesus Christ."

That is a strange way to describe God...
...especially that "seven spirits" part.[9]

John refuses to settle for boring words or vanilla descriptions. Instead, he wants to wake us up. This Apocalypse wants us to see. So familiar things are made as strange as possibly so that we'll see again. He starts with the word "God." Let's make that strange. As the book begins, a literal human being has been included in the definition of God. Before we examine anything else in Revelation (and there's some strange stuff in this book), we should name this oddity:

---

[7] Easy examples include subversive storytelling in the gospels (cf. Mk. 2.7), the entire narrative moment of John (Jn. 1.1 to 20.28), ancient hymns preserved in the New Testament (cf. Col. 1.15-20), and even directed statements within early Christian writings (cf. Rom. 9.5, Heb. 1.3).

[8] See, for example, Matt. 28:19; Mk. 1.10; Jn. 20.21-22; Gal. 4.6; 2 Cor. 13.14.

[9] As we read Revelation we begin to see that **John loves to use numbers to classify rather than count. Numbers are used to not to name quantity but quality.** So by saying "seven spirits"—and even by choosing "seven churches" (1.4)—John is evoking an ancient number of fullness and complete- ness and totality. *He's giving a quality more than a quantity.* John isn't saying, "one spirit, two spirits, three spirits..." Rather, he's saying something like "the full and complete spirit of God who is everywhere, always, animating everything."

A shamefully executed first-century Jewish peasant
is central to how Christians define God.

Forget anything else... that. is. strange.

It's ironic that the popular American way of interpreting Revelation gets things almost entirely backwards. We often assume that the future is the primary thing—the main thing, the real thing—and Jesus just happens to be somewhere in the future. Instead, the Bible ends with Jesus revealed as reality's center, and the future happens to be somewhere in him.

Revelation frequently talks about what we've heard a thousand times in a strange new way. And Revelation does this intentionally. *Revelation makes everything strange in hopes that blind eyes might begin to see.*

We've all experienced moments where we can suddenly see with new eyes. Whether the leaves, or the lights, or our loved ones, we've all experienced moments when suddenly the familiar becomes strange. And then suddenly— for just that moment—we can behold where we had been blind.

We see the beauty again.
We see the goodness afresh.
We see the world new.

The Rocky Mountains west of Denver and Colorado Springs are a prime example. My fellow Coloradians and I see them all the time, and we easily become blind to them. But there are times when they look strange, and those are the moments when we can see them again. When sunlight paints the back ranges gold, or when snow falls in an unusual pattern, or when low clouds hide the peaks. When the mountains become mysterious, we suddenly see them again.

This is what Revelation does: it makes thinks mysterious. "Too mysterious," we often think. Every sentence drips with oddity, intrigue, and strangeness. But that's part of its genius. What if the strangeness of Revelation is not something we need to entirely decode or un-strange? What if Revelation's oddness and intrigue mean to help us?

Revelation's strangeness is less about hiding things from us and more about revealing what we've stopped seeing. Revelation helps us see by being strange.

It starts with God. *Let's make God strange so we can see God as clearly as possible: this human, Jesus, defines what we mean by the word "God."* If you want to know what God is like, then look at Jesus. Read the gospels and you'll discover what God is like. Follow Jesus around, watch his kindness, and service, and mercy, and love. You'll see what God is always doing...God is speaking grace and peace. And, surprisingly to many, that's what Revelation does too.

Revelation is ultimately about God speaking grace and peace.

Verse 4 conveys "grace and peace" from the God defined by Jesus. That's what the book of Revelation is ultimately about—about God bringing salvation to our broken world and broken lives. This healing is going to be painful, but the God defined by Jesus is fully committed to it. He has devoted himself to our healing to the point of his own death. The world's healing is costly.

That's why verse 4 can announce "grace and peace" and then verse 7 can say "all tribes of the earth will wail on account of him."[10] *God's healing and our wailing are not at odds with each other.* We frequently assume grace to be wimpy and peace to be spineless. But God's grace causes groaning. Peace often means pain. When Love-in-the-flesh begins working love into our flesh, we wail.

---

[10] John is borrowing language from Zechariah 12:10 right here. And "in the Zechariah passage the mourning is quite evidently said to be penitential grief, which is followed by divine pardon, cleansing, and restoration" (Caird, 18). "Indeed, the nations in 1:7b do not mourn over themselves but Jesus, which fits better into an understanding repentance than judgment" (Beale, 197).

Most of us want healing with no wailing, but Revelation reminds us that it doesn't work that way. Ask anyone who has experienced deep and lasting healing in their lives. They'll tell you that grace and peace are frequently painful. Whether in relationships, or destructive patterns, or hard situations—deep healing almost always hurts like hell. And the sicker we are, the more the healing hurts.

Perhaps chemotherapy provides a helpful (if flawed) metaphor for the grace and peace of God revealed by Revelation. When someone is undergoing chemotherapy, it looks horrible. The treatment is violent, and our patient is hurting, throwing up, hairs fall from their heads like stars from the sky. It's like hail, blood, and fire raining down on their lives.

But the point of the chemo is not to kill someone. The aim of chemo justifies the pain of chemo. The treatment aims to heal by killing the deep and dangerous problem. *The point of chemotherapy is healing; its point is grace and peace.*

So too with the grace of God we call God's judgment. God does indeed judge, but his judgments always aim at destroying anything that destroys life.[11]

Think of the visions of Revelation like chemotherapy for all creation. But make no mistake about the aim—God is always speaking grace and peace. Even when grace causes groaning and when peace will mean pain. Even when we'd rather stay sick, God has committed himself to our healing.

And that is terribly good news.

---

[11] See Revelation 11.18 for an essential key for understanding language of God's anger, wrath, judgment, etc... not only in Revelation but all of scripture.

If healing for the entire world
required God himself to be pierced,
then healing in our lives will certainly involve some pain.

And so Revelation begins by confronting us: Are we tired of being blind? Are we ready to stop sleepwalking? Do we want to wake up and see? Really? Truly?

If we want to really be fully alive,
it's time to stop avoiding God's painful grace.

No more half measures. We must open ourselves to the painful process of receiving peace. Revelation is less like an extended forecast of the future and more like an anthem of allegiance to Jesus: "I will follow the Lamb wherever he goes and allow his cleansing blood to flood my veins and burn away my darkness."

And when we commit ourselves to this treatment, of course we're going to see the future differently. But we'll also see the present differently. And the past. And our suffering. And our shame. And our relationships. And our priorities, values, jobs, hobbies, everyday decisions. And basically everything.

//

Alpha and Omega, humble me with this ancient book that makes everything strange. Teach me to recognize Jesus as the faithful witness—that you yourself were pierced for me. I open my life to the painful healing of your grace and peace. Unblind me. I want to see. May I behold the beauty of your presence and the wonder of living in your world. Amen.

(Revelation 1v9-20)

I, John, your brother and companion in the suffering and kingdom and patient endurance that are ours in Jesus, was on the island of Patmos because of the word of God and the testimony of Jesus. On the Lord's Day I was in the Spirit, and I heard behind me a loud voice like a trumpet, which said: "Write on a scroll what you see and send it to the seven churches: to Ephesus, Smyrna, Pergamum, Thyatira, Sardis, Philadelphia and Laodicea."

I turned around to see the voice that was speaking to me. And when I turned I saw seven golden lampstands, and among the lampstands was someone like a son of man, dressed in a robe reaching down to his feet and with a golden sash around his chest. The hair on his head was white like wool, as white as snow, and his eyes were like blazing fire. His feet were like bronze glowing in a furnace, and his voice was like the sound of rushing waters. In his right hand he held seven stars, and coming out of his mouth was a sharp, double-edged sword. His face was like the sun shining in all its brilliance.

When I saw him, I fell at his feet as though dead. Then he placed his right hand on me and said: "Do not be afraid. I am the First and the Last. I am the Living One; I was dead, and now look, I am alive for ever and ever! And I hold the keys of death and Hades.

"Write, therefore, what you have seen, what is now and what will take place later. The mystery of the seven stars that you saw in my right hand and of the seven golden lampstands is this: The seven stars are the angels of the seven churches, and the seven lampstands are the seven churches.

02. All-Powerful Unstoppable Jesus

On the evening of October 30, 1938, panic gripped thousands across the United States as news reports began circulating that Martians had begun an invasion of the earth. Reports included the institution of martial law, speculation about Martian technology, the radio station itself suffering damage and casualties, and eventually reports of a devastating invasion of New York City.

Listeners who resisted scooping up their children and fleeing with food and rifles were eventually greeted with an announcer informing them that they were listening to a CBS dramatization of H.G. Wells' *The War of the Worlds*. The

audience had heard science-fiction being performed, not news being reported. *Listeners misunderstood the genre... and suffered because of it.*

Revelation is written as a particular genre with a distinct flavor. We get our first strong taste comes shortly after the book's opening, as John discloses why he is writing this document in the first place.

John is a man[1] who finds himself imprisoned on an island called Patmos, off the coast of modern day Turkey. He finds himself a political prisoner of the Roman Empire (1v9), separated from those he loves and likely to die in exile. In his isolation and suffering, John finds himself met by Jesus in some kind of vision (1v10).

John glimpses Jesus surrounded by lights—in the middle of **seven lamps on seven golden stands** (1v12). The setting disorients until John takes in the details. The seven golden lamps signal that we're in a holy setting like Israel's tabernacle or temple.[2] The figure in their midst wears a long, **foot-length robe**[3] (1v13), the sacred garb of a priest at work in that setting. It takes us a moment to get our bearings with John, but this is some kind of Temple. Jesus is present even in the prison of Patmos. God was in this place, and we did not know it.[4]

John's description of Jesus "just sounds like" Revelation—with vivid colors, weird phrases (e.g. "the keys of Death and Hades"), and the number seven beginning to appear repeatedly (1v11, 12, 20). Jesus is wearing his priestly robe with a golden sash (1v13). Wooly white hair crowns his head and his eye sockets blaze with balls of fire (1v14). His feet shimmer like Iron Man's boots, and his voice thunders with the life-giving, earth-shaping power of tumbling cataracts (1v15). And he's holding seven stars in his right hand (1v16).

---

[1] **On authorship**: Scholars debate the precise identity of John. I see very little difference whether he is the actual Apostle John or another early church leader named John (whom scholars designate "John the Seer" or "John the Divine"). Either way, the author experienced something of a transcendent vision that the Spirit helped him articulate, and it was subsequently accepted by the Church as inspired scripture.
[2] Exod. 25.31-40; 37.17-24.
[3] The **robe reaching down to his feet** is a *podērēs* a rather unique word used for the priestly vestment in Exodus 25.7; 28.4, 31; 29.5; 35.9 as well as Zechariah 3.5. See Beale, 210.
[4] Genesis 28.16.

This is no Jesus meek and mild; this is Jesus fierce and ferocious.

John calls him "one like a son of man" (1v13), which was one of Jesus's favorite titles for himself as he walked around Galilee. It's the name of a mysterious figure in the scroll of Daniel who vanquishes monsters, rides the clouds, and eventually rules the cosmos.[5] John has already alluded to this mysterious figure by saying that Jesus is coming with the clouds,[6] but now John stands before him. And the experience is terrifying.

With the way John has described him, Jesus is not a guy you want to meet in a dark alley. Or—even better—Jesus is the guy you want *with you* if you wind up getting mugged at midnight:

"Nice switchblade... but before I give you my wallet, I'd like you to meet my friend Fire Eyes. That's right... back up. He's got other tricks too. (Do the thing with your mouth.) Yeah, that's right!—You better run!— that's a sword coming out of his mouth!!" (1v16)

It's silly when we frame it that way, but that's the overall impression John conveys in his barrage of images. Revelation reveals Jesus through a first-century Jewish genre we call "Apocalyptic." We have lots of other examples of this genre,[7] and they all utilize loads of story, symbolism, and metaphor. Just as we know what to expect when we watch a science-fiction blockbuster, or noir detective film, or horror movie, *John's churches knew what to expect when they heard an apocalypse read.*

---

[5] See Daniel 7.13-14ff. The "beasts" (empires) rising from "the sea" (primordial chaos) are found in v2-8. **Side note: when you see an "ff" after verses... it means "and following."**
[6] Rev 1.7.
[7] **"Apocalyptic literature"** tends to center on someone being revealed hidden heavenly secrets through an angel (or heavenly messenger) in a vision. This vision critiques grand scale injustices in the present while promising grand-scale justice in the future. And this vision gets expressed with pictures, symbols, colors, numbers, Old Testament images (e.g. dragons) as well as popular mythological stories (e.g. the "Apollo myth" in Rev. 12). Examples of this literature within in the Bible include Dan. 7-12, Zech. 12-14, Mk. 13 (and parallels in Matt. 24; Lk. 21). Other ancient examples you could google include *1 Enoch, 2 Baruch, 4 Ezra,* and *The Apocalypse of Peter.*

Revelation reveals Jesus
in apocalyptic style.

So to clarify, when he describes Jesus, John does not give a literal physical description in the way we would describe a suspect to a police sketch artist.

Q - "Could you please describe the face that you saw?"
A - "Well, his face was like the sun shining in full strength."

That's not what John is aiming at.
Not even close.

We can be confident on this point because John shows his cards in verse 20. He lets us know from the outset that he's talking in symbols. He tells us:

> "Those seven lampstands are not (of course) literal lampstands. Those seven lampstands are the seven churches that I'm writing to. And those seven stars in his hand are not (of course) literal stars. Those seven stars are angels[8]—spiritual personalities of the churches."

John rarely gives this kind of up-front explanation for his images. But here he clarifies—perhaps for anyone unfamiliar with apocalypses—that he's not talking about literal lighting fixtures or actual intergalactic burning spheres of plasma.

So in his description of Jesus, John writes in a particular genre that everyone is familiar with. He employs metaphor, pictures, and symbols to describe the Jesus he encountered as overwhelming and powerful and unlike anyone he's ever encountered.

---

[8] The language of **"angels"** is an example of a detail no one can nail down. "Angel" literally just means "messenger" in Greek but is typically used of a messenger from God. These **seven stars** could be referring to "the messenger" leading each church (their overseer/pastor/etc) or it could be referencing a spiritual being responsible for and corresponding to an earthly reality. If that sounds wacky, Scripture makes veiled hints at these mysterious spiritual realities other places. "Angels" are assumed to correspond to groups of people (Dan. 10.13) and to individuals (Matt. 18.10; Acts 12.15). A gift of Scripture in general—and Apocalyptic in particular—is how it humbles us. There are dimensions of reality to which we are completely oblivious.

Revelation uses a lot of symbolism. That's part of the genre. And this comes as an immense relief because as slick as Iron Man's boots look on Tony Stark, they seem extremely odd on Jesus.

The knowledge that Revelation employs symbolism comes as *such* a relief that we're tempted to start following John's example. It's tempting to start trying to explain, decode, and de-mystify every single image in the book. We could start right here with John's description of Jesus, since he's already given us a jump-start with the "meaning" of the lampstands and the stars:

Golden Sash	Royalty - the anointed King/Christ/Messiah (Pss. 2, 72, 110)
Feet-length Robe	Priestliness
White Hair	Victory & purity & wisdom & looks like God (Dan. 7.9)
Eyes of Fire	Penetrating, perceptive, insightful vision
"Furnaced-burned" Feet of Bronze	Strength & stability especially in trials (Dan 3.21-26)
Waterfall voice	Godlike voice (Ezek. 1.24; 43.2) & life-giving (Ezek. 47.1-12)
Sword from Mouth	Piercingly effective words of truth
Face like Sun	Splendor, glory
Seven Lampstands	Local communities (as well as full-and-complete church)
Seven Stars	The spiritual personalities of local churches

A table like this sure makes us feel like we're making "progress" on understanding Revelation, doesn't it?

We can look at his **golden sash** and see something of ritzy royalty and priestliness. We can analyze his **snow white hair** and recognize white as a symbol of victory, purity, and wisdom...a resembling God himself in Daniel.[9] We find searching penetration in **eyes like fire**, strong purity of **metal feet**, divine life-

---

[9] Daniel 7.9, mysteriously called "the Ancient of Days."

giving power in a **waterfall-voice**, the **piercing effectiveness** of his words, and glorious splendor in a **solar face**.

But is this the heart of reading Revelation?
Decoding ciphers?

If so, now that we've got verses 12-16 neatly dissected, labeled, and de-mystified, perhaps we should just move on to the rest of Revelation. With a few more tables, some cultural background, and a little historical context, maybe we could finally crack Revelation once and for all.

We began last chapter by clarifying that Revelation reveals Jesus. But even when we recognize Jesus, not the future, as the center of Revelation, we can still fall into a trap with two problems. The trap involves thinking that we're really understanding Revelation only when we un-symbolize all of its symbols. We're tempted to think that we only really "get" the Bible's ending when we decode its images and dissect its details.

Don't misunderstand: we *do* need some kind of framework for understanding. Revelation was written when God meets John of Patmos in all his particulars of culture, history, language, etc. And so the tools of cultural background, historical context, language work, (etc.) *are* essential for illuminating what Jesus revealed to John. But when these tools begin to consume us—when we think that deepest understanding depends on our ability to dissect—we have fallen into a trap with two immense problems.

The first problem is obvious: the book becomes overwhelming. It would take years to understand Revelation... if ever. There are hundreds of details in Revelation and thousands of opinions about each detail. Who has the time to do all that research and dissect all those details? That would mean most normal Christians could never connect with Revelation.

Furthermore, a few details have been totally obscured by the centuries. Nobody knows their precise meaning. What do we do there? If Revelation "works" by decoding and dissecting all of the details, then there will be some parts of the book that will never "work."

But let's pretend for a moment that we could. Even if we *could* somehow nail down every detail, we would still run into a second problem. It's a deeper problem to which we would have become even more susceptible: pride.

Revelation seems carefully designed to humble us, to make the world mysterious, and to fill us with wonder. When we approach the book with the clinical precision of a biology lab, we're ultimately aiming for the control of a dissection—a control that ruthlessly eliminates surprise. And we need that when we dissect a frog or ferret or lion. We can analyze them *because* they no longer hop or scurry or roar. There are no surprises—there is no danger—because there is no life. We are in control because they are dead.

Revelation, however, continues to roar and cannot be tamed. We approach its details less like a dissection table and more like a safari. We are entering a new world. We need to observe the details—indeed, small details are essential—but we must remain keenly aware that we tread ground both wild and holy. We must admit that we're not in control. Until then, it will be hard to be humble.

Should we delude ourselves into thinking that we can finally nail down everything in Revelation, we would eventually become pride-filled people:

"Look, I've finally figured it all out—God, the world, the future, everything."
"Look how spiritual and dedicated and clever I am."
"Look, why can't others crack this code too?"

And once we manage to purge all mystery from Revelation, all wonder from the universe, and all surprises from God, we would become bloated brains boasting that we are finally in control. And this runs opposite to Revelation design. John's vision is not ultimately on the dissection table here; we are. As with the rest of Scripture, God aims to use Revelation to open us up, to analyze us, to crucify us... and to resurrect us.

No part of Revelation means to drive us to bull-headed predictions, or over-reaching analysis, or ever-changing flowcharts. All of Revelation means to drive us to our knees. We should remind ourselves early and often that Revelation is primarily meant to be absorbed not analyzed. When we slip into obsessive over-analysis of dissecting and decoding, we are slipping further and further away from the point of the book.

While this is especially true for Scripture and Revelation, it's also true for almost any work of art. Consider music for a moment. Music captivates us, transports us, and even changes us, in a way few things can. But does the music "work" because you analyzed it?

Does your favorite song captivate you
because you've nailed down music theory?

Does the musical score of your favorite movie
transport you because you've dissected its mechanics?

Let's get specific with our analogy for a moment. We all have different tastes in music, and I don't know what moves you—be it country, classical, or hip-hop. But there's one piece of music that universally captivates humanity: The Mission Impossible theme song.

You're humming it already.

Imagine asking someone to describe their favorite thing about that iconic spy music. And imagine, after a moment, if they drew the following table on a napkin as an objective, verifiable, technical answer to your question:

A balance between turmoil and sense
A two bar bass riff
A solid tonal centre
Short, repeating notes in melody
Held notes falling in semitones
Melodic patterns in each evolving bar

On some level these are all correct. All of those things *are* technically true about the music. And yet this table falls woefully short of the music itself. It's nothing like an adequate answer. Dissecting the details of the music might be helpful to a degree, but it's not the *purpose* of the music. The music is meant to be absorbed and caught up in, not merely analyzed. It quickens our pulse, elevates a movie moment, and helps Tom Cruise dangle off the world's tallest building (and other delightful nonsense).

We probably aren't in danger of missing the purpose of music because it effortlessly transports most of us. But when it comes to the Bible's final book, we're frequently in danger of missing its purpose. Revelation is not primarily meant to be decoded or dissected... it's meant to be experienced. It's meant to cause us to see God revealed as Jesus. It's meant to humble us before him and fill us with wonder at a mysterious, beautiful world under his reign.

We begin to "understand" Revelation
as we're driven to our knees in worship.

That's what happens to John. As the first person to experience the strange and grand vision of Revelation, he models the proper response. When he experiences this vision—when John sees Jesus—he falls at Jesus's feet as though dead (1v17). John sees Jesus of Nazareth with unlimited power, and finds it absolutely overwhelming

If you've ever seen the Disney movie *Aladdin*, there's a moment near the end when Jafar (the bad guy) becomes gigantic and all-powerful. Jafar becomes a human being with unlimited, unstoppable power. I remember sitting in the theater as a kid and sweating it. The climactic moment of that cartoon gives us a conception of what John sees.

His Spirit-inspired vision reveals Jesus—the human being—as all-powerful and unstoppable. Even though this is Jesus (not Jafar), and even though this is the perfect human being (not some creepy Grand Vizier), this is still terrifying.

But if there were one person that humanity could elect to the position of unlimited power, it would be Jesus of Nazareth, right? I mean, have you read the gospels? He feeds the hungry, heals the sick, raises the dead, comforts the afflicted, forgives sins, dines with sinners. Jesus is trustworthy with power.

But this raw power is still terrifying. We tremble when we see him in cosmic grandeur, even though this is Jesus of Nazareth. As we saw last chapter, the presence of his unfiltered life makes our sin-sick bodies wail (1v7).

John is the first person to "understand" Revelation. He's writing about something deeper than theological theories or fan-fiction about the future. He recognizes the person and power of God in Jesus, the nature of the universe, and his place within it. And John invites us to share his understanding. John falls at Jesus's feet as though dead. That's the reaction of anyone who really begins to see God. And that's the reaction Revelation aims to provoke.

But notice the words that thundering like Niagra Falls over John and the rest of us. They are words we hardly dare believe:

"Do not be afraid" (1v17).

That's what the book of Revelation is about.
That's how the book of Revelation works.

Revelation aims to overwhelm our senses—our seeing, smelling, hearing, everything—so that *we will realize how small we are* and *how strong Jesus is*. And then his divine voice tells us not to be afraid.[10]

If we're not falling down dead to be resurrected,
we're not understanding Revelation.

It doesn't matter how many details we can decode or dissect.

What happens when we finally begin to see Jesus this way? That God is in this place—yes, even here and now? When we begin to admit our smallness and weakness? When we begin to glimpse that Jesus is strong and full of love?

What happens is our lives change.

Recognizing Jesus as all-powerful and unstoppable often does not seem obviously practical or immediately helpful. It's not an easy bit of "application" that we can painlessly "apply" to our lives in five minutes. But this seemingly impractical reality—that the Crucified One is the Conquering One—happens to be the center of the gospel. And learning to believe this news is the only thing that will fundamentally change our lives. It is news to make our life new. We fall down dead only to hear the whisper of resurrection: "Be alive. You will live, my child. Do not be afraid."

This vision has already transformed John's entire outlook by the time he puts quill to parchment. The Roman government had exiled him and imprisoned him on the prison island of Patmos (1v9). He's lonely. He's quarantined away from civilization. He's separated from the churches and communities he loved. Distant, desperate, stranded, alone.

---

[10] If it feels like I'm playing fast-and-loose by calling Jesus both "God" and "the perfect human being," it's because both apply in equal measure to the person of Jesus. The human being Jesus shares the throne of God (Rev. 4.3; 5.6), functions as God throughout the book's narrative, and by the end of the Revelation Jesus explicitly speaks God's titles as his own (Rev. 1.8; 22.13).

Whatever our bad day (or month or year), John was likely experiencing something worse. But after this vision—after recognizing his smallness and Jesus's strongness—John's entire outlook on life has changed.

John realizes that he is not in this situation because of the power of Rome. There would be plenty to fear if the powers of chaos, violence, and death were that strong... but they are not. Rome doesn't rule the kings of the earth; Jesus does (1v5). John recognizes that ultimately his current situation falls under the providential care of the word of God (1v9), not the word of Rome.

Jesus reigns. Even when things are hard. Even though life hurts right now. Even when we are drowning in tribulation, turmoil, and suffering.[11] Even though life requires patient endurance. Notice what's growing between **suffering** and **patient endurance**: God's **kingdom** (1v9). What an odd place for "the kingdom" to be. In spite of everything, God is good, God is here, and God is at work. And this good news saturates every chapter of the Apocalypse.

God is actually at work. Right now. On your Patmos. In your loneliness, in your pain, in your struggle, in your exile. The word of death cannot out-speak the word of God.

Despite all appearances, despite our doubts and desperation, despite the pain of prison and Patmos, Jesus and his kingdom are in the middle of everything and stronger than anything.

If we allow the Spirit to open our eyes to this revelation, the outlook of our life will change... just like John's.

The only one to fear is Jesus.
And Jesus says, "Fear not."

---

[11] The NIV's "suffering" in verse 9 is the same word frequently glossed "tribulation" in other translations and even by the NIV in 7.14.

"Don't fear… just follow. I've already experienced everything you fear. I've already died but I'm alive forever (1v17). Just keep following. There is nothing to fear. I will show you life. I will make you alive. Follow me, my love."

That's what Jesus said to John.

That's what Jesus says to all of us.

//

All-powerful, unstoppable Jesus, may you teach me how to absorb the Scriptures even as I learn to analyze them. May you reveal your living presence to me to the point of making me afraid—I want to know your strength. And may I hear your gentle whisper of love that banishes all fear. Amen.

(Revelation 2v1-7)

"To the angel of the church in Ephesus write:

These are the words of him who holds the seven stars in his right hand and walks among the seven golden lampstands. I know your deeds, your hard work and your perseverance. I know that you cannot tolerate wicked people, that you have tested those who claim to be apostles but are not, and have found them false. You have persevered and have endured hardships for my name, and have not grown weary.

Yet I hold this against you: You have forsaken the love you had at first. Consider how far you have fallen! Repent and do the things you did at first. If you do not repent, I will come to you and remove your lampstand from its place. But you have this in your favor: You hate the practices of the Nicolaitans, which I also hate.

Whoever has ears, let them hear what the Spirit says to the churches. To the one who is victorious, I will give the right to eat from the tree of life, which is in the paradise of God.

(Revelation 3v14-22)

"To the angel of the church in Laodicea write:

These are the words of the Amen, the faithful and true witness, the ruler of God's creation. I know your deeds, that you are neither cold nor hot. I wish you were either one or the other! So, because you are lukewarm—neither hot nor cold—I am about to spit you out of my mouth. You say, 'I am rich; I have acquired wealth and do not need a thing.' But you do not realize that you are wretched, pitiful, poor, blind and naked. I counsel you to buy from me gold refined in the fire, so you can become rich; and white clothes to wear, so you can cover your shameful nakedness; and salve to put on your eyes, so you can see.

Those whom I love I rebuke and discipline. So be earnest and repent. Here I am! I stand at the door and knock. If anyone hears my voice and opens the door, I will come in and eat with that person, and they with me. To the one who is victorious, I will give the right to sit with me on my throne, just as I was victorious and sat down with my Father on his throne. Whoever has ears, let them hear what the Spirit says to the churches."

03. THE SEVEN CHURCHES

The early chapters of Revelation remind us that John has written *a letter*. That might be easy to overlook. Last chapter we recognized that John is writing in a particular style: the genre we call "first-century apocalyptic." That's *how* he writes. But *what* he writes is a letter.

When John turned "to see the voice" speaking to him (1v12), he caught glimpse of all-powerful, unstoppable Jesus (1v13-20). And what that voice told him to do was write a letter. To seven local churches (1v10-11).

Seven personalized letters comprise Revelation 2-3, reminding us that this entire book—with its strange, symbolic language—was originally heard by specific people of another place, time, language, and culture.

Revelation is ancient mail.

Ancient mail from Jesus, through an angel and guy named John (1v1), to a cluster of local Jesus communities in the western half of Asia Minor—the present-day country of Turkey.

It's worth remembering this is ancient mail when we see wild, cartoonish characters, or hear patterned uses of colors and numbers, or feel overwhelmed with strange scenes. This book is a letter—a letter written in a style and genre *that those in the first-century would recognize.*

Jesus tells John, "I want you to write to seven churches in a particular corner of the Roman Empire." These seven communities are geographically close together, forming a rough path or circuit. Whomever John recruited to carry this letter would have carried this letter from one church to the next. They would have sailed from Patmos into Ephesus and then hit the bustling sea-port of Smyrna before heading inland and trekking to the towns of Pergamum, Thyatira, Sardis, Philadelphia, and Laodicea.

Revelation is ancient mail.

Easy to lose sight of, but it's well worth remembering. Because whatever Revelation is, it's something that these seven churches would have (mostly!) understood.[1] Jesus didn't send a coded puzzle originally meant for comfortable Christians in the twenty-first century. Jesus sent a stylized letter originally meant for struggling Christians in the first century. *If we cannot imagine the original hear-*

---

[1] We should note, however, that John has crafted a document so dense, intricate, and layered that it could serve as lifelong meditation literature for a community. John is aware he is writing Scripture in the majestic tradition of Israel. Evidence points to early Christian communities having teachers trained to were well-versed in Israel's Scriptures who could help guide others in their meaning. John likely expected these teachers—who could tease out the sophisticated subtleties of the TaNaK (i.e. the Old Testament) as well as Paul's letters or the gospels—to be engaging with his vision for a lifetime.

ers of *Revelation* understanding our interpretation of this letter, then our interpretation probably needs to be rethought.

We need to rethink our reading skills. The unlikely alternative is that Jesus needs to rethink his writing skills... as if Jesus started writing Revelation to local, historic communities but then got carried away talking in secret code about the threat of Soviets or microchips. I find that unlikely. Jesus knows how to write a focused letter.

It's far more likely that the original churches understood this letter far more easily than we do. An incredible amount of work has to happen before any of us can read this letter. First, it has to be translated (or we have to learn Koine Greek). After that, we undertake the monumental task of learning about apocalyptic literature, studying Greco-Roman culture, reading up on history, piecing together life at that time, etc. By contrast, the original hearers of this letter *just heard it*. They didn't have to learn a new language or get a crash course in first-century Greco-Roman culture. They didn't need to brush up on their history to understand this letter. They were simply living it.

The church in Ephesus simply knew who the group called "Nicolaitans" were (2v6). We don't.[2] That's an easy example of a detail we'll never decode with absolute certainty. Don't misunderstand, we can make really good guesses. It's likely they were a group advocating small compromises with Roman culture so that Jesus followers could fly under the radar, avoid persecution, and live more comfortably.

But where we have to bend over backwards to piece together cultural and historical clues, they just heard the letter. Where we have to make guesses, they just understood. Where we hear ancient riddles, they heard current events. Where we hear tantalizing puzzles, they heard everyday details—the frequently boring, everyday details of their lives.

---

[2] That lets the cat out of the scholarly bag, but it's the truth. We don't know with certainty.

For example, when we read the Laodicean's mail (3v14-22), it requires a history lesson for us to realize their city was in a great location for economic trade but a terrible location for water. Their city boomed with all kinds of business—from finance and banking to specialized textiles and clothing. They were even on the cutting edge of medicine and known throughout the region as a go-to place for ophthalmology and eye health.

"Eyes bothering you? Can I interest you in some Laodicean eye salve?"

Seriously, it was a hot commodity.[3]

They considered themselves rich—almost without need (3v17). Lack of good water was their only problem. Their neighbors in Hierapolis had access to therapeutic hot springs. And their other neighbors in Colossae had access to clean, cold water. But the only local water in Laodicea was a small spring of lukewarm lime water that made people sick. All that wealth and they couldn't quench their thirst.

To this local church Jesus says,

> "You're behaving like that wretched lime water that makes you sick. If you were hot, you would be therapeutic. If you were cold, you would be quenching. But you're neither, and it's nauseating."

All their wealth has blinded them to the truth: they're actually pitiful, naked, blind. For all their wealth and fashion, the need true riches, true clothing, and true eye salve from Jesus (3v17-18). We have to do bunches of background research to recognize points that landed immediately for them. These were the sometimes boring, frequently infuriating, everyday details of their lives. Much of our monumental task involves seeing their mundane.

The book of Revelation is ancient mail, and we need to approach it that way. *When we read all of Revelation, we need to remember God is speaking to more*

---

[3] Beale, 305-6

than us. In the first century, God spoke through this document to seven historic communities. And if we're reading the book in a way they couldn't possibly understand (i.e. in ways concerned only with twenty-first century Western Christians), we're probably not reading it the best way.

Revelation is ancient mail
that reveals Jesus
in apocalyptic style.

But this ancient mail does not *only* address first century Christians in Asia Minor. We know this because Jesus (or John[4]) has chosen the number of his communities carefully. This is written to *seven* churches, and seven is a loaded, symbolic number in Revelation.

We mentioned it in a footnote in chapter one, but it's worth saying explicitly here: *Revelation frequently uses numbers to classify more than to count.* **Numbers name quality more often than quantity.** By choosing to write to "seven" churches John chooses a symbolic number as robustly complete as creation itself.[5] By writing to seven historic churches, John clues us in that his letter addresses *more* than just these historic churches. Jesus addresses the whole church—the full and complete church—in this letter. Wherever or whenever people are following Jesus, those are the people to whom Revelation speaks.

That intentionally includes us.

Entire books have been written exploring these seven personalized letters and lessons to be gleaned from them. They challenge us to consider our calling to Jesus as a counter-cultural allegiance that will often put us at odds with prevailing culture. They invite us to welcome the Spirit's refining work within us even

---

[4] Throughout Revelation, it's frequently impossible to disentangle who exactly is "authoring" a passage. A literal historic man (John) writes this book with incredible and careful literary prowess. AND the living Jesus ungirds and animates both the book and the vision from which the book sprang.
[5] The primordial creation poem preserved in Genesis 1 frames the crafting of cosmos as being completed in **seven**.

when it's painful and costly. But all of these potential lessons actually form one big lesson—a large pattern, a constellation of lessons—that we need to name:

The local church
is at the heart
of how Jesus saves.

The local church is central—not only in the book of Revelation but throughout all of the New Testament. The witness of earliest Christians never presents us with a privatized, atomized, individualistic faith. As true as it is that Jesus cares about and relates to each of us individually, the early church placed less emphasis than we often think on having "personal relationship with Jesus."[6]

Central to salvation for the earliest Christians
was participation in the community of God's people.

They insisted that God is accomplishing the rescue/healing/salvation of the world in and through Jesus. And Jesus works this rescue/healing/salvation most directly through a particular group of people.

The questions for the earliest Christians were more along these lines:

- Do you want to be a part of that people?

- Will you allow the Spirit of God to include you in this?

- Are you willing to be grafted into the people of God?

It's common today to hear people bemoan how they like Jesus but don't really care for the church. Even those of us who consider ourselves devout Christians, committed to serving with a local church, frequently adopt this mindset.

---

[6] That phrase, of course, never occurs in the New Testament. It's true that Paul's statement in Galatians 2:20 ("I live by faith in the Son of God, who loved me and gave himself for me"; notice the singular "me") provides us with a poignant window of a personal dimension present in the early church. But the personal grows out of being included in God's people (Gal. 2.15-16), and God's people are not formed by a quorum of the personal.

We often think:

> "The REALLY important thing is my internal, private, personal relationship with God. My reading the Bible, my prayer time, my singing worship in the car, my feelings and experiences, my helping the poor, my personal choices and morality. But vulnerable, committed service to and with a particular local community? Well, that's an optional add-on. I mean, I do it… but it's not exactly central. It's an awkward extra—like a Christian club I'm sometimes involved in."

But this way of thinking was completely foreign to the earliest Christians.

Jesus addresses *communities* in Revelation, not *individuals*. The lampstands shining light into the world are Churches, not Christians. Not even particular superstar Christians *du jour* like Billy Graham or Mother Theresa or Martin Luther King Jr.—take your pick—not even they are THE light of the world. It is the Church, in all its local expressions, that illuminates the world.

The book of Revelation begins with a grand vision of Christ telling John not to be afraid (ch1), and Revelation ends with a grand vision of heaven transforming the world (ch21-22). Those are the bookends of the good news found in Revelation. We recognize our smallness—that we can't save the world or even ourselves. Jesus, however, is strong and coming to save. But sandwiched between the grand vision of Love himself and the vision of Love coming to remake the world, we find something we wouldn't expect. We find the seemingly unimportant, obviously imperfect, frequently infuriating, local church.

But the local church is something we would rather skip past.

Eugene Peterson gets honest for all of us:

> We want a Christ who is pure goodness, beauty, and truth. We prefer to worship him under a caress of a stunning sunset, or with the inspiring tonalities of a soaring symphony, or by means of a penetrating poetry. We would like to put as much distance as possible between our worship of Christ and the indifferent hymn singing and fussy moralism which somehow always get into the church. We are ardent after God

but cool towards the church. It is not irreligion or indifference that keeps many away from the church, but just the opposite: the church is perceived and experienced as a carcinogenic pollutant in the air of religion. Many people, wanting to nurture faith in God, instead of entering the company of saints who look and act a lot more like sinners, take a long walk on an ocean beach or hike a high mountain or immerse themselves in Dostoyevsky or Stravinsky or Georgia O'Keeffe.

But to all this aspiring asceticism the Gospel says No: "Write to the seven churches." We would prefer to go directly from the awesome vision of Christ (Rev. 1) to the glorious ecstasies of heaven (Rev. 4, 5) and then on to the grand victorious battles against dragon wickedness (Rev. 12-14) but we can't do it. The church has to be negotiated first. The only way from Christ to heaven and the battles against sin is through the church.[7]

Peterson provides spot-on insight. The gateway we must pass through—from the grand vision of all-powerful, unstoppable Jesus (ch1) to the world's salvation (ch21-22)—is the church. *John has structured his letter on the macro-level in such a way to say:*

The local church
is at the heart
of how Jesus saves.

The centrality of the church on the *macro*-level of Revelation's structure is also reflect on the *micro*-level of how of each of these seven letters. Each letter embodies the same structure of 1) Jesus, 2) local church, 3) saving future. Each begins with a backward embrace of the vision of all-powerful, unstoppable Jesus.[8] Then comes the practical particulars of encouraging and challenging the local church. And finally each ends looking forward, anticipating the future of

---

[7] Peterson, 44-45.

[8] In the letters to Ephesus and Laodicea, we find Jesus walking among his lampstands holding their essence (2.1) and also Jesus as the faithful and true witness/martyr (3.14). The other five occurrences can be found in 2.8, 2.12, 2.18, 3.1, and 3.7.

heaven transforming the world.[9] Be it on the macro-level to the micro-level, John's letter falls apart without the local Jesus community.

It's also telling that these communities get to eavesdrop on the other's letters. Just as individual Christians need each other, local churches need each other. Each community glimpses different pieces of the complete vision of Jesus, and each anticipates God's restoration of all things in different ways. But the differences between them do not divide them. *Each local church is a place where individual Christians participate in a Kingdom bigger than any of us can fully see. And each local church can learns glimpses more of the Kingdom by humbly listening to how Jesus is speaking to other churches.*

From the grandest to smallest of levels, and across a diversity of communities, the local church is where Jesus works salvation into the world.

Not only that, Jesus works salvation into *us* through the church. God works salvation into us—and we work out that salvation—through community. *The life of salvation does not happen in isolation. It cannot. By definition. Being drawn into the life of God means being drawn more deeply into love... and love requires relationship.* I cannot love in isolation, and love is what God is.[10] We remember with the church the mystery that God is himself a community—Father, Son, and Spirit. The heart behind our universe is eternal dance of self-giving, others-embracing love. And the church is where God invites us to participate in the dance of love that God already always is.

This doesn't mean, of course, that our relationship with God as individuals persons does not matter. Of course it does! The church, however, helps us recognize and remember that our "personal relationship with Jesus" involves more than just our person. We were made for relationship—to serve and celebrate and love each other.

---

[9] Ephesus hears promise of the tree of life (2.7) while Laodicea hears promise of sharing a throne with Jesus (3.21). The other five occurrences are found in 2.10-11, 2.17, 2.26-28, 3.5, and 3.12.
[10] 1 Jn. 4:16.

Dietrich Bonhoeffer writes, "Let him who cannot be alone beware community. Let him who is not in community beware being alone."[11] He recognized how God forms us alone into lovers and puts us together to practice love. We *do* need solitude and silence, retreat and reflection, and times of quiet—they center us in God's love and allow his Spirit to permeate us. But if we stay in solitude too long, we risk sinking into selfish isolation. Jesus calls us frequently to solitude but never calls us to isolation. Jesus transforms our deepest selves so that we can be involved with all those whom Jesus loves. Dancers, after all, only truly become dancers when they join the dance. The local church is the theater where love gets embodied, practiced, and performed.

Anyone who has performed anything—music, theater, sports—knows how important practice is. Practicing scales, rehearsing lines, or repeating layups can seem tedious or trivial. But repetition is how we are formed into musicians, performers, or athletes. So too with love. We rehearse love with one another in the church. It is in the boring details of the seemingly trivial local church where Jesus forms us into lovers who can love the unlovable. The church is how Jesus brings his kingdom in our lives as it is heaven. That's what we see in all seven of these letters: Jesus at work. In varying degrees and ways, we find Jesus affirming, correcting, challenging—making us like him.

Make careful note that Jesus does not correct or challenge "the world" or "people in general." *Revelation, with all its encouragement and warning, addresses the Church.* When Jesus calls out that he "stands at the door and knocks," he's talking to the church.[12] Despite the way this verse is often evoked at church altar-calls, Jesus is not addressing non-Christians. It is we, as the local church, who are often in danger of shutting Jesus out. Jesus wants intimacy with us. He wants to share a meal with us.[13]

---

[11] Dietrich Bonhoeffer, *Life Together* (New York: HarperCollins, 1954), 78
[12] Rev. 3.20.
[13] See Revelation 10 for the surprise meal.

Jesus yearns to come in, be with, and dine with us (together!). Jesus desires for us (together!) to become lovers who can live in life instead of death. The primary place where Jesus works out his salvation is in us (together!). Jesus talks to us together, saves us together, disciplines us together.

Yes, even discipline. And Jesus disciplines us for the exact same reason my wife and I discipline our daughters when they get too close to an electrical outlet or play with wires. Jesus disciplines us because he loves us.[14] He doesn't want us wandering into death.

Jesus wants us fully and forever alive.
And "together" is where Jesus promises to make this happen.

As Peterson mentioned, those of us who yearn deeply for the spiritual life often to want it "pure" and "untainted." We see the boringness or ugliness of the local church and think, "That cannot be it. That cannot be where Jesus is at work." We quietly assume the local church to be something like a "pollutant." At best it seems an awkward optional thing. At worst it seems like a bug in the software of spirituality—something "in the way" of a spiritual life more pure and powerful. But what if we need to rethink what we're looking for? What if the church is a feature not a glitch?

What if the local church is not *in the way of* spiritual formation?
What if the local church is *the way into* spiritual formation?

I confess that my desire to feel spiritual often outweighs my desire to actually be Christlike. I would rather hike in the mountains, listen to music, read poetry, and talk about theology at a coffee shop. I would rather do this with people who are like me, and I would like to feel spiritual while I'm doing it. Joining with other people as the local church doesn't always *feel* spiritual. Who am I kidding? It's inconvenient. It's often boring. It's sometimes ugly. It's frequently

14 Rev. 3.19.

frustrating. There are dozens of details that we'd rather not deal with. Interacting with people often doesn't *feel* spiritual. And worse, it often exposes parts of me that I'd rather ignore. And this is precisely why we need it.

The local church is vital because it's bones and blood—indisputably real.

The inconvenient, boring, ugly, frustrating details of the local church—of actually joining with those who aren't like us, towards whom we wouldn't naturally gravitate—this is the primary place where the Spirit works *to make us Christlike*. This is the place where Jesus begins to strip us of our selfishness and make us like himself. It doesn't always feel spiritual, but I'm not sure where we got the idea that it should. This is where our real lives are exposed, and it's where Jesus draws us into life that's even more real.

The seven personalized letters of Revelation 2-3 remind us that this book cannot be about escaping into an imagery world of ideas or theology or the future. Instead, Jesus addresses us—together—in the mundane details of our lives (together!) as the local church. And he promises that the real world of our lives will be the theater of his salvation.

As we'll continue to see, *the local church is the gateway to everything else in Revelation.* And that's because the local church is always at the heart of how Jesus saves.

//

Light of the Lampstands, teach me to hear your voice that talks to more than just me. May I be built together with others as the local church. May we (together!) glimpse a vision of you that trains us for your never-ending kingdom of love. May I realize that the boring, ugly, dumb details are how your Spirit makes me like you... even when life doesn't feel spiritual. Amen.

(Revelation 4)

After this I looked, and there before me was a door standing
open in heaven. And the voice I had first heard speaking to
me like a trumpet said, "Come up here, and I will show you
what must take place after this." At once I was in the Spirit,
and there before me was a throne in heaven with someone
sitting on it. And the one who sat there had the appearance
of jasper and ruby. A rainbow that shone like an emerald
encircled the throne. Surrounding the throne were twenty-
four other thrones, and seated on them were twenty-four
elders. They were dressed in white and had crowns of gold
on their heads. From the throne came flashes of lightning,
rumblings and peals of thunder. In front of the throne, seven
lamps were blazing. These are the seven spirits of God. Also
in front of the throne there was what looked like a sea of
glass, clear as crystal.

In the center, around the throne, were four living creatures,
and they were covered with eyes, in front and in back. The
first living creature was like a lion, the second was like an
ox, the third had a face like a man, the fourth was like a flying eagle. Each of the four living creatures had six wings and
was covered with eyes all around, even under its wings. Day
and night they never stop saying:

"'Holy, holy, holy
is the Lord God Almighty,'
who was, and is, and is to come."

Whenever the living creatures give glory, honor and thanks
to him who sits on the throne and who lives for ever and
ever, the twenty-four elders fall down before him who sits on
the throne and worship him who lives for ever and ever.
They lay their crowns before the throne and say:

"You are worthy, our Lord and God,
    to receive glory and honor and power,
for you created all things,
    and by your will they were created
    and have their being."

04. BACKSTAGE OF THE UNIVERSE

Something new begins in Revelation 4. After addressing the seven local Jesus-communities in a personalized way, John begins to recount in earnest the mysterious vision he experienced.

John describes his transcendent experience as a story—an intricate, ever-modulating narrative—that runs through the rest of the letter. It's a bigger story than a *conservative emphasis* on individuals getting saved, being "good and moral" and going to heaven after death. And it's a grander vision than a *liberal emphasis* on acts of mercy, social justice, and a humanistic utopia. John tells us the story of the universe's salvation. It's a vision that includes both the salvation of individuals *and* the salvation of cultures, economies, societies, and nations. Anything and everything we can imagine gets included in God's great rescue. Revelation promises salvation on a grander scale than we can imagine.

The local church will play a pivotal role in this story, but this story does not begin with us. Salvation does not hinge on humanity. The rescue, healing, and transformation of all things hinges on God. Divine shoulders bear the weight of the world remade by love.

We should put it bluntly: we are not the realest real thing. There exists something more real than us, gathering us up in its gracious gravitational pull. That's why Revelation 4 begins the way it does—with a tractor beam.

John suddenly sees a door (4v1). An open door. John then finds himself drawn upward through this door and marveling at the realm of elemental realty, what we call "heaven."

This door didn't come out of nowhere. In the last letter to the seven churches, we hear Jesus saying how he stands at the door and knocks (3v20). Jesus longs for intimacy with every one of his people. Jesus wants to pass through the doorway so his church can share a meal with him. But when the door opens, John also passes through.

What if Jesus comes in our door
to invite us out of ourselves?

That's the provocative suggestion that God grants the lonely prisoner of Patmos. The triumphant trumpet-voice heard in chapter one (1v11) now invites John to rise through a door (4v1-2). And once we pass through this door with him... well, we need no convincing that we're in the strange new world of Revelation. Imagery breaks loose in wild, untamed ways. And a scene in heaven confronts us.

When we hear the word "heaven," almost all of us have a particular kind of image that jumps to our mind. Perhaps something like Gary Larson's delightful *The Far Side* comics. My conscious mind knows that heaven doesn't look like this, but my subconscious offers up the image anyway. Bright, puffy clouds float through my mind. Lazy white cumulus against a bright blue sky with a gentle

breeze blowing. Perhaps a few quaint harpists quietly strum somewhere un-
seen. And, hey, now that I think of it, the bored guy
wishing for a magazine doesn't seem far off.

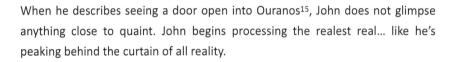

Our minds default to cartoonish images of "heaven"
like electronics slipping into sleep mode. We have
to vigilantly fight for other images. We need to name
this fluffy, boring image of heaven so we can move
past it. John's vision shatters every assumption we have
about heaven.

When he describes seeing a door open into Ouranos[15], John does not glimpse
anything close to quaint. John begins processing the realest real... like he's
peaking behind the curtain of all reality.

Heaven is like going backstage of the universe.

John's upward plunge into *Ouranos* feels less like arriving at some stiff country
club in the sky and more like a sea-weary sailor finally sinking their toes into
terra firma. He finds something solid—the deepest and most foundational layer
of existence. The dimension of reality where we "see" the Source of the universe, the Mystery at the heart of all things—the Good, the True, the Beautiful.

This is Ouranos. Heaven. Backstage of the universe.
The dimension of reality totally transparent to God.

And we need to pay close attention:

John's experience of this God-filled-dimension is in the present... not future.[16]

We popularly conceive of "heaven" as a reality exclusively in the future after we
die. But this conception will blind us to what John experienced, where heaven is

---

[15] Maybe the Greek word for "heaven" will help it feel strange again.
[16] "This is not a vision of the ultimate 'heaven,' seen as the final resting place of God's people. It is,
rather, the admission of John into 'heaven' as it is at the moment. The scene in the heavenly throne
room is the present reality..." (N.T. Wright, *Revelation for Everyone*, 44).

the God-reality parallel to our present. This deeper reality exists side-by-side with—or better, undergirds—reality on earth. All of this becomes abundantly clear as Revelation unfolds.

To be certain, the trumpet-voice does tell John that he will see "what must take place after this" (4v1). Revelation *will* offer us glimpses into the fullness of time, but those glimpses are not here.[17] Before he can see plans for the future, John must see the one who holds the future.

The technical word for John's experience is "theophany" or "revealing of God." God's Spirit (4v2) has gifted John with a picture of God's very self. And it's an experience ultimately beyond description.

We've all had experiences so powerful, or overwhelming, or wonderful that we're at a loss for words trying to describe it. Mystical experiences certainly fit the bill. But even more common experiences frequently escape our descriptions. We start to tell someone about our child being born, or swimming with dolphins, or the intensity of a car accident... and suddenly we're at a loss. Words fail. We find ourselves searching, straining, stretching for words to describe something beyond description. We raid our verbal warehouse, hunting for fresh metaphors, or analogies, or images to express the inexpressible.

That's John's challenge throughout Revelation.

As he searches for words worthy of his vision, John finds a robust arsenal in his verbal warehouse: the language of the Old Testament. The words, images, and metaphors of the Jewish scriptures are the most powerful language John possesses. Like nearly all of the earliest Christians, John has a Jewish background and a single-minded commitment to the God of Israel, Israel's Messiah, and

---

[17] Beale considers "what must take place after this" to be an intention parallel with Daniel 2.29 & 45 that affirms the "subsequent visions of the book are further visions concerned with an explanation of the 'latter days,' which are both 'realized' and 'unrealized,' set in motion but not consummated (as ch. 1 affirms), including the eschatological past and present as well as the future" (317-318). It could also mean something more like "here's what is coming next in this vision" (cf. Rev. 1.19).

Israel's scriptures. *The images of the Old Testament, therefore, become John's native tongue to describe what it's like to peek behind the curtain and glimpse the heart of the universe.*

Almost every image in John's account of heaven can be traced back to other parts of Scripture. One scholar called John's account of heaven "a symphony of Old Testament theophanies."[18] The various Old Testament visions, stories, and moments where God revealed himself have now been woven into seamless concert with each other. In his efforts to describe the indescribable, John decides to pour us a Scripture smoothie—a cocktail of worship—siphoning every sip of sacred writ to express the inexpressible:

> "Man oh man, what I experienced... it was like three parts Daniel, two parts Isaiah, mixed with some Ezekiel and a splash of Exodus. Those prophets sure had a clue. Heaven is nowhere close to fluffy or quaint or boring—it's the most alive place I've ever seen.

> "Energy like you've never seen. Like a nuclear reactor. Like the heart of a star. **Lightning** and **noise** and **peals of thunder** (4v5), like the energy, lightning, and fire on Mount Sinai when God appeared to Moses and a ragtag mass of former slaves.[19]

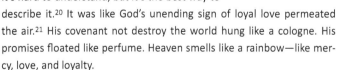

> "I remember there was **a throne**. And Someone sitting on it (4v2). Someone who reminded me of beautiful gems (4v3). And something like a **rainbow**, bright and beautiful like an emerald, encircled the throne and this Someone (4v3). Ezekiel once described God that way, and I know it's hard to understand, but it's the best way to describe it.[20] It was like God's unending sign of loyal love permeated the air.[21] His covenant not destroy the world hung like a cologne. His promises floated like perfume. Heaven smells like a rainbow—like mercy, love, and loyalty.

[18] Gorman, 106 citing Jean-Pierre Prévost's *How to Read The Apocalypse.*
[19] See Exodus 19.16-18.
[20] See the strange vision of Ezekiel 1 (specifically Ezek. 1.28).
[21] Gen. 9.16. This primal promise of mercy and loyal love is to all creation... not just the people of God.

"All around this Someone were other people. *Elders*—other kings (4v4). I'm pretty sure they were kings since they had golden crowns. I think they may have been a picture of all God's people because there were *twenty-four* of them—like the twelve sons of Jacob meeting the twelve apostles of Jesus. They were like a picture of all of us... the entire people of God. As difficult and painful and sometimes terrible as life sometimes looks, we're actually royalty. Even right now.[22]

"But we're not proud or pompous or pushy kings... nothing like Alexander or Domitian or Donald. God is making us humble kings. Lowly kings. Serving kings. Kings like Jesus. Because that's what I saw those twenty-four elders doing... they followed the lead of all living creatures (4v9) and worshipped that Someone on the throne.

"It's like God's people were learning to do what all creation was meant to do... worship. Maybe that's what was going on with the *four*[23] *living creatures* at the center (4v6-8). The prophets have seen these kinds of strange things before,[24] and here it was like all a picture of all creation fully present, fully alive,[25] and fully alert[26] before the throne.

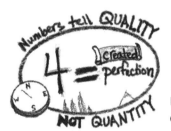

"All living things were practicing their purpose: praising the Lord God Almighty (4v8). And then we, the people of God, followed creation's lead with our own song (4v9-11). The limitless, gracious, seven-fold Spirit of God (4v5) was drawing us all there.

"It's impossible to do it justice... it was just beautiful."

That is something like John saw. The vision he experienced during the Lord's Day on Patmos was unspeakable. And yet he's been told to speak it. So he

---

[22] See Ephesians 2.6

[23] The **number four** represents another case of quality not quantity. Four seems to represent wide-sweeping, inclusive completeness *within creation*. Think of the "four corners" of the world (7.1, 20.8) and the cardinal directions of north, south, east, and west.

[24] **The living creatures** of Revelation 4 resemble the earthy cherubim of Ezekiel 1.4-11 but with the number of wings of the fiery seraphim from Isaiah 6.2. Much ink has been spilled speculating about these creatures, but they seem to be best understood as creatures representing all of creation. Animals wild (lion), domesticated (ox), flying (eagle), and human... from all the world

[25] The moving of the creatures with their wings reflects the visions of the seraphim in Isaiah (6.2).

[26] Perhaps creation is saying "I'm all eyes."

stretches language to its breaking point: Just backstage of the universe there's Someone on the throne, crackling with energy and life, surrounded by mercy, and endlessly praised by creation and the people of God. This Someone is so alive, so powerful, so joyful, so serene, that even primordial forces of chaos and confusion like "the sea" quiet before him (4v6).

In this vision, we glimpse that reality has a center. The universe has a nucleus. A pulsing heart behind all things—creating, sustaining, ordering.

John recognizes that there is a Someone
around whom everything orbits...
and it is not him.

And it's not you. And it's not me. We do not sit on the throne. The world does not orbit around us. We did not create the world, nor do we sustain it. Forget everything else for a moment, we don't even create or sustain our own lives. We don't even keep ourselves breathing.

We are not the center of the universe.

This might seem like the most obvious statement in the world, but we don't know it. Not in our guts. We're not the center of the universe. We don't really remember that... not often. Consider whatever is frustrating or angering us at the moment. How much of our anger—if we really got honest—is actually anger that the universe refuses to orbit around us?

This is the common denominator between a parking space stolen from us and the most complicated relationship problems we face:

> "No one seems to realize that all of creation orbits around me and my needs. What a disturbance in the universe. What an anomaly in space-time. People argue with me, disrespect me, and refuse to bend to my will. And on a daily basis! Don't they realize they should be centered around me, bowing to me, singing my praises?"

I wonder how much anger and pain, struggle and sin, worry and anxiety, insecurity and arguments—how much human suffering comes from our constant surprise that creation doesn't orbit around us? How much of human sin stems from our constant desire to sit on the throne that is not ours?

We live our lives *convinced* that if others would just do what we want, *then* there would be peace. *Then* the sea would be calm. If *they* would just do what we want, *then* we could forgive them. *Then* we would be able to sing.

"Don't they know that my needs are the realest real?"

A lot of times we quietly even think about God this way. We talk about "asking Jesus into our heart" as if the goal is to graciously give God a part of our life: "I'll make Jesus a part of my world because my life—my world—my heart—is the realest real thing." But Revelation sabotages all of this thinking.

We've heard Jesus say, "I stand at the door" (3v20) but when the door opens (4v1), it's less like we invite God into our lives and more like God pulling us into his life—into the life of heaven.

Frequently I want maintenance-man-Jesus to help all things work rightly in my small, selfish world. I demand that God fix this financial struggle, or solve the crisis of the day, or satisfy my cravings... and can you do it right now please? Most of the time I want God to confirm me as the center of the universe. And I am furiously frustrated that God never seems to do that.

I mean, I invited Jesus into my life...
so why isn't he fixing everything?

But maybe Revelation shows us something different. Maybe Jesus is asking us into *his* life. Maybe Jesus is inviting us—drawing us—into *his* heart. To take up a cross, to love others, to forgive others, to serve others when it's painful. Maybe a voice is calling all of us, "Come up here, I'll show what must take place... it looks like losing yourself in a new world."

Right now in your life—really, the conditions on the ground right now—God is painfully pulling you into his world. He's already opened the door, drawing you into a world where you're not on the throne, where you're not the center, where your selfishness doesn't win, where the world doesn't orbit around you. And that world is heaven; it's the best place any of us could possibly be.

Jesus inviting us into his life is harder than us inviting Jesus into ours. It takes a longer time. It's more painful. It requires us to surrender our fantasies about the throne. It means giving up our delusions that one day the world or that person or circumstances will orbit around us. It requires us to throw down every one of our crowns (4v10)—all our ambition, and accomplishments, and pride, and self-preoccupation—at the feet of Someone else.

The invitation of Jesus is difficult because Jesus invites us to die. Not physically. If it were only that easy God would slay us all. We've got to surrender our lives, die daily to our self-obsessed selves, and permit our pride to be crucified. And we do this so that truest Life can raise us.

Jesus knows that until we die to ourselves, we can never join the undying song behind the curtain. Until we answer Jesus's knock to exit our ego, our lives will never experience peace like crystal glass, or smell the fragrance of mercy, or behold the beauty of heaven, or enter the freedom of the children of God. We will forever be waiting for others to sing our praise, and forever we will be disappointed. It's time for the beauty backstage life to take centerstage.

//

Jesus, may I hear you knocking and trust that you want me. May I see the ways that you are drawing me into your life. Help me recognize the parts of my life where I claim the throne, expecting others to orbit me. Help me join your Church in following creation's in worship: Teach me how to daily sing the song of self-giving love. Amen.

Then I saw in the right hand of him who sat on the throne a scroll with writing on both sides and sealed with seven seals. And I saw a mighty angel proclaiming in a loud voice, "Who is worthy to break the seals and open the scroll?" But no one in heaven or on earth or under the earth could open the scroll or even look inside it. I wept and wept because no one was found who was worthy to open the scroll or look inside. Then one of the elders said to me, "Do not weep! See, the Lion of the tribe of Judah, the Root of David, has triumphed. He is able to open the scroll and its seven seals."

Then I saw a Lamb, looking as if it had been slain, standing at the center of the throne, encircled by the four living creatures and the elders. The Lamb had seven horns and seven eyes, which are the seven spirits of God sent out into all the earth. He went and took the scroll from the right hand of him who sat on the throne. And when he had taken it, the four living creatures and the twenty-four elders fell down before the Lamb. Each one had a harp and they were holding golden bowls full of incense, which are the prayers of God's people. And they sang a new song, saying:

"You are worthy to take the scroll
    and to open its seals,
because you were slain,
    and with your blood you purchased for God
    persons from every tribe and language and people and nation.
You have made them to be a kingdom and priests to serve our God,
    and they will reign on the earth."

Then I looked and heard the voice of many angels, numbering thousands upon thousands, and ten thousand times ten thousand. They encircled the throne and the living creatures and the elders. In a loud voice they were saying:

"Worthy is the Lamb, who was slain,
    to receive power and wealth and wisdom and strength
    and honor and glory and praise!"

Then I heard every creature in heaven and on earth and under the earth and on the sea, and all that is in them, saying:

"To him who sits on the throne and to the Lamb
    be praise and honor and glory and power,
for ever and ever!"

The four living creatures said, "Amen," and the elders fell down and worshiped.

05. THE INSIDE JOB OF THE LAMB

John's unspeakable vision began with all-powerful, unstoppable Jesus. This is a vision that never leaves him. We will see in Revelation 5 that as John's back-stage tour of the universe continues, the One who conquers by being crucified becomes *more* central, not less.

In Revelation 5, the importance of Jesus
gets amplified by a locked safe
that opens up a cosmic revolution.

You'll see.

Until this point, the identity of the Someone on the throne has been left vague and undefined (4v2-3). Many other apocalypses also do this, presumably out of reverence for the Holy Mystery that is God. We've seen that all of creation (*four living creatures*) continually worship... Someone. The people of God (*twenty-four elders*) follow creation's lead, bowing down to... Someone.

Someone is on the throne.

If Revelation 4 wanted us to realize we're not on the throne, then Revelation 5 wants us to recognize who is. Naming who is on the throne will eventually be the cosmic revolution. But before we discover the identity of this Someone, we're tantalized with a locked safe. And, as it turns out, this mysterious detail will play a critical role in John's entire story.

We join John in his vision, standing with him before the throne, and looking straight up—way up there—in the right hand of that mysterious Someone who sits on the throne. In that Someone's hand... we see a scroll (5v1).

This scroll is the locked safe of John's story.

A scroll that no one can open.

Wait—what's the big deal? A scroll in someone's hand would surprise no one in the ancient world. Scrolls were the equivalent of books or moleskin journals or three-ring binders. There was nothing exotic about scrolls; they were just where you wrote stuff down. What exactly is going on? Why draw attention to this scroll? No, you didn't miss anything, and, yes, this is the first time we're hearing about this scroll. John doesn't explain what this scroll is. Whatever it is, however, it's important.

It's a scroll sealed shut... sealed with **seven seals** (5v1).

Perfectly sealed.

At first glance this scroll resembles *an ancient will*. Under the Roman legal system, you needed six witnesses to sign and seal your will before you died.[1] You would write it, sign it with six other people, then roll it up and seal it shut with a glob of hot wax. All six witnesses would make their own unique impression in the wax using a ring or a stamp. And once you added your own unique glob of wax, you would have your legal Roman will complete... sealed with seven seals.

Other scholars have speculated that it could be *some kind of a legal document*. Since the vision of a heavenly throne room is a government setting on the

---

[1] Bauckham, *The Climax of Prophecy*, 248.

grandest scale, a nicely-sealed government document would fit nicely. And it is sealed with a symbolically-loaded number.

Still other scholars have thought *this scroll might be the Old Testament*. That would be a LOT of writing to squeeze onto just one scroll. But notice that this scroll has writing on both sides of it—inside and out.[2] Maybe someone has crammed the Torah, the Prophets, the Writings. And maybe the true meaning of the Old Testament is "locked up."

John doesn't explicitly tell us what this scroll is, but we have firm footing to think that this scroll is important. Attention gets drawn to it, it has lots to say (with writing on both sides), it is perfectly sealed (with seven seals), and it is resting in the right hand of the Center of the universe.

We gaze straight up at this scroll with John and an angel joins us in our staring (5v2). The angel cries out: "**Who is worthy** enough—significant enough—who is capable, deserving, fit enough—to break off these bits of wax and open this scroll? Who's got the security clearance to open this classified document? Who holds the combination to the safe?" This angelic question is yet another clue that the scroll is important.

The suspense builds. The silence deafens. The tragedy crushes because no one can open the scroll (5v3). No one in this entire epic throne room. No one "in heaven or on earth or under the earth." No one anywhere can open this scroll.

Whatever this scroll is, it has now graduated to super-duper important.[3] Evidently this scroll absolutely *must* be unsealed, opened, and understood. The scene acts like the fate of the universe depends on it.

---

[2] John either had a vision like Ezekiel's (Ezek. 2.8 - 3.4), or perhaps John is describing the indescribable by borrowing that image. The scroll in Ezekiel is the hidden declaration and plan of God that will be made known through his words and actions.

[3] That's highly technical language, I know.

We can see the gravity of the situation in John's reaction when he hears that the scroll is locked. He has a nervous breakdown (5v4). He "wept and wept." Think about that. John loses it... in the middle of heaven. This is a big clue that John has not time-traveled to the future. Tears don't make sense there. But John is now behind the curtain of the present reality, and he loses himself to despair because things are not as they should be yet. God's kingdom has not yet come on earth as it is in heaven. John's loved ones are still suffering. His churches are still struggling. Violence, evil, and darkness are still terrorizing the world. Tears aren't gone yet.

John is sobbing in heaven over this scroll.

Whatever this scroll is, it's not coupons for Kroger or an ad from Dennys. This scroll is not junk mail. Whatever it is, it's important.

This scroll will only escalate in importance as John's story continues. In chapters to come, we will see all hell breaking loose—the four horsemen of the apocalypse bursting forth—as the seals of this scroll are broken (6v1-8). And after the scroll is finally opened, we will see an angel hand it to John (10v2,8) and tell him to eat it (10v9-10). But you didn't miss anything. John never explicitly tells us what this scroll is or what it symbolizes.

The storytellers of modern, serialized television (i.e. *Mad Men* or *Breaking Bad*) often don't spoon-feed their audiences with ham-fisted, flat-footed explanations. And neither does John. Master storytellers expect a lot from their listeners—to follow the clues, to keep up, to connect the dots. Everyone reading Revelation has to make a decision—an educated guess, an intuitive leap—about what this scroll is. And when we do, the rest of Revelation begins to fall into place.

Remember that John has been drawn into God's dimension of reality. He has been beckoned to see "what must take place after this" (4v1). Since John hasn't time-traveled to the future, a really good guess would be that this scroll contains "what must take place." That's why this is such a classified document. This scroll seems to be the one sealed up way back in the book of Daniel.[4] There it contained God's purposes and how he would establish his kingdom.

This scroll contains the biggest answers to the biggest questions. Questions like: What is going on? Will it always be this way? Can it be otherwise? What's in store for the world? What are God's purposes in the world? How does Israel's story end, and how will God sort out history?

In short, this scroll seems to answer
the most important question of them all:
"How will God save the world?"

One of the world's leading Revelation scholars describes it this way:

> "The kingdom of God is to come on earth, as it already exists in heaven... It is a reasonable conclusion, then, that the scroll which the One who sits on the throne holds in his right hand (5:1) is his secret purpose for establishing his kingdom on earth... the scroll will reveal how it is to come."[5]

You're right—John includes no flat-footed exposition that says, "God's plans to save the world are sealed up in the scroll." Much like our theories about a TV series we love, we will have to hold this theory with open hands to see if it makes sense of the rest of Revelation. But the implied content of the scroll

---

[4] Scholars largely agree that John imagery draws on Daniel 8:26 and 12:4, 9 (and maybe 7:10). There the scroll explained the mysteries of God's coming kingdom of cosmic judgment and redemption.
[5] Here's the context for those curious: "...chapter 4 already enables us to understand, in a general sense, what the scroll's content must be. Chapter 4 is primarily a revelation of God's sovereignty, as it is manifest and acknowledged in heaven. Only a little acquaintance with prophetic-apocalyptic literature is required for a reader to infer that this vision prepares for the implementation of God's sovereignty on earth, where it is presently hidden and contested by the powers of evil. In other words, the kingdom of God is to come on earth, as it already exists in heaven. This is in fact strongly implied in Revelation's version of the song of the living creatures (4:8), who instead of proclaiming, like Isaiah's seraphim (Isa 6:4), that the earth is already full of God's glory, proclaim God as the One 'who was and who is and who is to come' — i.e. to the world to establish his kingdom. It is a reasonable conclusion, then, that the scroll which the One who sits on the throne holds in his right hand (5:1) is his secret purpose for establishing his kingdom on earth. From chapter 4 we know that God's kingdom must come:the scroll will reveal how it is to come." (Bauckham, *The Climax of Prophecy*, 249).

seems to be this: ***"How God will save the world?"*** This educated guess scores a point here because it makes sense of why John would have a nervous break-down in heaven. Right now, no one has a clue how God will save the earth.

John glimpses a scroll that—if someone could only open it—would give us the answers and show us the future. If someone could just understand it, we would discover God plans for rescuing human history, judging evil, bringing justice, healing wounds, and making all things new (20v5).

These are God's plans on a global level. How will God right the wrongs of Alep-po and Auschwitz, or famine and food shortages, or human trafficking and racism, or all the untold human suffering throughout the centuries. For every time we've read a headline or history book and asked: "How could things possi-bly be made right? Is there a future? Is there hope? How can these hurts be healed? Can this too be made new?"

These are also God's plans on a personal level. All of our individual stories par-ticipate in the sad saga of human history. Those same questions we ask about the world become excruciating when they're focused onto the intimate wounds of our own lives: "How could things possibly be made right? Is there a future? Is there hope? How can these hurts be healed? Can this too be made new?"

We usually distract ourselves away from these questions
because we share John's despair that no one can answer them.

This scroll answers our questions,
and John is weeping our tears.

We ask:

> "How *could* there be healing? The die has been cast, the decision made. Things have gone from bad to worse. There is no solution. The cancer is back. The holocaust happened. My loved one has already died. The wounds are too deep. What future could there be? How could anything be made new?"

72

We don't dare ask the hard questions or hope the hard hopes. We avoid them if at all if possible. Because (let's be honest) these questions are too heavy for us. If we went to some places, opened some memories, explored some wounds, or asked some questions, we feel we would weep forever. We can't open the scroll. Seemingly no one else can. So we choose distraction over despair.

...but then something happens.

Good news arrives through the people of God. The church speaks the gospel. One of the twenty-four elders says, "Do not weep" (5v5). (This is always the task of the Church: to speak good news into a heavily distracted, quietly despairing world.) The elder says:

> "Do not weep. Someone *can* make sense of the world, of history, of the future. There *is* someone who is Strong: the King from whom all hopes for a king grow.[6] Someone has conquered.[7] The Lion of Tribe Judah. He can make sense of our world and breathe hope into our lives. Weep not, someone *can* open the scroll."

"Thank goodness," we can almost hear John say, "that there's a Lion who is strong enough to open the scroll and tell us how God saves the world." And he looks to see this Conquerer, this Strong One, this Lion. But he's shocked at what he sees. He doesn't see a Lion... he sees a Lamb.

*We **hear** of a **Lion** (5v5),*
*but we **see** a **Lamb** (5v6).*

An unusual Lamb—freaking us out—with both its location and appearance. First, this Lamb seems to be standing in two places at once. Literally the Lamb is standing "in the middle" of the throne and "in the middle" of the *elders* (5v6).[8] English translations smooth out John's description in a variety of ways, but this

---

[6] That is, the "root" of David (5.5).

[7] The NIV unhelpfully switches its translation for *nikaō* right here to "triumph" (cf. 12.11, 17.14) but it's the same word that also gets translated as "victorious" (2.7, 11, 17, 26; 3.5, 12, 21; 15.2, 21.7), "conquer" (6.2; 13.7), and "overpower" (11.7). It's a theme that runs through John's vision that a more formal equivalent translation can help you see.

[8] The same word *mesō* ("in the midst" or "among") is used twice. Scholars debate exactly what John means. For my money, we're seeing the mind-bending reality of Jesus, fully God and fully man.

Lamb seems to be at the center of heaven's throne and also among the elders—among us.

Second, the Lamb has an odd appearance. Taken as literal description, this poor animal seems radioactive, with **seven horns** and **seven eyes** (5v6). This is where we need to remember that numbers and images in this style of writing are symbolic, not literal. **Eyes** are an ancient symbol of seeing, perception, and knowledge. **Horns** are a symbol of vitality, power, and strength. And this Lamb has **seven** of each. This Lamb is perfectly knowledgable and perfectly strong.

But the description gets stranger. This Lamb looks "as if it had been slain." The NIV's translation ("slain") makes it sound clean and clinical. The greek is more graphic... a better translation might be "slaughtered." It's messier. And that's the picture. Violently killed. Butchered.

This Lamb is slaughtered and still standing.

The strangeness climaxes as we combine location with appearance: this slaughtered lamb shares the center of heaven. The throne—that place where only God should be—is where we find the Lamb worthy to open the scroll (5v6).[9]

Now we've arrived at the cosmic revolution:

God has revealed Godself
in love willing to bleed.

The mysterious Someone on the throne has revealed himself.[10] Fog does not forever shroud the throne; God is no longer an unknowable Mystery. Jesus was already included in the definition of God at the beginning of chapter 1, so per-

---

[9] A careful reading of the text, of course, reveals a distinction between the Lamb and the Divine Throne-sitter. The Lamb both shares the center of the throne (5.6) AND ALSO receives the scroll from "him who sat on the throne" (5.7). There is simultaneously a *shared essence* AND a *distinction of identities*. The Lamb shares—and reveals!—God's essence while also having a recognizably distinct identity (5.13). Another essential instance can be seen by comparing 1.8 and 21.6 with 22.13, where the "Lord God" and "I, Jesus" (see 22.16) both express their identity as "Alpha and Omega" and "beginning and end." Jesus in John's gospel states it simply enough: "If you've seen me, you've seen the Father" (14.9).
[10] "Peek-a-boo—! Apocalypse—! This is what I'm like!" -God

haps the Lamb's presence on the throne shouldn't take us by surprise. But it always does.

The ultimate power of the universe is self-giving love.

Love willing to bleed
can open the scroll.

This does not give us a quick answer to our hardest questions. This is certainly not an easy answer. But the triumphant suffering of God's cross makes sense of everything... especially how God will save the world.

Humble, suffering, triumphant love
sits on the throne and opens the scroll,
showing us both who God is and how God saves.

God is a Giver, generously granting existence to everything (4v11).

God is a Lover, to the point of pain, suffering, and slaughter (5v6).

God is a Servant, to the point of death, even death on a cross.[11]

This is precisely why the four living creatures and the twenty-four elders bow down before him (5v9). This is why everything in existence gives him "praise and honor and glory and power" (5v13). This is why the scene grows stupidly big, with the circles around the throne expanding exponentially (5v11-14). God is holy, holy, holy ("other, other, other"). Beyond anything we expected. At the center of all reality we find crucified and resurrected Love.

I'm certain we'll never make *intellectual* sense of all the suffering in the world. We cannot even rationally comprehend the suffering of our own individual

---

[11] Philippians 2.6-8.

lives, much less the collective horrors of human history. There's so much pain, suffering, slaughter that all our efforts to cognitively parse it out are doomed to despair. To our heaviest questions and deepest wounds, the gospel offers us a *relational* answer instead of an *intellectual* answer. There are no easy answers... just the cosmic revolution that the healing heart of Heaven bears our wounds of violence and continues to stand in triumph—in the middle of the throne and in the middle of us.

Revelation shows us
a God who makes everything new
by healing it from the inside.

This cosmic revolution shows us a God who is never detached or disinterested or far away. Instead we glimpse a God who has felt our every pain, who knows our every weakness, who has experienced our every temptation, and who chose to die in our darkness. And then he burst out the other side and promises to carry us with him.

This is how God works in the world, how God heals history, how God saves us. It's a slow, patient, inside job driven by love-filled crucifixion and resurrection.

If we're honest, the decisions of this God don't strike us as having "seven eyes" or "seven eyes." We think, "surely there was a better way." And it's precisely in this thought that we're challenged to rethink our definitions of "perfect knowledge" and "perfect strength."

Evidently this is a better, deeper kind of rescue than we could imagine. God plunges into the worst of pain, sinks into the grossest of injustices, suffers the deepest of tragedies—to heal it all from the inside. Humanity is not alone in the slaughter. And after absorbing it all, the center holds.

God is still standing.
And we will too.

As we struggle to make sense of all our aching questions, Revelation invites us to trust that salvation is an inside job. God's victory does not avoid the slaughter but bears it, passes through it, transfigures it.

*How many of our doubts stem from
looking for a different kind God
and a different kind of victory?*

Most days of the week, I wish God would leap out from his hiding to make sense of the world. Why doesn't God just charge the battlefield and use his "horns" (strength) and "eyes" (knowledge) to overpower my circumstances, deliver a death-blow to my enemies, and arm-wrestle the world into compliance? I wish God would fix everything from the outside. And do it now please.

But that's not how God works.

Most of my frustration comes from desiring "a victorious life" that looks different from God's victory. In almost every area of our lives, we want our victories proud, immediate, and obvious. And painless. Don't forget that.

*We want the Lion's success
with none of the Lamb's suffering.*

But there's no "success" or "salvation" outside of the Lamb.

The *Lion's power* arrives in the *Lamb's patience.*

The *Lion's success* arrives in the *Lamb's surrender.*

The *Lion's supremacy* arrives in the *Lamb's service.*

*Patience. Surrender. Service.
Love—even when it means suffering.*

Those paths don't feel like victory. But Jesus assures us that they are. Even when they look like weakness—like an absurd dead-end—like a bloody mess—they are the path of deepest healing and hope and conquering.

The Lamb on the throne invites us to rethink the entire world. God uses his limitless knowledge and power to get inside and save—slowly, patiently, painfully. John recognizes the gospel with crystal clarity: the triumphant suffering of Jesus is how God saves the world.

Love willing to bleed
is how God saves the world.

And, as we are going to see, this is why the local church is so important. The people of Jesus join Jesus in the brutal, beautiful task of bleeding love for the sake of the world. We follow him in this. We keep trusting him. And one day we will see the scroll opened, our questions answered, and the world made new.

//

Lion of Judah, teach me to bring my hard questions to the throne. I want to learn to weep so I can learn to love. Surround me with the witness of the Church to remind me that hope is real and salvation is an inside job. Give me faith to trust your presence in my suffering. Help me follow you patiently, O Lamb of God, on the conquering path of surrender and servanthood. Amen.

I watched as the Lamb opened the first of the seven seals. Then I heard one of the four living creatures say in a voice like thunder, "Come!" I looked, and there before me was a white horse! Its rider held a bow, and he was given a crown, and he rode out as a conqueror bent on conquest.

When the Lamb opened the second seal, I heard the second living creature say, "Come!" Then another horse came out, a fiery red one. Its rider was given power to take peace from the earth and to make people kill each other. To him was given a large sword.

When the Lamb opened the third seal, I heard the third living creature say, "Come!" I looked, and there before me was a black horse! Its rider was holding a pair of scales in his hand. Then I heard what sounded like a voice among the four living creatures, saying, "Two pounds of wheat for a day's wages, and six pounds of barley for a day's wages, and do not damage the oil and the wine!"

When the Lamb opened the fourth seal, I heard the voice of the fourth living creature say, "Come!" I looked, and there before me was a pale horse! Its rider was named Death, and Hades was following close behind him. They were given power over a fourth of the earth to kill by sword, famine and plague, and by the wild beasts of the earth.

When he opened the fifth seal, I saw under the altar the souls of those who had been slain because of the word of God and the testimony they had maintained. They called out in a loud voice, "How long, Sovereign Lord, holy and true, until you judge the inhabitants of the earth and avenge our blood?" Then each of them was given a white robe, and they were told to wait a little longer, until the full number of their fellow servants, their brothers and sisters, were killed just as they had been.

I watched as he opened the sixth seal. There was a great earthquake. The sun turned black like sackcloth made of goat hair, the whole moon turned blood red, and the stars in the sky fell to earth, as figs drop from a fig tree when shaken by a strong wind. The heavens receded like a scroll being rolled up, and every mountain and island was removed from its place.

Then the kings of the earth, the princes, the generals, the rich, the mighty, and everyone else, both slave and free, hid in caves and among the rocks of the mountains. They called to the mountains and the rocks,

"Fall on us and hide us from the face of him who sits on the throne and from the wrath of the Lamb! For the great day of their wrath has come, and who can withstand it?"

After this I saw four angels standing at the four corners of the earth, holding back the four winds of the earth to prevent any wind from blowing on the land or on the sea or on any tree. Then I saw another angel coming up from the east, having the seal of the living God. He called out in a loud voice to the four angels who had been given power to harm the land and the sea: "Do not harm the land or the sea or the trees until we put a seal on the foreheads of the servants of our God." Then I heard the number of those who were sealed: 144,000 from all the tribes of Israel...

...After this I looked, and there before me was a great multitude that no one could count, from every nation, tribe, people and language, standing before the throne and before the Lamb. They were wearing white robes and were holding palm branches in their hands. And they cried out in a loud voice:

"Salvation belongs to our God, who sits on the throne, and to the Lamb."

All the angels were standing around the throne and around the elders and the four living creatures. They fell down on their faces before the throne and worshiped God, saying:

"Amen! Praise and glory and wisdom and thanks and honor and power and strength be to our God for ever and ever. Amen!"

Then one of the elders asked me, "These in white robes—who are they, and where did they come from?"

I answered, "Sir, you know."

And he said, "These are they who have come out of the great tribulation; they have washed their robes and made them white in the blood of the Lamb. Therefore, "they are before the throne of God and serve him day and night in his temple; and he who sits on the throne will shelter them with his presence. 'Never again will they hunger; never again will they thirst. The sun will not beat down on them,' nor any scorching heat. For the Lamb at the center of the throne will be their shepherd; 'he will lead them to springs of living water.' 'And God will wipe away every tear from their eyes.'"

When he opened the seventh seal, there was silence in heaven for about half an hour.

06. SEVEN SEALS

In our last chapter, John introduced a central, symbolic detail in his story: a mysterious scroll (5v1). This locked safe at the center of heaven seems to be "the will of God" in parchment form. It holds answers to the toughest questions that humanity can ask about the world or our individual lives. Questions like:

"When will God do something about a broken world? When will God do something about human suffering—especially the suffering of those who love God? When will God do something to make everything right?"

There's a theme emerging:
"When will God do something?"

Every single one of us long to read this scroll. Most of us have experienced terrible moments or excruciating seasons where we've cried out: "When are you going to do something, God? And things are such a mess, what could you possibly do to make things right?"

John began despairing when he realized that these questions are so heavy—this scroll is such a classified document—that no one could ever be able to read it. Imagine opening your mailbox to find an envelope with life-changing contents, but somehow it's impossible to open. That's the picture. In the ancient world, before you could read a scroll, you had to break off the bits of wax sealing it shut. But no one is "worthy" or weighty or strong enough to break these seals and make sense of the scroll.

But then John was told, "Do not despair! Do not weep!" Someone *can* open this scroll. And he saw Jesus, the Lamb. The crucified King can make sense of the world and our lives. And now Revelation 6 and 7 will describe the process of breaking the seals to "open" this scroll.

"When will God do something?" we ask.

"Just you watch," John answers.
"Jesus will make sense of the world."

Chapter 6 begins with possibly the craziest cluster of verses in the Bible. As the Lamb begins breaking into the scroll to reveal God's plan for the world, all hell starts breaking loose. This unassuming scroll quickly becomes a blockbuster set-piece. As the first four seals are broken, the four horsemen of the apocalypse materialize. Four colorful horses gallop forth, devastating the world on a massive scale.

Since most of us are unfamiliar with the genre of this letter (first-century apocalyptic), we keep reminding ourselves that Revelation is full of pictures and symbolism. *These are not literal horses or riders.* Scholars, both liberal and conservative, blessedly agree on the broad meaning of these symbols. *The seals seem to represent evils and struggles within human history.* And this makes sense on an intuitive level: before anyone can read the scroll, someone needs to confront everything keeping the scroll shut. These "seals" stand in the way of God's purposes in the world.

Before we can arrive at God's purposes, we have to honestly address our frequently nightmarish world. The Lamb must confront the miserable misadventures of human history before anyone can read the scroll. That's the seals.

The first four seals go together. They are "horses" charging against God's purposes. These horses (and their riders) embody some of the world's most profound, persistent, painful problems. And almost all human weeping can be traced back to their evils.

In the **white horse** (6v2), we find the human desire to dominate other human beings— everything from office gossip around the water cooler to the ambition of Alexander the Great, Napoleon, and Hitler.[1] And what happens when this desire to dominate, conquer, and win grows out of control? How do people eventually triumph over others? Why, with the **red horse** (6v3-4), of course! The horse of blood and fire; the hatred of war.

Then, once in power, conquerors often don't concern themselves with the scales of justice—with careful, sustainable systems to make sure everyone's needs are met. And so the **black horse** of economic injustice (6v5) follows. When the prices of food (like wheat or barley) skyrocket to twelve times the normal cost,[2] the greed of those in power says, "As long as it doesn't touch my luxury—the oil and wine—the new iPhone and stock prices—I don't care about rampant inflation or food shortages or the plight of others" (6v6).

Eventually comes the **pale green horse** (6v7-8) with its rider "Sickness" or "Death."[3] Notice that Death has been personified. Death is riding a horse with his sidekick Hades—the Greek underworld and prison of the dead—following closely behind. And they are allowed to bring death to **one-fourth** of the earth.

---

[1] It's sometimes thought that perhaps the first rider could be Jesus (or "the gospel") riding forth since Jesus is later depicted riding a white horse (19.11). This is, however, ultimately unsatisfying, because it breaks up a fourfold, thoroughly negative unit. It makes more sense to see Jesus appearance later as the "true and better" conquerer.

[2] Beale, 381: "The prices listed here are about eight to sixteen times the average prices in the Roman Empire at the time." That's like milk costing $25 a gallon or bread costing $36 a loaf.

[3] "Thanatos" is Greek for "death" but was also the word used for a pestilent disease. We do this too in English when we call the medieval bubonic plague "The Black Death."

These are the first obstacles that the Lamb confronts. We're getting closer to the scroll being opened—our questions closer to being answered—but things are getting worse. We see conquerings and war, economic injustice and pestilent death running amok.

What seems most troubling is how God himself seems to be ushering in these horrors. The Lamb is breaking the "seals," bringing them forward. And creation itself seems to welcoming it too. Did you notice how the four living creatures around the throne keep saying "come"?[4]

The Lamb seems to welcome the Horses.

If this isn't our lived experience, I don't know what is. God—who ought to be healing the world—frequently seems to be allowing the opposite. *Why would those around the throne welcome the worst?* We'll have to address this in later chapters... it's simply a hanging question mark at this point in John's story.

As the Lamb begins to open the scroll,
it's like all the heartache of human history
begins to unfold before us.

Which eventually begs the question: "What in the name of heaven and earth is going on? Sweet and merciful God, how much longer?" And that leads us to the next seal, where we see human confusion and collateral damage.

When the **fifth seal** is broken (6v9), we don't get a fifth horse. We see something different. The horses stop appearing after the wonderfully symbolic number of *four*. Now instead he sees the souls of those committed to Jesus under some kind of altar in heaven. They're asking "God, when are you going to judge? When will you right the wrongs of the world?" *Instead of a symbolic picture of evil's perpetrators, we see a symbolic picture of evil's victims.* True humanity gets crushed by evil.

---

[4] Revelation 6.1, 3, 5, 7.

Christians killed by tyrants or various local persecutions are pictured as under an altar in heaven. This seems a strange place for them to be until we remember where the blood of sacrifice would drain: it would pool under the altar. Those who have faithfully followed Jesus even to death are pictured as a sacrifice *for* the Lamb and *with* the Lamb.

But they won't be at peace until justice is done in the world.[5] Despite the fact that they are safe in God's reality, they are restless. Not all is right in the world. So they continue to do what the people of God must always do: pray through the world's toughest questions. Bring tough questions to God. And they sound like the psalms[6]:

"How long, Sovereign Lord? What is going on?
How do we make sense of this? What will you do?
When, O Lord, are you going to show up and do something?"

This, by the way, is the task of every local church. We must cultivate spaces like this altar. Spaces that are ruthlessly vulnerable, brutally honest, fearlessly realistic. There are no questions off-limits within the church. The saints are nothing if we not honest about our confusion and truthful about the world. And, in prayer, we courageously explore what seems to make no sense, offering it in faith to God.

As these "martyrs" (or "witnesses") ask their tough questions, we arrive at the wild and wooly **sixth seal.** When this seal gets broken, it sounds like we're approaching the end of the world. We're told of all manner of cataclysm—a great earthquake, the sun blackening, the moon reddening, stars falling like fruit from trees, the sky rolling up like a scroll, mountains fleeing, islands vanishing (6v12-14). It sounds like the end of the world, but these pictures are like the horses. These images are symbolic.

---

[5] This is more evidence that John's vision of heaven is not in the future but more like "backstage" occurring simultaneously with history. Christians who have been killed (6.9) by cruel tyrants or local persecution are "in heaven" but not at peace yet. These martyrs await universal justice.
[6] See especially Psalms 6, 13, 74.

If we try to read these images as literal happenings or predictions, logic unravels immediately. We cannot even read side-by-side verses in chronological sequence. The images conflict with each other. People hide in the mountains (6v15), but the mountains were just removed (6v14). On a strictly literal level these images don't make much sense.

The language sounds like the end of the world because this is frequently how the prophets of Israel talked about God getting ready to "show up and do something."[7]

When Ezekiel or Joel or Isaiah talk like this—and they do—they weren't talking about the end of space-time. They used earth-shattering, world-falling-apart kind of language to talk about God getting ready to act decisively *within* history. Isaiah, for example, uses this kind of language to talk about the imminent collapse of the Babylonian Empire and God's hand in it.[8] Here John seems to be raiding his Old Testament verbal warehouse for adequate language to describe God on the verge of acting. The Lamb is *about to* finally open the scroll.

But this earth-shattering language of God can be used another way. Jeremiah uses these kinds of images as anti-creation language.[9] He poetically describes the effect of human evil on God's good world. The kind of evil we see in the first four seals causes creation unravel—to fall apart at its seams. That is another layer to how John is using this language. Evil causes the world to disintegrate *and so* the Lamb is about to act.

The final barrier to God's purposes in this sixth seal can be glimpsed in people's reaction to the God about to act. People are resisting God—resisting his good and loving judgment that casts out evil, forgives sin, and restores what is bro-

---

[7] If you're looking to explore this, check out Isa. 24.1-6, 19-23; 34:4; Ezek. 32.6-8; Joel 2.10, 30-31; 3.15-16; Hab. 3.6-11. Most of the wild images in these prophetic passages "refer to the historical end of a sinful nation's existence occurring through divine judgment" usually through military conquest of one nation against another (Beale, 397). The strong language conveys the seriousness and imminence of God's work.

[8] Isaiah 13:10-13.

[9] Jeremiah 4:18-28.

ken. They don't want the Lamb to open God's purposes. They look around at a world falling apart and blame God—slandering his character as hateful and destructive. "It's that awful Lamb on the throne, he's trying to kill us!" (6v16-17).[10] They echo the cry of rebellious Israel, asking the mountains and rocks to *"fall on us and hide us."*[11] They don't realize that God has always been a God who brings judgment in order to restore.[12]

This symbolic language of the sixth seal points us toward the baffling reality that we, as humanity, would often rather cling to the death-filled world of Horses instead of receiving the life offered by the Lamb. God casting evil out of the world will inevitably also involve God casting evil out of us. And we continue to cling to our favorite scraps of sin and death. We consider the death we know preferable to the life that we don't.

We are afraid of the self-giving Lamb.
We fear Love remaking us.

Let's quickly recap. The ***first four seals*** show us the evils of human history. Then in the ***fifth seal*** we find a group of people crying out to the God of self-giving love, asking him to heal the world. And in the ***sixth seal*** we find another group who doesn't want that healing to come. They don't want the Lamb to burn away everything that is not love. You couldn't guess who they are—they are all of us, coming from all walks of life.[13] But they would rather live in a world full of war, economic injustice, and death than see Love remake the world. They prefer the Horses over the Lamb, a world of death over a world of life. As we look see everything blocking God's purposes in the world, this sixth seal—the hardness of the human heart—might be the most difficult to break through.

We often would rather hide than be healed.

---

10 See discussion of "wrath" in chapter 12.
11 Hosea 10:8.
12 Hosea 6:1-2; 10:1-2; 11:1-4, 8-11.
13 Revelation 19:18-19 depicts this same group of people as being allied with "the beast." They seem to be a cross-section of the "all kinds of people" who prefer death (the horses, the Beast, etc) to life.

Hard-hearted humanity shouts: "The judgment of God! The wrath of the Lamb! *Who can withstand this*!?" (6v17). And then John's vision immediately gives us an answer. It's an answer in super symbolic language, but it's definitely an answer. A group of angels, in preparation for the seventh seal and the final "breakthrough" of God, cries out: "You know, we really should 'seal' those who are going to make it" (7v2-3).

We're back to globs of wax. In the ancient world, a personalized mark stamped in wax could do a lot of things. As we've seen, it could seal a scroll shut. But it could also simply show ownership. For example, a king might put his unique, royal seal on a public decree so everyone knew it to be legitimate. We suddenly overhear a group of angels saying, "You know guys... let's mark out those who *are* going to make it. We should glob them, stamp them, seal them.[14] Because there *are* a lot of people who *will* withstand this."

So we hear them globing, stamping, and sealing a super-symbolic number: one hundred forty-four thousand (7v4-8).

12 x 12 x 1,000 = **144,000**

It's like the people of God counted on crack.[15] And the "counting" of this group sounds like one of those ancient military roll-calls we find in the Old Testament.[16]

Heaven hears our twisted question: "Who can **withstand** Love remaking the world?" So Heaven replies, "There's an entire army of people who will be able **standing** before the Lamb."[17]

---

[14] The stories of both Exodus 12 (marking doorposts at Passover) and Ezekiel 9 (marking foreheads) seem to be in John's background here. Like Passover, those who are marked seemed protected from the plagues against evil and "the Destroyer" (9.11, cf. Exod. 12:23, Heb. 11:28).
[15] The **number 12** is used to represent God's people (especially in a complete sense), while **1,000** (and its multiples) serves as a symbolic multiplier. The complete people of God... and make it bigger.
[16] The list here resembles **a military census** of the kind we see in Numbers 1-2. When the 144,000 reappear in 14.1, they are described symbolically as a victorious, ritually pure army (compare the comment about "virgins" in 14.4 to Deut. 23.9-10, 1 Sam. 21.5; 2 Sam. 11.8-11).
[17] The verb for "withstand" in 6.17 and "standing" in (*histēmi*)?

If we need any convincing that 144,000 is a symbolic number, we should pay careful attention to the difference between what John hears and what John sees.[18] John **hears** 144,000 being sealed (7v4) but what he actually **sees** is more people than anyone could count (7v9). More people are being saved than he thought. There is a massive, uncountable army of people who long to see a world remade by Love.

This is an army of the truly victorious. They wear **white robes** and anticipate a world with no hunger or thirst, with no tears or death (7v15-17). A world ruled by the Lamb and not by Horses. They know they have nothing to fear form the Lamb so they refuse to hide. On the contrary, they sing the Lamb's praises.[19] And they have actually joined in his suffering love. They have worked through **"the great tribulation,"** immersing themselves in the Lamb's very life and finding themselves made clean and victorious by his blood (7v14).[20]

And now we've finally reached what should be *the* decisive moment: the breaking of the **seventh seal** (8v1). There's been a dramatic interlude between the sixth and the seventh, introducing us to the army of martyrs. It's almost like John wants to build our anticipation to the breaking point. But now we finally arrive at the seventh seal... and we're surprised.

Because we have to wait.

> (8v1) "When he opened the seventh seal, there was silence
> in heaven for about half an hour."

With every barrier to God's purposes finally broken, we expect sound and fury, shock and awe.

But what we get is silence... and waiting.

---

[18] John has already used this technique of upending our expectations in 5.5-6, where he *hears* about the Lion of Judah but *sees* a slaughtered-but-standing Lamb.

[19] Their song is a remix of two of Isaiah's prophetic songs (Isa. 49.9-10 and Isa. 25.7-8).

[20] The first two horses (6.2-4) shows our depraved instinct about victory. We want to wear white so we resort to making others bleed red. Here, the Lamb makes us truly victorious (white) by plunging into the self-giving love of the Lamb's blood (red). The symbolism shocks us, because blood is not bleach.

There's something genius about this. It's just like our lives. We reunite with people waiting, longing, and asking, "God, how long until you do something!?" We all live it. We see chaos galloping all around us, and we trust that God is going to do something. We expect him to work at a certain moment in time, in a certain kind of way...

...and then God surprises us.

We expect God to save our world immediately—what's taking so long?— the scroll is unsealed!—surely everything is ready!!—and then we're left hanging. There's silence. We've got to wait... a little... longer. *The unfolding of God's plan takes a bit longer than we anticipated.* Even the souls under the altar in heaven longing for justice are told to wait a little longer while a few more Christians die (6v11). That's certainly not what we expected.

"But make no mistake," Revelation insists, "God IS saving the world."
It's just never HOW we expected or WHEN we expected.
Faithfully following Jesus frequently means waiting a little longer.

Frequently, the life of faith involves waiting in silence.
Following Jesus means we're called to live faithfully, to
pray faithfully, and to die faithfully. There are no shortcuts.
Our lives must be lived. And life frequently demands staying
the course even as heaven seems to "wait."

If that's where you are right now—like your world is getting worse, like heaven is silent, like God's plans are forever coming and never arriving, take courage. God has better plans than we can imagine. And we won't be in silence forever. In the grand scheme of things it's not long... only half an hour.[21]

---

[21] "The term **'half-an-hour'** has no obvious mystical or symbolic meaning, although Henry Swete's simple explanation is attractive: 'Half-an-hour, though a relatively short time, is a long interval in a drama and makes an impressive break between the Seals and the Trumpets.' We can perhaps imagine the lector pausing at this point for dramatic effect: the hearers naturally want to find out what will happen next. While time may be scrambled in the Apocalypse, it still rehearses a story, like our own lives, a sequence of happenings that can only be lived and told in time." (Mangina, 118)

Frequently, the life of faith also involves sitting in suffering. Intricate theories about Revelation and the end of the world argue that God will spare his people from "suffering" (or "the tribulation"). But it's worth noting that everyone in that uncountable singing army comes out of **the great "tribulation"** (7v14). If anyone ever implied that giving devotion to Jesus could help you escape all suffering, they were dead wrong. In fact, Revelation seems to imply that God may be most deeply at work when our world appears most falling apart.

When **the great "suffering"** arrives in our lives, we can run, hide, and rebel. Or we can trust that Love is actually at work. We can enlist in his singing army of love who builds for the Lamb's new world before it has fully arrived.

Through silence and suffering, the Lamb works the purifying fire of his love into the otherwise inaccessible places of our souls. Jesus is ever-present and committed to our cure... even when it means the path to wholeness will be hard. Lean into the waiting, for he is there. Lean into the silence, for he is loving. And he is patiently at work in all things to make us more like him (i.e.the definition of salvation).

This is the sacred mystery and severe mercy: *Jesus does not save us from suffering; he frequently saves us through it.* He pierces our pride, crucifies our self-sufficiency, breaks through our defenses, and then... resurrects us. Even when horses are galloping, earth suffering, and heaven silent. "Make no mistake, " insists Revelation, "God is already at work... God is already saving."

And you will not wait forever before you see it.

//

Lamb on the Throne, may I long for your good judgment to break every barrier into the world. Come quickly and banish the galloping forces of evil. Burn away all that is not love. Teach me through silence and suffering, giving me eyes to recognize your always-surprising rescue. May my life be shaped into praise by the news that you claim me. Amen.

When he opened the seventh seal, there was silence in heaven for about half an hour.

And I saw the seven angels who stand before God, and seven trumpets were given to them.

Another angel, who had a golden censer, came and stood at the altar. He was given much incense to offer, with the prayers of all God's people, on the golden altar in front of the throne. The smoke of the incense, together with the prayers of God's people, went up before God from the angel's hand. Then the angel took the censer, filled it with fire from the altar, and hurled it on the earth; and there came peals of thunder, rumblings, flashes of lightning and an earthquake.

Then the seven angels who had the seven trumpets prepared to sound them.

The first angel sounded his trumpet, and there came hail and fire mixed with blood, and it was hurled down on the earth. A third of the earth was burned up, a third of the trees were burned up, and all the green grass was burned up.

The second angel sounded his trumpet, and something like a huge mountain, all ablaze, was thrown into the sea. A third of the sea turned into blood, a third of the living creatures in the sea died, and a third of the ships were destroyed.

The third angel sounded his trumpet, and a great star, blazing like a torch, fell from the sky on a third of the rivers and on the springs of water— the name of the star is Wormwood. A third of the waters turned bitter, and many people died from the waters that had become bitter.

The fourth angel sounded his trumpet, and a third of the sun was struck, a third of the moon, and a third of the stars, so that a third of them turned dark. A third of the day was without light, and also a third of the night.

As I watched, I heard an eagle that was flying in midair call out in a loud voice: "Woe! Woe! Woe to the inhabitants of the earth, because of the trumpet blasts about to be sounded by the other three angels!"

The fifth angel sounded his trumpet, and I saw a star that had fallen from the sky to the earth. The star was given the key to the shaft of the Abyss. When he opened the Abyss, smoke rose from it like the smoke from a gigantic furnace. The sun and sky were darkened by the smoke from the Abyss.

And out of the smoke locusts came down on the earth and were given power like that of scorpions of the earth.They were told not to harm the grass of the earth or any plant or tree, but only those people who did not have the seal of God on their foreheads. They were not allowed to kill them but only to torture them for five months. And the agony they suffered was like that of the sting of a scorpion when it strikes. During those days people will seek death but will not find it; they will long to die, but death will elude them.

The locusts looked like horses prepared for battle. On their heads they wore something like crowns of gold, and their faces resembled human faces. Their hair was like women's hair, and their teeth were like lions' teeth. They had breastplates like breastplates of iron, and the sound of their wings was like the thundering of many horses and chariots rushing into battle. They had tails with stingers, like scorpions, and in their tails they had power to torment people for five months. They had as king over them the angel of the Abyss, whose name in Hebrew is Abaddon and in Greek is Apollyon (that is, Destroyer).

The first woe is past; two other woes are yet to come.

The sixth angel sounded his trumpet, and I heard a voice coming from the four horns of the golden altar that is before God. It said to the sixth angel who had the trumpet, "Release the four angels who are bound at the great river Euphrates." And the four angels who had been kept ready for this very hour and day and month and year were released to kill a third of mankind. The number of the mounted troops was twice ten thousand times ten thousand. I heard their number.

The horses and riders I saw in my vision looked like this: Their breastplates were fiery red, dark blue, and yellow as sulfur. The heads of the horses resembled the heads of lions, and out of their mouths came fire, smoke and sulfur. A third of mankind was killed by the three plagues of fire, smoke and sulfur that came out of their mouths. The power of the horses was in their mouths and in their tails; for their tails were like snakes, having heads with which they inflict injury.

The rest of mankind who were not killed by these plagues still did not repent of the work of their hands; they did not stop worshiping demons, and idols of gold, silver, bronze, stone and wood—idols that cannot see or hear or walk. Nor did they repent of their murders, their magic arts, their sexual immorality or their thefts.

07. SIX TRUMPETS (JESUS IS NOT BATMAN)

Is everyone keeping up? Have we lost anyone? Now might be a good time for a recap: Revelation aims to reveal something—for us to see Someone. John's letter is an Apocalypse not an Almanac. It's more a game of peekaboo than a list of predictions. Revelation aims to reveal God through the person of Jesus.

Revelation is ancient mail
that reveals Jesus
in apocalyptic style.

John experiences a mystical vision of God-revealed-as-Jesus (ch 1),
and Jesus addresses seven ancient communities that he loves (ch 2-3).

Then John is drawn "behind the curtain" into heaven
where he glimpses God's mysterious plan to save the world (ch 4-5).

And although this plan looks unknowable and impenetrable,
Jesus can break through everything blocking God's purposes
and will show us how God is going to save the world (ch 6-7).

That's the story so far.

When we ended last chapter, arriving at the seventh and last seal, we expected God's purposes to be finally be revealed. Maybe we even expected the end of the world. But instead we were met with a surprising silence.

We have to wait
a little longer.

As the seals were broken, our eyes watched the earth—seeing the horrors of human history (seals 1-4), the confusion and collateral damage (seal 5), and the hardheartedness of humanity as God prepares to act (seal 6).

John now draws our attention away from the tragedy unfolding "on the stage" of earth and directs it toward what is happening "backstage" in heaven. Like a lecturer pausing mid-sentence or a teacher quietly waiting, *the silence of heaven commands our attention.* The thunderous, pulsating, music of heaven has all stopped with the seventh broken seal. What will happen?

Well, a couple of things happen during heaven's silence. First, **trumpets** get handed out to seven angels (8v2). Second, another angel with some kind of container for burning incense (i.e. *a censer*) approaches an altar in heaven (8v3). While the brass section of heaven begins receiving instruments, this angel is gathering a cupful of prayers to bring before the throne. This altar seems to be the same one towering above the slaughtered people of God (6v9).[1] Now the gut-wrenching questions of the saints ("How Long?") are pictured as incense rising up before God (8v3-4).[2] From a narrative perspective, the silence seems to allow the prayers to be heard.

These are the prayers of the martyred; the prayers of the murdered. The prayers for justice in the world... for all things to finally be made right.

---

[1] Although ancient Israel had two altars—the altars of Burnt Offering outside the tabernacle/temple and the altar of incense inside—John's vision seems to combine the two. "...the heavenly altar combines aspects of both the incense altar and the altar of of burnt offering in the earthly temple" (Beale, 455).
[2] The image was firmly established by John in Revelation 5.8. He's drawing on an ancient image (cf. Ps. 141.2) that was still used by contemporaries like Paul (Eph. 5.2, Phil. 4.18).

The suspense has been mounting—the silence deafening—but suddenly, in a flash, we see this container of prayers get mixed with fire and thrown to the earth.[3] Heaven launches a prayer bomb, shattering the silence with an explosive light show—thunder, rumblings, lightning, an earthquake (8v5).[4] Heaven has cleared its throat as it prepares to respond.

If we thought the breaking of the seventh seal to be a little anticlimactic, perhaps we should reconsider. It seems like everything from here forward flows from this broken seventh seal.[5] In imagery from both Exodus[6] and Joshua,[7] trumpet blasts will now begin shaking the world.

These trumpets usher in some of the most notoriously difficult reading in the book of Revelation. *Suddenly John's vision begins to look like unbridled chaos. In the **first four trumpets** alone we see:*

- *one-third of grass and trees* incinerated by **fiery, bloody hail** (8v7),
- *one-third of the sea **turned to blood*** and *one-third of ships and sea life destroyed* by **a fiery mountain** (8v8-9),
- *one-third of the rivers poisoned* by **a falling blazing star** (8v10-11), and
- *one-third of every light in the sky blotted out by **darkness*** (8v12).

Boy... that escalated quickly.

These first four trumpets arrive as a packaged set just like the four seals (the horses). A lot is happening all at once. One, two, three, four. Land, salt water,

---

[3] Ezek. 10.1-7 (cf. Beale, 459).

[4] This is a repetition of the events found 4.5. This repetition is included and escalated every time a cycle of seven ends—after the seals (8.1, 5), after the trumpets (11.15, 19) and after the bowls (16.17-21).

[5] "Thus the formula [see note above] serves to anchor the divine judgments of chapters 6-16 in the initial vision of God's rule in heaven in chapter 4. It also creates a particular kind of relationship between the three series of seven judgments. The judgment of the seventh seal-opening, the climax of the first series, described by this formula in 8:5, encompasses the whole course of the judgments of the seven trumpets, and similarly the judgment of the seventh trumpet, described by this formula in 11:19b, encompasses the whole series of bowl judgments, climaxing in the final, fullest elaboration of the formula in 16:18-21." (Bauckham, *Climax of Prophecy*, 8)

[6] Exodus 19 tells the wildly significant story of YHWH's fiery appearance before Israel at Mount Sinai. The story includes an odd, recurring detail: as God arrives there is a "sound" like a "trumpet" that perpetually increases in intensity (Exod. 19:16, 19; 20:18, cf. Deut. 4:12). It is the mysterious "sound" of God arriving. We have already seen this "God-arriving image" in Jesus's voice (1:10, 4:1).

[7] Seven-fold trumpet blasts eventually make the promised land secure from enemies (Josh. 6:1-21).

fresh water, sky. Every base covered. Every direction of creation. That's the symbolism of *"four."* These trumpets touch the entire world.

Although it may feel like unbridled chaos, from a storytelling perspective these trumpets are as controlled as a thermostat. In the transition from the "seals" to "trumpets," the chaos has only increased moderately: *from one-fourth to one-third.*[8] It might feel like we're crash-landing but this is actually "a controlled descent into chaos."[9] And perhaps there's a good reason for the pilot making this descent.

The *seven seals* revealed a God who breaks through all barriers to achieve his purposes. These *seven trumpets* reveal a God who answers the prayers of his people. These trumpets are a picture of prayers rising before God that detonate change in the world. God *always hears* the cries of his people.[10] And heaven *will answer* with trumpet blast.[11] God will liberate his people (Egyptian plagues) and shatter the power of evil (Jericho trumpets).

If we read Revelation straight through looking for chronological, literal predications, the trumpets will baffle us. We'll find ourselves wondering how only one-third of the sea could turn into blood? I mean, wouldn't it mix together with the other two-thirds? And—wait a second—I thought the sun and stars disappeared with seal six (6v12-13)? Weren't the heavens rolled up? Didn't the sun turn black like goat hair while stars fell like figs?[12]

Those would be valid and baffling questions *if* John were giving us chronological and literal descriptions of future events. *The book of Revelation, however, is an Apocalypse not an Almanac*—it's not predicting how many inches of rain or blood we should expect. This book makes little sense as literal predictions about the future's weather. If that's what we're looking for, we will be continually confused when we approach Revelation. That's simply not what the book is.

---

[8] In 6.8 (the fourth seal/horse), we're told that Death is given power over one-fourth of the earth.
[9] Mangina, 119.
[10] The motif of God hearing his people's cry also sets off the story of the exodus (Exod. 2.23-25).
[11] Trumpets are also an image in Zephaniah accompanying "the great day of the YHWH" (1.14-16).
[12] See Revelation 6.12-13.

But if you're looking for *promises about God's character*, you begin realizing the artistic genius at work here.[13] He's revealing what God—what Jesus—is like. This is the language of peekaboo more than prediction. The symbolic language of the trumpets reveal what God and his kingdom are like.

What is God like? God answers prayer. And one day heaven's answers to our biggest requests will be undeniable. Old-Testament-powerful. Plagues-of-Egypt-spectacular. God is going to overthrow evil.

These first four trumpets sound vaguely familiar because they are a remix of the Exodus story.[14] In that iconic story, we're told of God sending ten spectacular plagues to warn the Egyptians and their king (Pharaoh) to turn from evil. And these plagues also serve to rescue God's people from suffering in slavery. With these first four trumpets, we see three of those plagues returning—fiery hail, water turned to blood, and darkness blotting out the daylight.[15]

What God is like? God rescues us from slavery and suffering. He breaks through everything blocking his purposes—everything opposed to love. God will answer the gut-wrenching prayers of his people with an explosive answer like the ultimate Exodus. A day is coming when God will rescue the world from sin, death, and the devil. God will confront and conquer all the powers of darkness that enslave his people. God will destroy everything killing creation (11v18).

Peekaboo!—this is what God is like! And it's really good news.

---

[13] "[The trumpets and bowls] form a highly schematized literary pattern which itself conveys meaning. Their content suggests, among many other things, the plagues of Egypt which accompanied the exodus, the fall of Jericho to the army of Joshua, the army of locusts depicted in the prophecy of Joel, the Sinai theophany, the contemporary fear of invasion by Parthian cavalry, the earthquakes to which the cities of Asia Minor were rather frequently subject, and very possibly the eruption of Vesuvius which had recently terrified the Mediterranean world. John has taken some of his contemporaries' worst experiences and worst fears of wars and natural disasters, blown them up to apocalyptic proportions, and cast them in biblically allusive terms. The point is not to predict a sequence of events. The point is to evoke and to explore the meaning of the divine judgment which is impending on the sinful world... [John's structure] makes a wonderfully varied but coherent evocation of the biblical and theological meaning of the divine judgment... but if we try to read it as prediction of how that judgment will occur we turn it into a confused muddle and miss its real point." (Bauckham, *The Theology of Revelation*, 20-21)
[14] See Exodus 7-11.
[15] The plagues in Exodus are as follows: fiery hail (9.23), water to blood (7.20-21) and poisoned (7.24), selective darkness (10.21-23).

That's what John seems to say with the first four trumpets. But as the trumpets continue, the thermostat of chaos keeps climbing... and makes for disturbing reading. And we get a warning that the heat is rising.

An eagles soars into the scene—into a world shaken by answered prayers. He announces **three "Woes"** to everyone who wants nothing to do with Love or Truth or Goodness (8v13).[16] The three remaining trumpets will be "woes"—the verbal version of big red stop signs for all who hate.[17] The eagle knows that haters face rough waters and wants to spare them. And as we hear of the next trumpet, we discover how right he was.

The **fifth trumpet** blows and we get our **first woe:** a "star" falling out of the sky. This "star" is a spiritual personality—an angel according to verse 11—falling to earth.[18] That sounds a little foreboding in itself, but then this personality is given "the keys" for opening up "the Abyss" (9v1-2).

You know... **the Abyss**? Picture a blackhole—you know, the kind in space? Now picture a primordial, evil blackhole... in the ocean. That's kinda what the ancients meant by "the Abyss." A watery heart-of-darkness-sort-of-thing where evil is imprisoned.[19] And this "fallen star" is given "the keys" to open it up. Presumably by heaven. Presumably by Jesus himself. Because last we checked, Jesus was the only one with keys (1v18). So... why on earth is heaven allowing keys to go to a **"fallen star"**[20]? Handing over this key doesn't appear to bring

---

[16] The eagle's warning addresses the **"inhabitants of the earth"** (8.13). This actually does *not* simply mean "all human beings." Instead "inhabitants of the earth" or "earth-dwellers" seems to be a "semitechnical description for the human race in its hostility to God" (Mounce, 48). Whenever people are described this way in Revelation, they are living in a hardened pattern of hatred toward God (cf. 11.10; 13.8,12; 17.2,8).

[17] "...the eagle's cry sounds hopeful in context. Though the heavenly bodies above be darkened, the eagle still soars *en mesouranēmati* (literally, "in the middle of heaven"), declaring that the earth-dwellers' future is no fixed law of the Medes and the Persians. Fate does not rule; God rules. There is still time to repent and to live" (Mangina, 121-122).

[18] We've seen this already in Revelation 1.20.

[19] "The Abyss," *The Anchor Bible dictionary: Volume 1: A - C.* New York: Doubleday, 1992.

[20] Revelation 9:11 gives this star two names: **Abaddon** and **Apollyon**. Tomes have been written exploring these, but seems like the most significant observation we could make in short space: "Many commentators have seen in the name Apollyon a reference to the god Apollo who may sometimes have been symbolized by a locust. Apollo's name originated from the same Greek word that is behind Apollyon... If there is such an allusion in mind here, then the point might be to show that the devil himself is behind Domitiian and all other rulers who claimed to be an incarnation of Apollo. Augustus enjoyed playing the role of Apollo in private dinner plays, and Romans sometimes referred to Apollo as the "Tormenter"...This would also be a further hint that the figure in v 11 is Satanic and that evil angels are to be identified with sinful rulers and peoples" (Beale, 504).

about anything good. It sounds like hell itself creaks open to release a swarm of demonic, monster locusts (9v3-11). And this "fallen personality" leads haters of God into a tortured-kind-of-existence.[21] It's horrible. The only silver lining is that it doesn't last forever. The life-cycle of actual locusts is a brief but devastating five months. And this is like that. Limited.[22]

All of this, by the way, is still plague imagery. It's like the eighth plague of Egypt[23] and the prophetic warnings of Joel[24] have mutated into a swarming, destructive army of locusts on LSD led by the devil himself.

The woes continue to arrive. The echoes of the eagle's voice remind us that two more trumpets are on the way—two more "woes" yet to come for haters (9v12). So the **sixth trumpet** blasts and we see the **second woe**. More chaos erupts in a notoriously-difficult-to-interpret passage: **four angels** dry up the Euphrates River allowing an unstoppable invading army of inconceivable size[25] to **kill one-third of humanity** (9v13-19). An army clothed in smoke and flame[26] riding demon horses with lion heads. That breathe fire. Oh, and they have snake tails. Yeah... stuff of nightmares.

It seems this sixth trumpet combines Egypt's final plague with first-century fears and turns them to eleven. The final plague of the Exodus story involved the "destroyer"[27] or "destroying angels"[28] arriving to slay Egyptians. That's the picture here—evil angels unchained (9v14) and leading an army. That army was, of course, a first-century fear. Terrorism and global viruses haunt twenty-first

---

21 Rev. 9.11 calls him this personality "the Destroyer" in a few languages.

22 Wright, *Revelation for Everyone*, 87.

23 Exodus 10.1-20

24 A central image of the prophet Joel is that of a vast—likely symbolic—**army of locusts** that decimates Israel's land of promise (Joel 1.4ff). Despite all the damage done by these "locusts," Joel hears Yahweh promising that he will restore the people of God (e.g. Joel 2.25).

25 "Myrias" (or **myriad**) is 10,000, and it is the largest number in the Greek language. When John says 10,000 x 10,000 x 2, he's making the size and scope super-massively big and then doubling it. He's trying to overwhelm us, not give us a math problem.

26 The **colored breastplates** of horse and rider correspond to the "plagues" they inflict: fire (red), smoke (dark blue), and sulfur (yellow). (See Mounce, 196.) It's as if these horsed riders are embodiments of destruction (cf. Gen. 19:24; Rev. 14.10-11; 18.18; 19.3; 20.10; 21.18).

27 Exodus 12:23.

28 Psalm 78:49.

century imaginations in the way that an invasion from the East haunted first century imaginations. Everyone in the Roman Empire held their breath about the mysterious Parthian Empire over the Euphrates River. They even had horse-back archers who could attack as they approached or even after they had passed—harming from both "mouth" and "tail."[29]

But the sixth trumpet—with its grotesque details—adds downright hellish images to this final plague and this military fear.[30] Scholars don't agree on their precise meaning,[31] but multiple threads connect the fifth trumpet. Trumpets five and six both seem concerned with the cancerous growth of wickedness.[32] And even this evil is not beyond the sovereign sphere of God—he permits it only for a time. The picture portrays how evil distorts, harms, and consumes the human race... especially when we worship anything other than the Lamb.[33]

What is God thinking? Why did creation itself welcome the horsemen (6v1-8)? Why does Jesus allow spiritual personalities to rebel, deceive, and torture (9v2-11)? Why permit mass destruction to loom large over the idolatrous human race (9v13-19)? The "problem of evil" grows ever larger in John's vision, and there's nothing like an answer in sight. It's still hanging there.

How exactly should we understand God allowing evil room to roam to be an answer to prayers? We will have to wait for the **seventh trumpet** (also called "the seven bowls") for an answer. And besides, we already have enough here to fill out the rest of a chapter.

Let's state the obvious: the trumpets are incredibly difficult to interpret. They qualify as some of the most sophisticated (i.e. hard to understand) symbolism in the entire Bible. The fog is thick here, and there is no scholarly or saintly con-

---

[29] Caird, 122.

[30] "...the impact of the vision is diminished by speculative attempts to provide theological equivalents for specific items. Better to experience the vision as a whole than to trivialize it by excessive interpretation of details" (Mounce, 195-196).

[31] N.T. Wright with typical candor comments on "a whole spectrum of speculation" from futuristic battles with tanks and helicopters to spiritual allegorization (Wright, *Revelation for Everyone*, 91).

[32] The hellish imagery, the escalation from a tortured existence to an ended existence, and these trumpets as a couplet escalating the stakes of the first four.

[33] "The hordes of demons who fairly swarm through these chapters exercise their power only to the extent that we worship them, 'construct' them, and so endow them with life" (Mangina, 126).

sensus. So if the church lacks consensus, can these images tell us anything? What can these images point us toward? What do they tell us? Can we make some kind of general (if tentative) decision about these things?

I think we can; and I think we must. We must realize something about God's endgame in answering prayer. Sometimes God directly orchestrates the over-throwing of evil (*first four trumpets*). And other times God allows evil to consume itself (*fifth and sixth trumpets*). But what is God's goal? What is God working toward whenever and however he answers prayers?

The end of Revelation 9 is worth reading again:

> (9v20-21) The rest of mankind who were not killed by these plagues still did not repent of the work of their hands...they did not stop worshiping demons, and idols of gold, silver, bronze, stone and wood—idols that cannot see or hear or walk. Nor did they repent of their murders, their magic arts, their sexual immorality or their thefts.

Can you hear the ache behind these verses? "Ugh... they're still choosing death... what will it take for people to choose life?" Despite God beginning to overturn evil—pictured in plagues of Egypt, eagles shouting stop signs, a tortured existence opposing God, and allowing evil to consume itself—despite it all, people are still refusing to repent. Still. Ugh.

Human repentance is the aim of heaven's activity—that people would turn from death and choose life. Because when we harden ourselves against obedience to Love, we choose a plagued life. Existence becomes tortured. We eventually long to die even with death eluding us (9v6). But the Lamb longs for humanity to be full of life. Even when answers to prayer are fiery, painful, and surprising, the aim is always mercy, healing, and new creation.[34]

---

[34] "The Apocalypse narrates these events not in order to explain the way things are now, however, but to hold out the hope that *things will not always be like this*. Revelation's concern with cosmic happenings is strictly framed by its concern for the covenantal relationship between God and humankind. The world as we know it is beset by evil, sin, death, and the devil's reign of terror. The Apocalypse employs the idiom of cosmic catastrophe to describe the overturning of the present order and the coming of God's kingdom. Judgment is ordered toward mercy: thus the waters of bitterness (Rev. 8:10-11) will be sweet and by 'the river of the water of life, bright as Crystal, flowing from the throne of God and of the Lamb' (22:1)" (Mangina, 121).

Whatever these trumpets point us toward, they're not about Jesus with his pockets full of painful tricks, enjoying the rush of beating up the bad guys. And that's what we're tempted to think about passages like this, isn't it? I have heard some sermons actually explicitly teach this. They make it sound like a personality change has taken place in Jesus. It's as if the Jesus of the gospels has been brooding darkly over every injustice inflicted on him, and now—here, in Revelation—he's finally returning to deliver dark vengeance.

Sometimes influential pastors even present it this way:

> Revelation fills in the gaps of Jesus's personality that we don't find out about when we read the four gospels. Revelation tells us about Jesus the cage-fighter. Jesus who delights in delivering body blows to other people (never us). Jesus coming back with a utility belt full of tricks to sadistically inflict fear and pain on his enemies. One day Jesus will make the bad guys bleed and by *their* stripes the world will be healed."[35]

But that doesn't sound like the Lamb. That sounds like Batman. As we read these hard passages in Revelation, we become tempted to think that Jesus is coming back with a dark alter ego. We're tempted to think that God will one day answer prayers for mercy with punishment.

And that's why (quick Bible interpretation lesson) it's of utmost importance that we remember: *We interpret what is unclear in Scripture through what is clear in Scripture.*

These are controversial, notoriously difficult passages full of sophisticated symbolism. So we must interpret them through what is uncontroversial, plain, and literal. And we look at the life of Jesus to find that.

---

[35] That is a paraphrase of Mark Driscoll. His actual, verbatim written statement is: "In Revelation (the last book of the New Testament), Jesus is a prize-fighter with a tattoo down His leg, a sword in His hand and the commitment to make someone bleed. That is the guy I can worship. I cannot worship the hippie, diaper, halo Christ because I cannot worship a guy I can beat up." Father, forgive us all.

The hard parts of Revelation
do not guide us to
the identity of Jesus.

The identity of Jesus
guides us through
the hard parts of Revelation.

We know Jesus.

Jesus is the one feeding the masses and healing ungrateful lepers, forgiving sins and dining with sinners, welcoming children and loving every single person to the point of death.[36] Jesus is the One who dies for us while we're his enemies. He is the One who prays "Father forgive them" while he's being killed. Jesus is the one who loves, loves, loves to the point of death, and even after he's dead, the grave can't stop his love. He has the gaul to come sauntering out of the tomb on Easter so he can love some more.

The backstage pass of Revelation 4-5 went to extraordinary lengths to build suspense and then reveal that Jesus, the Lover of lovers, sits on the throne.

The center of all reality is the Lamb on the throne.
The Crucified One. Self-giving Love.

Jesus hates sin precisely because Jesus loves sinners. The reason you hate the cancer is because you love the person. The reason you hate a snake in the crib is because you love a baby in the crib. Jesus hates sin because he loves sinners. Sin is what is killing people—and God endlessly loves people. If you need to hear it: God's singular, eternal, unending disposition towards you—yes, you—is love. God always already loves you. And the trumpets point us toward a God who vanquishes sin—directly and indirectly—precisely to set sinners free.

---

[36] Romans 5.8 + 1 John 2.2

God nurses no grudges. Every bit of sin and curse, all wrath and suffering, has always already been absorbed by God in Jesus. That's central to what the cross is about; that's central to the gospel. The Lamb has absorbed every plague and grants us pardon. God suffers our violence to give new life. The gospel itself is at stake if we mistake Jesus as Batman.

When we get to the hard parts of Revelation we interpret them through the Lamb sitting on the throne (5v6). **The Lamb is our North Star**—our compass needle, our guiding light—helping us navigate thick fog and difficult terrain.

Revelation does not reveal a Jesus different from the gospels. Revelation reveals that the Jesus of the gospels will crucify all sin in order to resurrect the cosmos. The God revealed in Jesus was, and is, and will always be the Crucified Lover. Revelation tells us (in images frequently too hot to handle) that Crucified Love wins. The God who always already loves everyone to the point of death—this God wins. God accomplishes salvation through death and resurrection. But make no mistake, the violence of the cross belongs to humanity not God.

Christians believe that Jesus saves us by enduring our violence on the cross. And this is the Jesus we follow. We yield to this Jesus—to Love willing to bleed — accepting his claim on us, participating in his death, and sharing in the divine nature of his indestructible life.[37] That's our hope. That's the gospel.

God himself recreates us through the cross. And these trumpets foreshadow that reality on a cosmic scale: God will one day answer the groaning prayers of all creation by recreating all things through his cross. The trumpets point to a day coming—ready or not—when Jesus will share his cross with the entire world, crucifying evil and resurrecting everything else. There's a day coming when all creation will be carried through Calvary. The cosmos itself will pass through the cross into resurrection.

---

[37] Galatians 2.20; Philippians 3.10-11; 2 Peter 1.4; Hebrews 7.16.

We must be clear about God's character: *God's goal is never to destroy the world but to recreate it.* Jesus intends to destroy all evil and set all creation ablaze with love. The prayers of the saints will rise like incense and return like fire. And what we call "the wrath of God" is simply the love of God burning away all that is not love.[38]

Our general (tentative) decisions about the thick fog of the trumpets must be guided by this: *Love is what God always does because Love is who God always is.* We can say this with confidence, because we interpret the unclear part of the Scripture through the clear. And Revelation is crystal clear: the Lamb is on the throne.

When *Revelation* is hard to understand, cling to this.
Cling to Love. Cling to the Lamb.

And when *life itself* is hard to understand, cling to this.
Cling to Love. Cling to the Lamb.

We cling to the reality that *God is answering our deepest prayers*, be they for justice, or hope, or relationship, or healing, or provision, or freedom, or new life. *God is answering our deepest prayers even when the answers are often hard to recognize.* They return like fire—burning away parts of our world, crucifying bits of us... and igniting resurrection life.

//

Jesus, help me cling to your love made known in the cross. Teach me to cling especially when things are hard to understand. Help me pray with confidence and trust that heaven will answer my prayers in purging and powerful ways. Help me hunger for the day when you make all things new and practice your fiery resurrection today. Amen.

---

[38] Notice the way Jesus talks in Luke 12.49-50: "I have come to bring fire on the earth, and how I wish it were already kindled! But I have a baptism to undergo, and what constraint I am under until it is completed!" Jesus says his goal is to **bring fire** to the earth (purify and recreate the world) and the way he "kindles" this fire is through the cross.

Then I saw another mighty angel coming down from heaven. He was robed in a cloud, with a rainbow above his head; his face was like the sun, and his legs were like fiery pillars. He was holding a little scroll, which lay open in his hand. He planted his right foot on the sea and his left foot on the land, and he gave a loud shout like the roar of a lion. When he shouted, the voices of the seven thunders spoke. And when the seven thunders spoke, I was about to write; but I heard a voice from heaven say, "Seal up what the seven thunders have said and do not write it down."

Then the angel I had seen standing on the sea and on the land raised his right hand to heaven. And he swore by him who lives for ever and ever, who created the heavens and all that is in them, the earth and all that is in it, and the sea and all that is in it, and said, "There will be no more delay! But in the days when the seventh angel is about to sound his trumpet, the mystery of God will be accomplished, just as he announced to his servants the prophets."

Then the voice that I had heard from heaven spoke to me once more: "Go, take the scroll that lies open in the hand of the angel who is standing on the sea and on the land."

So I went to the angel and asked him to give me the little scroll. He said to me, "Take it and eat it. It will turn your stomach sour, but 'in your mouth it will be as sweet as honey.'" I took the little scroll from the angel's hand and ate it. It tasted as sweet as honey in my mouth, but when I had eaten it, my stomach turned sour. Then I was told, "You must prophesy again about many peoples, nations, languages and kings."

I was given a reed like a measuring rod and was told, "Go and measure the temple of God and the altar, with its worshipers. But exclude the outer court; do not measure it, because it has been given to the Gentiles. They will trample on the holy city for 42 months. And I will appoint my two witnesses, and they will prophesy for 1,260 days, clothed in sackcloth." They are "the two olive trees" and the two lampstands, and "they stand before the Lord of the earth." If anyone tries to harm them, fire comes from their mouths and devours their enemies. This is how anyone who wants to harm them must die. They have power to shut up the heavens so that it will not rain during the time they are prophesying; and they have power to turn the waters into blood and to strike the earth with every kind of plague as often as they want.

Now when they have finished their testimony, the beast that comes up from the Abyss will attack them, and overpower and kill them. Their bodies will lie in the public square of the great city—which is figuratively called Sodom and Egypt—where also their Lord was crucified. For three and a half days some from every people, tribe, language and nation will gaze on their bodies and refuse them burial. The inhabitants of the earth will gloat over them and will celebrate by sending each other gifts, because these two prophets had tormented those who live on the earth.

But after the three and a half days the breath of life from God entered them, and they stood on their feet, and terror struck those who saw them. Then they heard a loud voice from heaven saying to them, "Come up here." And they went up to heaven in a cloud, while their enemies looked on.

At that very hour there was a severe earthquake and a tenth of the city collapsed. Seven thousand people were killed in the earthquake, and the survivors were terrified and gave glory to the God of heaven.

The second woe has passed; the third woe is coming soon.

The seventh angel sounded his trumpet, and there were loud voices in heaven, which said:

"The kingdom of the world has become
    the kingdom of our Lord and of his Messiah,
    and he will reign for ever and ever."

And the twenty-four elders, who were seated on their thrones before God, fell on their faces and worshiped God, saying:

"We give thanks to you, Lord God Almighty,
    the One who is and who was,
because you have taken your great power
    and have begun to reign.
The nations were angry,
    and your wrath has come.
The time has come for judging the dead,
    and for rewarding your servants the prophets
and your people who revere your name,
    both great and small—
and for destroying those who destroy the earth."

Then God's temple in heaven was opened, and within his temple was seen the ark of his covenant. And there came flashes of lightning, rumblings, peals of thunder, an earthquake and a severe hailstorm.

08. EAT THE SCROLL (REVELATION'S REVELATION)

We started our last chapter by reminding ourselves that Revelation tells a story that transports us from prison to paradise—from the island of Patmos (ch1) to the gardens of New Jerusalem (ch21-22). It's a good-news-kind-of-story. John's vision tells the story of the world's salvation. The vision ends with the kingdom of God finally and forever arriving on earth as it is in heaven.

It's easy to lose sight of the story
especially as seals break,
trumpets sound,
and images overwhelm.

We've been trying to remind ourselves that this story is *not* an Almanac giving literal predictions about weather patterns in the future. The story John tells is an Apocalypse revealing what God is like. And, so far, one of the primary "revelations" about God has been that God actually *does* have a plan to save the world.

We first saw this plan in the form of *a sealed scroll* (5v1). With all the strange scenes unfolding since, it's easy to forget about this scroll. We may have forgotten, even though John had a nervous breakdown in heaven worrying that it would not be opened (5v4). We might have forgotten even though every creature in existence (5v13) praised Jesus that he alone could open the scroll and make sense of it (5v9). And even though John's vision devoted significant story space to its opening (6v1 - 8v1), if you're anything like me, that scroll may have slipped your mind.

Perhaps we're simply not used to reading apocalyptic literature. Perhaps it's our attention spans. Perhaps we think God, or John, or the Bible, should spoon feed us the deepest mysteries of universe in a more easily-digestible, immediately understandable form. (I'm doubtful that is even possible, but I often wistfully wish for it.)

It's easy to lose interest in the slow, patient work of God's salvation. We're frequently more dazzled by disaster movies than artistic masterpieces; maybe that's why we change Revelation from the latter into the former. Images of carnage grab our attention. With all the special effects that go along with the seven seals (6v1 - 8v1) and seven trumpets (8v6 - 11v15), who cares about a boring old scroll?

The "boring old details," however, often hold the key to unlocking a story's trickiest mysteries. Just ask Sherlock Holmes. When a detail quietly returns, that detail is probably important... perhaps critical.

With the images of **six trumpets**, John has been assuring us that God actually does answer the prayers of his people (8v3-6ff) with answers sometimes painful and often surprising. But John's earliest listeners would have been on pins-and-needles for the seventh trumpet—for the final answer—especially after he made them wait for the seventh seal (8v1). Surely the seventh trumpet will usher in the salvation of the world.

John is a master-storyteller who knows what his listeners are clamoring for... and he keeps building the suspense. The great blast of the **seventh trumpet** won't arrive for almost two more chapters (11v15). And between the sixth and seventh trumpets, we discover the return of the scroll—now unsealed. A towering angel now arrives from heaven carrying **an open scroll** (10v2).

After the painful images of the first six trumpets, this angel is a sight for sore eyes. Here we have someone who looks, smells, sounds like heaven—his body robed with cloud, his head perfumed with a rainbow, his face shining, his legs like pillars of fire (10v1). From head to toe this figure reminds us of all the love, delight, peace, and energy that animates the universe backstage.

Yet this angel doesn't stand backstage in heaven. This angel has planted his feet on-stage in this world—one foot on the earth, the other planted on the sea.[1] Suddenly we're filled with hope in the midst of demonic armies. Seeing this angel is like suddenly seeing an Allied Tank in the middle of Nazi-occupied territory. Heaven's tank conveys strength, authority, and hope—more help is surely coming.

In fact, when the angel speaks (10v3), he's *like a lion roaring* over the radio requesting air support. "Could you send in the *seven thunders*?" he shouts. The Lamb's scroll seems meager—a little small[2]—now that it's finally open. Surely now we need some Lion power. The seven thunders squadron answers his roar. Upgraded firepower is on the way... but then, all of a sudden, HQ calls off the air support. The authority of heaven issues overriding orders: "That bit from the seven thunders... don't include them, John. We don't need them. They're not part of the story" (10v4).

What is this all about?

Well, the chaos thermostat has been steadily rising. We've seen an escalation of judgment, like a steady increase of chemotherapy. We watched hurt and horror gradually increase on the earth from **one-fourth** (6v8) to **one-third** (8v7-12,

---

[1] Interestingly his foot is ON the sea, not IN the sea. While this angel doesn't seem to be Jesus himself, he definitely embodies Jesus's strength and authority. The blurring of an angel's identity with the identity of God occurs frequently in the Old Testament (for instance, see Exod. 3.2-4)

[2] The word used in verses 2, 9, and 10, *biblaridion*, is slightly than the earlier word for "the scroll" (*biblion*) in chapter 5 and 10:8. *Biblaridion* is *biblion* in diminutive form (i.e. "pig" and "piglet" in English). We shouldn't let the slight lexical change distract us. Richard Bauckham makes the exhaustive, technical, and conclusive argument for the scrolls of chapter 5 and 10 being identical in *Climax of Prophecy* (243-257). Perhaps by calling it a "scroll-let" here, John helps us visualize the scroll as "bite-size" for what comes next.

9v15). All of the pain has been permitted (even surgically used) for the ultimate purpose of healing. Heaven's ultimate aim is for people to turn from evil and choose life (9v20-21). In more theological language, every bit of God's permissive and active will serves the purpose of salvation not damnation.

God always intends to save not destroy.

But after six trumpets, the hard-hearted humanity has refused to turn from evil. They refuse to be healed, to choose life. This angel seems to think that what is needed is a stronger dose of the same painful medicine. If things kept going the same way, we would expect another painful cycle of seven... this time affecting **one-half** of the earth.

But, suddenly, the seven thunders are silenced—put on mute.

"Don't write that down. Don't pass that along to your churches, John. This story is not simply ever-increasing judgments of pain and suffering. That's not the way this story goes. That's not the message I want the churches to hear."

The angel takes this gentle rebuke in stride. He remains confident that soon— very soon in fact—God's mysterious, saving purposes will be accomplished. The mysterious purposes of God will be enacted soon in these days before the seventh trumpet sounds. There will be no more delay (10v5-7). God's plan to make everything new will finally appear... but without thunderous air support.

Heaven's strategy is wiser than ever-increasing firepower. The Great Physician calls for a deeper therapy, not higher doses of the same medicine. And here we approach one of the chief revelations of Revelation: heaven's wiser strategy will involve John; God's deeper therapy involves us.

The local church
is at the heart
of how Jesus saves.

Much of John's vision has unfolded from the vantage point of heaven.[3] But now he's being summoned back to the earth: "It won't do for you to live with your head in the clouds; go to the place where the mysteries of heaven, the everyday of earth, and the chaos of oceans all converge.[4] Meet that angel who has carried the mysterious plan of God into the world. Go there. Take the scroll (10v8)."

So John takes the scroll.

"Now eat it" (10v9).

Maybe that's worth a pause. John is told to eat a scroll with writing on both sides of it. This has happened before in Scripture. It's a wonderful symbolic image borrowed from the prophet Ezekiel.[5] When Ezekiel was first charged to speak God's words to God's people, Ezekiel had a vision of a remarkably similar scroll... which he was told to eat. It's an ancient image that conveys:

"The words of God are not to be merely studied, analyzed, or agreed with. This scroll isn't merely for reading; it's for ingesting. Receive this into yourself. These words are to become part of you. Eat the scroll."

The Spirit gives this image to both Ezekiel and John of Patmos. In the midst of hardship, isolation, and suffering, John hears God inviting him to take in—to ingest, eat—the saving plans of heaven.[6]

The scroll passes out of sight into John's mouth. This is a thrilling, climactic moment in John's story. This is what we've been waiting for. It's what the world desperately needs. It's what John despaired might never be known. God's plan to save has arrived on a silver platter. It's kind of a big deal. Here at Revelation's midpoint, God's plan to save the world will finally be put on dazzling display.

---

[3] Rev. 4.1.

[4] This angel, rather significantly, bridges heaven, earth, and sea (10.5).

[5] Ezek. 2.8 - 3.4.

[6] "As with Ezekiel's scroll, [the scroll's] contents cannot be revealed until ingested by the prophet John" (Bauckham, *The Climax of Prophecy*, 250).

We wait with bated breath. How John will describe the secrets of the universe to us? We've all wondered about this scroll, this plan—what is it like? John swallows. Now he speaks (10v10):

"God's plan is for ultimate good..." (it tastes sweet)
"...but it's also tough medicine" (he's a little nauseated).

Argh!! Tell us more, John! Can you be more specific? We're halfway through a book called "Revelation" for crying out loud! Can you finally reveal it?! Tell us about more than just the flavor!! How will God save the world?!

At this point, we've got to pay careful attention. What comes next is a touch confusing. But if we grasp this moment of eating the scroll, we're close to grasping all of Revelation.

At first glance, the transition from Revelation 10 to Revelation 11 feels like a complete change of subject.[7] When you read it, John seems to abruptly change topics. Suddenly we're hearing about what seems like entirely different things... the tabernacle, olive branches, two witnesses, who knows!? (And, let's get real. Most of the time we are nowhere close to understanding what's going on, so we don't really care.)

But, in actuality, John has begun telling us
about "more than just the flavor."

John isn't changing subjects. He's telling us the scroll itself:

"Behold, God's plan to save the world."

If that seems like a stretch, we should look back at Ezekiel to get a clearer picture of what's happening. Right after Ezekiel eats the scroll, he immediately

---

[7] Seriously... look up the transition (or lack thereof) between 10.11 and 11.1.

began to convey God's message. Through visions, through stories, through performance art, through haircuts—I kid you not.[8]

Ezekiel eats his scroll
and immediately does everything he can
to communicate that message.

The pattern holds true with John.

John is told that he's got to prophesy to the world—to the people God loves and intends to make fully alive. Prophesy to peoples and nations and languages and kings (10v11). And as chapter 11 begins, that's exactly what John does. John eats the scroll and immediately does everything he can to communicate that message.[9]

Buckle up!—get ready!—this is exciting! John is telling us God's plan to save the world! But it's not what we expected. Not at all. Because John starts by telling a short story:

It begins with **the Temple** being measured (11v1), and **the holy city** getting trampled (11v2). And then we meet our main characters... **two witnesses** who put on quite the spectacular show until they get killed (11v3-10). For, you see, **the beast** from **the Abyss** makes war on them—attacks them, overpowering and killing them. A monster from that primordial, evil blackhole in the ocean kills them, transforming these "two witnesses" into "martyrs" or "witnesses unto death." (The Greek word for a witness is "martus.")

But then the impossible happens. God's witnesses are rescued from the grave... raised from the dead (11v11-12). These martyrs are vindicated. They were witnessing to something wildly true.

---

[8] That haircut comes in Ezekiel 5.

[9] "Everything which precedes John's consumption of the scroll is preparatory to the real message of his prophecy" (Bauckham, *The Climax of Prophecy,* 255).

It's a tightly constructed story. These "two witnesses" cling faithfully to truth even to the point of death... and then are rescued. And this is crucial: notice what happens because of these "two witnesses." The impossible happens. Again. People finally begin repenting of sin. Because of their witnesses and faithfulness to death people turn away from their wickedness (11v13).

Remember, we are in the middle of the **sixth trumpet**. We have focused on trumpets as heralding divine responses of plague-like power, but trumpets are also Jericho imagery. Trumpet six is the moment in Joshua right before that great city collapsed from sevenfold trumpet blasts.[10] But here, because these two witnesses, only "one-tenth" of "the great city" (11v8,13) collapses. And love finally breaks through human hardness of heart.

A symbolically small remnant of people die,
but the vast majority of people survive and find life.[11]

Those who had previously rebelled against God are now gripped by the beginning of wisdom—by the "fear" of the Lord—and they begin "giving glory" to the God of heaven.[12]

So in a short little parable—spanning only 10 verses—John tells us of something that achieves what raw power cannot. Think about that. The faithful lives of these "two witnesses" accomplish what the plagues of Egypt could not: compelling people to turn from death and choose life.[13]

This story of the two witnesses
seems to be a parable about the Church.

---

[10] Joshua 6.1-21

[11] "The remarkably universal, positive result of the witnesses' testimony is underlined by the symbolic arithmetic of 11:13. In the judgments announced by Old Testament prophets a tenth part (Isa. 6:13; Amos 5:3) or seven thousand people (1 Kgs. 19:18) are the faithful remnant who are spared when the judgment wipes out the majority. In a characteristically subtle use of allusion, John reverses this. Only a tenth suffers the judgment, and the 'remnant' (*hoi loipoi*) who are spared are the nine-tenths. Not the faithful minority, but the faithless majority are spared, so that they may come to repentance and faith." (Bauckham, Theology of Revelation, 87)

[12] The language of "fear" and "giving glory" is exclusively used as the proper posture before God (cf. 14.7; 15.4; 19.5-7).

[13] Glance back at 9.20-21.

God saves the world through Jesus...
and the world meets Jesus
through the witness of the local church.

It's an intricate story—a genius sort of parable—and space doesn't allow us an exhaustive examination. But here's what's going on under the parable's hood squeezed into one dense sentence: Like Ezekiel, John eats a scroll and speaks God's plans that involve a metaphor from Zechariah[14] garnished with Moses and Elijah[15] imagery to fulfill prophecies of Daniel[16]. Whew—that's a snapshot under the hood. And the point is this: the Church must faithfully follow Jesus in self-giving love.

John raids his verbal warehouse and presents a greatest-hits-remix of prophecies, stories, images and language to communicate what the scroll has revealed to him: *the local church is at the heart of how God saves.*

So John tells us a story of two witnesses.[17] These witnesses live and die faithfully proclaiming truth. It's a stylized thumbnail sketch of the church's task in history. For some period of time in history[18] the church points the world to Jesus in word and deed. The fire from the witnesses' mouths is just as symbolic as a sword coming out of Jesus's mouth.[19] We're not talking about literal fire-breath-

---

[14] The images of **lampstands** and **olive trees** are from Zechariah 4.11-14. There they symbolize the governor (Zerubbabel) and high priest (Joshua) of Zechariah's own time (4.14). It's noteworthy that lampstands have already been clearly established as a symbol for the Church in Rev 1.20. Here we have two lampstands instead of seven… evidently to match Zechariah's olive trees and to dovetail with the two symbolic figures of Moses and Elijah.

[15] The figures of Moses and Elijah became something of an embodiment of Scripture (Moses = the law, Elijah = the prophets) and are also the two closest witnesses to Jesus's transfiguration (Mk. 9.2-13 and parallels).

[16] The way John first communicates the scroll is something like "inside baseball" for the earliest readers familiar with Daniel 8.11-14 & 12.7. The prediction of Daniel 8.13 plays an especially significant role in this parable, with its concern for the Temple. Daniel's vision of the "trampling underfoot of the Lord's people" gets embodied in Revelation's images of the temple (11.1), holy city (11.2), and the life of the witnesses (11.3-12). (Bauckham, *The Climax of Prophecy,* 266-273.) John seems to be claiming Daniel's prophecy as a picture of the church's ever-present vocation.

[17] You need at least two or three witnesses to trust a testimony in the ancient world.

[18] The language in these verses of **three and a half years** and **42 months** and **1,260 days** are all the same amount of time. The symbolic nature of this expression seems to originate from both half of "fullness" (seven) and also Daniel 12.7 (a time = 1, times = 2, half a time = 1/2).

[19] Revelation 1.16; 2.16; 19.15, 21

ing any more than a literal monster from a literal abyss. John is saying that the church's proclamation of Jesus in the world is powerful (11v5). The church's deeds of love, mercy, truth in the world are just as miraculous as anything done by Moses or Elijah (11v6).[20]

What changes the world—what saves the world—is when the Church faithfully witnesses to self-giving love of the Lamb. Even when it's hard. Even when the world despises truth. And even when forgiveness and mercy are overpowered by hatred and violence.

The church's joyous task involves faithfully following Jesus in self-giving love even when it means joining him on the cross. We may get attacked—possibly even killed (11v7)—for witnessing to Love. *But our witness must happen because that's God's plan.* The "temple" (11v1) has got to be handed over to the nations. "The Holy City" (11v2) may have to get trampled to save those from "the Great City" (11v8,13).[21]

Even when it means our discomfort, or embarrassment, or literal death, the Church is called to love. We're called to witness to Jesus. In our word and deed. In all we say and do. This love, this truth, this life—it may not always be popular. It may torment people (11v10) and feel like hot coals on their head.[22] But that's our task: to love Jesus and love all.

---

[20] The plagues and waters into blood (11.6) are obvious allusions to the work of Moses (Exod. 7-11) and prophesying drought to Elijah (1 Kgs. 17).

[21] The reference to "the Temple" and the "holy city" in verses 1-2 both seem to be symbolic representations of the people of God like the "two witnesses" (cf. Eph. 2.21-22, 1 Pet. 2.5) rooted in the prophetic images of Daniel 8.13 (see note 14 above). Likewise "the great city" (11.8) and its collapse (11.13) are symbolic as well. John explicitly names Sodom, Egypt, and anti-Jesus Jerusalem as embodiments of "the great city." In the Old Testament, the "great city" can refer to include Nineveh (Gen. 10:12, Jonah 1:2; 3:2; 4:11) and Jericho and Ai (Deut. 1:28; 9:1-3). It was an archetypal way of talking about those opposed to YHWH and his purposes. The notorious, quintessential example is, of course, Babylon (Gen. 11:1-9), which will be introduced to embody this "great city" in the coming chapters (14:8; 16:19; 17:5; 18:2; 18:10; 18:21). It's worth noting that John is careful with his numbers, and the word "Babylon" is used precisely six, not seven, times.

"The great city, then, is neither one particular city (Rome, say) nor all cities in all times and places. It is rather the name we give to all those particular stories in which human beings rise up in opposition to the rule of God, seeking to dispose of God (and safeguard their own autonomy) by murdering his appointed messengers... The narrative does not, however, assign direct responsibility for the witnesses' death to the inhabitants of the city. The one who does the actual killing is 'the beast that arises from the bottomless pit.'" (Mangina, 140).

[22] Rom 12.20-21.

And that includes them... whoever our "them" is.

"Them" that don't deserve it.

"Them" that are the problem.

"Them" that started it.

Love them. Always. Relentlessly. Fiercely. Courageously. Love them to death. That's the secret on the scroll. Love willing to bleed is God's plan to save the world. Love is the only thing that truly changes people. We are invited to ingest the self-giving life of Jesus for the sake of the world.

The Lamb's inside job of salvation
gets into the world by getting into us.

We're called to share in the sufferings of Christ and also share in Christ's resurrection.[23] *That's the story of the witnesses, and that's our story.* Until the end of history—until the seventh trumpet sounds—the Church fulfills the mysterious purposes of God (10v7).

We join Jesus's life of love willing to bleed.
That, my friends, is God's secret plan to save the world.
That is Revelation's revelation.

After John eats the scroll and tells this parable of the two witnesses, we hear the eagle's voice again in our ears. It tells us that now we are finally done with the sixth trumpet... only one final answer remains. Two woes have passed; a third is coming (11v14).

Then the **seventh trumpet** sounds (11v15), but watch carefully! Instead of a **third woe**—because of these witnesses—we find worship. Instead of more pain, we get a party. We hear an army of people singing in celebration about

---

[23] Phil 3.10-11.

the end of history (11v16-18). That is, of course, because what Christians mean by "the end" is only the terminus of humanity's history of hatred. "The end of the world" actually signals the arrival of The Great Beginning. At the final trumpet, God will make good on all of his promises[24] and make all things new.[25]

When the seventh trumpet sounds, people celebrate that God's kingdom has finally arrived. The God of goodness has judged the world (11v17-18). It's time to destroy whatever destroys life. And the end of history is only "a woe" for those who want absolutely nothing to do with real life.

We're only halfway through Revelation, but it seems like we've arrived at the end of the world.[26] That's not incorrect. In fact, everything else that happens in Revelation could be thought of as an *unfolding of* and *reflection on* the church's role until "the seventh trumpet." In its coming chapters, Revelation will begin circling back and reflecting on God's purposes—and the church's role in them—from different angles.

But for us—here living before the final trumpet—perhaps we need remind ourselves that God's purposes are meant to be eaten not read, ingested not intellectualized, lived not analyzed. The often painful love of the cross is meant to be corporately embodied, not merely cognitively understood.

We frequently struggle with God because we can't figure out certain parts of our lives. We often feel like characters in a novel, and we want to know the full plot. We want to analyze and understand the novel while we're living the mid-

---

[24] There are **theophatic ("God-revealing") "light shows"** that signal literary transitions in Revelation. These "light shows" are bright symbols of God's presence in heaven (4.5) making itself known on earth. These "light shows" occur three more times in escalating intensity—at the end of the seals (8.5), trumpets (11.19), and bowls (16.18). It's significant that during this "light show," we catch a glimpse of the **ark of the covenant**, reminding us that Revelation points us toward the climactic completion of God's great covenant promises to bring blessing to a broken world (Gen. 12.2-3), to make a people for himself (Exod. 19.5-6), and to establish a human king forever (2 Sam. 7.16).

[25] Rev. 21.5.

[26] The **seventh trumpet** seems to signal the end of the world and the arrival of the future because in 11.17 God is no longer praised as the One "who is to come." God is simply "the One who is and who was." The "is to Come" has arrived. The second half of Revelation seems to be further exploring the redemptive task of the church in an oppressive world before this "seventh trumpet" sounds. The "seven bowls of God's wrath" (Rev. 16) could be thought of as an unfolding of the seventh trumpet.

dle of it. A few chapters back was really dark... what was that about? Why does this painful thread keep popping up again and again? Where will this plot line go? What's going on in this story?

We want to read our own scroll. But when we try, there are so many parts that don't make sense. We don't understand how God could sort this out, how there could be any healing, how any of this works. We can't read the scroll.

And that's ok.

We're not invited to *read* the scroll; we're invited to *eat* it. We're invited to participate in God's purposes even when we don't fully understand all of those purposes. We can follow Jesus when we don't know what the next chapter holds. We can love even when we can't figure out all the details. Even when very little makes sense, there is something we can do: we can feast on love. This, after all, seems to be the meal that Jesus was always intending to share with us (3v20).

We're always invited to feast on love—to receive the powerful, self-giving love of Jesus, making it more and more central to our lives. The purposes of God are meant to be eaten, to be embodied, to become part of us.

Feast on cruciform love,
for we are what we eat.

By the free gift of God, we are continually invited to receive—and become— love willing to bleed. The kind of love willing to suffer rather than inflict suffering. The kind of love willing to speak truth even when it may get us hurt. Eat and embody the love that seeks the good of others even to the point of pain and death.

This kind of love—this kind of life—is Resurrection Life. It's True Life. It's the life of Jesus... which is to say, the life of God himself. It's the gift that heaven eternally holds before us and commands us: "Take and eat." And when we do, salvation gets into the world through us.

The Divine Life cannot be examined from a distance. Nor can it be analyzed from the outside or even always understood in the moment. But make no mistake: relentless, revolutionary, self-giving love to the point of death... that is God's own life. And it is God's secret plan to save the world.

And some wonderful weekend—I know not when—we'll sip coffee together at dawn in New Jerusalem and perhaps understand a little more how our own scrolls worked.

//

Feast of Love, feed me your scroll. Until the seventh trumpet announces a new beginning, I want to receive your relentless love into my bones and become a witness to it. And may I become what I eat—your world-saving love—even when the beasts of darkness seem to be winning. May your love be my love; your death, my death; your resurrection, mine as well. Amen.

(Revelation 12)

A great sign appeared in heaven: a woman clothed with the sun, with the moon under her feet and a crown of twelve stars on her head. She was pregnant and cried out in pain as she was about to give birth. Then another sign appeared in heaven: an enormous red dragon with seven heads and ten horns and seven crowns on its heads. Its tail swept a third of the stars out of the sky and flung them to the earth.

The dragon stood in front of the woman who was about to give birth, so that it might devour her child the moment he was born. She gave birth to a son, a male child, who "will rule all the nations with an iron scepter." And her child was snatched up to God and to his throne. The woman fled into the wilderness to a place prepared for her by God, where she might be taken care of for 1,260 days.

Then war broke out in heaven. Michael and his angels fought against the dragon, and the dragon and his angels fought back. But he was not strong enough, and they lost their place in heaven. The great dragon was hurled down—that ancient serpent called the devil, or Satan, who leads the whole world astray. He was hurled to the earth, and his angels with him.

Then I heard a loud voice in heaven say:

"Now have come the salvation and the power
    and the kingdom of our God,
    and the authority of his Messiah.
For the accuser of our brothers and sisters,
    who accuses them before our God day and night,
    has been hurled down.
They triumphed over him
    by the blood of the Lamb
    and by the word of their testimony;
they did not love their lives so much
    as to shrink from death.
Therefore rejoice, you heavens
    and you who dwell in them!
But woe to the earth and the sea,
    because the devil has gone down to you!
He is filled with fury,
    because he knows that his time is short."

When the dragon saw that he had been hurled to the earth, he pursued the woman who had given birth to the male child. The woman was given the two wings of a great eagle, so that she might fly to the place prepared for her in the wilderness, where she would be taken care of for a time, times and half a time, out of the serpent's reach. Then from his mouth the serpent spewed water like a river, to overtake the woman and sweep her away with the torrent. But the earth helped the woman by opening its mouth and swallowing the river that the dragon had spewed out of his mouth. Then the dragon was enraged at the woman and went off to wage war against the rest of her offspring—those who keep God's commands and hold fast their testimony about Jesus.

09. THE FAIRYTALE THAT'S TRUE

Have you ever been watching a movie when suddenly, in the blink of an eye, everything changes? The film's actual appearance, I mean. You're captured by the story, following the main characters, the movie *looks* one way, but suddenly it *looks different*?

The live-action streets of London are suddenly replaced by animated dancing penguins as Mary Poppins teaches the children how to use their imaginations with sidewalk pictures. Or spooky, surreal animation descends as Hermione tells the legend of the Deathly Hallows. Or cloudy, black-and-white images float into view as Captain America's memories fill the screen.

We watch movies and have seen this. When a movie does it well, it doesn't confuse. *We understand that the abrupt change in appearance is granting us new perspective.* The storyteller (i.e. the director) wants to help us experience what a character is feeling, or fill in backstory, or let us glimpse the protagonist's daydreams. A change in lighting, color palette, or film style is used to signal to the us (the audience) that something has changed.

John of Patmos doesn't have modern technology of film, computer animation, or fancy lighting. But he does possess the versatile and reliable technology of rhetoric. Words—the magic of storytelling before the magic of Hollywood.

For the first half of Revelation, John has conveyed the vision he experienced with a fairly consistent style. His story has trucked along in a steady way. (It might have been a strange film to watch, but it's had a certain kind of flow.)

John caught a glimpse of all-powerful, unstoppable Jesus (ch1) urging him to write to his churches (ch2-3) before finding himself swept backstage of all reality (ch4) where he saw God's top-secret plan to save the world (ch5). That was the way it all started, right?

This setup led to the action-packed sequences of opening God's top-secret plans of salvation (ch6-7, *the seven seals*) and eventually the nail-biting scenes of God beginning to answer the prayers of his people (ch8-9, *the seven trumpets*). It all climaxed with the now-opened plans of God brought to John on a silver platter (ch10).

Lo and behold—that's exactly what John told us his book was about in his opening lines. He began with a spoiler, exactly what was coming::

> (1v1-2) The revelation of Jesus Christ, which God gave him to show his servants what must soon take place. He made it known by sending his angel to his servant John, who testifies to everything he saw—that is, the word of God and the testimony of Jesus Christ.

The angel has been sent. John is testifying. We've reached the point where the "revelation of Jesus Christ" has become clear as both an "about" and a "from."

Revelation ABOUT Jesus...
God loves the world to the point of death.

Revelation FROM JESUS...
God invites the church to join him in this love.

That's the secret plan of God to save. But it can't be intellectually analyzed or examined at a distance. God's plans must be ingested and embodied. Salvation must be lived into. The scroll must be eaten.

John symbolically acts out this "eating" (ch10) and immediately tells a parable to communicate the point—the two witnesses. This biblical remix offered a stylized picture of what happens when a community of people faithfully point to Jesus by embodying his love to the point of death. When this happens, it's more powerful than all the plagues of Egypt. *The faithful witnesses to sacrificial love accomplishes what fear and coercion never could.*

Love willing to bleed can change lives.
That's the "revelation" of Revelation.

Love willing to bleed is *the good news* of Revelation.

> You are loved. By God. To the point of death.

Love willing to bleed is *the summons* of Revelation.

> Join God's life. Join this love. To the point of death.

John is saying, "You churches who are facing persecution, you Christians who are tempted to give up on Jesus—don't walk away from your faith. Don't abandon Jesus. Don't compromise in a world full of hatred and evil. Cling to Jesus even when it's hard. Embody his life even when it's painful. Remember... love to the point of death."

We might not have understand every detail of symbolism in every frame of the movie, but there's been a flow. It's all felt pretty consistent.

Revelation 11 ended with **the seventh trumpet** finally sounding.

> (11v15)
> The seventh angel sounded his trumpet, and there were loud voices in heaven, which said:
>
> "The kingdom of the world HAS BECOME
>   the kingdom of our Lord and of his Messiah,
>   and he will reign for ever and ever."

God gives the final answer to prayer, and the of history has finally arrived. People sing about the arrival of the end like it's already here:

> (11v17-18)
> "We give thanks to you, Lord God Almighty,
>   the One who is and who was,
> because you have taken your great power
>   and HAVE BEGUN TO REIGN.
> The nations were angry,
>   and your wrath has come.
> The time has come for judging the dead,
>   and for rewarding your servants the prophets
> and your people who revere your name,
>   both great and small—
> and for destroying those who destroy the earth."

It's kind of weird, right? The final judgment of God arrives in the middle of Revelation. On one level, it's as if the Church joining Jesus in his sacrificial love signals history reaching its destination. On another level, it's as if the **seventh trumpet** signals the arrival of Jesus "in glory to judge the living and the dead."[1]

Um... so... what exactly is the rest of this book about?

The "final trumpet" arrives in chapter 11,
but there are still 11 chapters left.

Well, the rest of Revelation unpacks the witness of the church and final coming of Jesus in new ways. Now we're going to get a new perspective, a closer look at what we've already seen. For the next few chapters (**ch12-14**), we're going to see John circling back around and exploring that parable of the two witnesses— the role of the church in the world—from different angles.

---

[1] In the words of the Nicene Creed.

John is a master storyteller in the ranks of filmmakers like Walt Disney, or Steven Spielberg, or Wes Anderson. And as we enter Revelation 12, John employs all his storytelling skills in service of God's Spirit. The color palette changes, the lighting shifts, and the style becomes exaggerated—cartoonish even. Suddenly we're swept up in mythic-kind-of-language. The style shift feels as drastic as live-action film suddenly shifting into animation.

As we begin Revelation 12, John's story suddenly starts resembling something like an exaggerated, mythical cartoon. We're introduced to a couple of new characters: *a dazzling Woman* (12v1-2) and a terrifying *seven-headed Dragon* (12v3-4). The Woman is terrorized by this Dragon and gives birth to *a male child.* And by the end of the chapter we find a chase scene reminiscent of a Roadrunner cartoon.

You remember those cartoons, right? Wile E. Coyote does everything he can to catch the Roadrunner, opening ACME crates and hatching all kinds of diabolical schemes. But no matter how he tries, it never works. Everything conspires against the Wile E. Coyote... often even the laws of physics.

The Roadrunner always gets away.

That's the kind of scene we find in Revelation 12. Many scholars think this may even be a bit of comic relief. The Dragon tries to catch the Woman (12v13)—but she's given eagle wings[2] (12v14), flying away to a safe place in the wilderness. So the dragon tries sweeping away the woman (12v15) with a flood of chaos and water from his mouth,[3] but a sinkhole swallows the flood (12v16). It's like the earth has sided with this Woman. Everything, including the laws of nature, conspire against the Dragon.

The Woman always gets away.

---

[2] John's imagery has overtones of *the history* of God's people (Exod. 19.4) as well as *the future* of God's people (the new exodus/rescue promised in Isa. 40.31).
[3] The **torrential water** (a symbol of chaos in Revelation) seems to perhaps be symbolic of chaotic lies (cf. 12.9) and accusations (cf. 12.10) flowing from the Accuser.

Looking ahead, John will weave these new larger-than-life cartoon characters—the Dragon, the Woman (Rev 12), as well as two additional Monsters (Rev 13)—back into his main story around Revelation 15. He'll return to his primary storytelling style with one last cycle of sevens and throw these over-the-top characters into the mix. Maybe that's the ancient equivalent of CGI special effects.

John, master storyteller, uses the next few chapters—exaggerated, dreamlike, cartoonish as they are—to give different perspectives. He wants to reflect on the faithful witness of the church from new angles. He wants to give us a deeper sense of the church following Jesus—its magnitude and importance, its scope and significance, its daring and danger.

And so John begins by telling a popular story that we're all familiar with:
The child destined to destroy evil who is threatened at birth.

It's a popular story because it's a good story. Countless versions of this story have circulated through the centuries, with *the most popular modern retelling being **Harry Potter***. Millions of readers have been swept up in the story of "The Boy Who Lived," who is destined to destroy the evil snake-like Voldemort and who is protected by the ancient magic of love until he's old enough to do so.

If Harry Potter is the most popular modern retelling of the story, *the most popular ancient retelling is **the story of Apollo***. We talk about Harry Potter, they talked about Apollo. All seven of John's churches in first-century Asia Minor would have been familiar with this story. The goddess Leto was pregnant with Zeus's son, Apollo, the baby destined to kill the great dragon Python. Python attacked Leto, but Zeus carried her away on the wind and enlisted his brother, Poseidon, to hide her on an underwater island for four days. Those four days gave enough time for Apollo to be born, grow up, and be ready to slay the dragon.[4] (Imagine how turbulent Apollo's puberty must have been.)

---

[4] Beale, 624.

John retells a popular, compelling story and immediately signals that he knows he's talking in mythological language. Notice how when he introduces these new characters (the Woman and Dragon), he immediately tells us they're symbolic (12v1,3). They're signs. They signify something.

For John's listeners familiar with the Old Testament, these symbols would have evoked **the Garden of Eden,** signifying Eve and the Serpent. Read in light of that story, this symbolism stirs up primal holy hope. The images evoke the earliest memories of the biblical witness that promise how evil will one day be vanquished by the woman's offspring.[5]

The tale of a heroic, chosen child may entertain us with a smashing story... but that's what stories do. They entertain. *What makes John's story any different from the mythic sagas of the ancient campfire or the modern movie?*

Well, notice that there's one character John doesn't call symbolic: **the male child** born to rule the nations (12v5). Rather significantly, this child born to vanquish evil isn't called "a sign." He's not an apocalyptic cipher or a mythological image. This baby is the literal real deal. He's not a sign pointing to anything. All the signs serve him.

And John names the child. The mythic language of Revelation doesn't gesture vaguely toward an abstract defeat of evil or unknowable redemption. No. John joins the great cloud of witnesses pointing to a Galilean rabbi. The story we're telling is the story of **Jesus of Nazareth** (12v17). John tells a sweeping, mythic story about a person in living memory—a person someone in his churches could have glimpsed or met when they were a child.

Mythological language helps John communicate the gravity of the church's good news, but the Christian hope also goes far beyond legends or folklore. Our hope grows from a scandalously particular historic events. We look at a verifiably real *Jewish* peasant in first century Palestine and the transformative

---

[5] Genesis 3.15.

shockwaves he sent through history. Our hope for the future involves riding those waves. We can look *forward* in real hope because we can look *backward* and name a particular person. John is drafting his own version of the popular mythic story with one extraordinary difference: he insists that it's true. Spiritually, physically, eternally historically true. To borrow language of C.S. Lewis, in Jesus we find the myth that actually happened.[6]

Jesus gets named at the end of this episode (12v17), but only appears in it for a flash (12v5). That feels right though, because that feels like human history. Jesus only arrives for the blink of a few decades before he ascends to heaven. The entire life of Jesus—his birth, growth, life, teaching, healing, miracles, suffering, death, resurrection—all four gospels—fits squarely in verse 5 between "she gave birth to a son" and "her child was snatched up."

Revelation 12 tells the Christmas story. It's just the strangest Christmas story ever told. Obviously this is not John giving us a literal rendering of Jesus's birth. No one thinks Mary (the literal mother of Jesus) literally dodged fireballs or waterfalls from a literal dragon in a literal desert. Some parts of this telling may reflect historical memories—like evil threatening Jesus at the time of his birth[7]—but this is a mythic, highly-stylized telling of Jesus's birth. But if you want to tell the fullest truth of what happened in Jesus, you have to tell the story like this at some point.

The arrival of Jesus has changed the world. His birth has won a war (12v7-12).[8] With the life, death, resurrection, and ascension of Jesus, you could say that the armies of heaven—led by the archangel Michael from Daniel's visions[9]—have defeated the forces of evil. The Author of Life has written himself into the story, birthed himself into his own people, and defeated darkness from the inside. And because of God's decision to become human, the Dragon has lost his place

---

[6] "Now the story of Christ is simply a true myth: a myth working on us in the same way as the others, but with this tremendous difference that it really happened" (C.S. Lewis in a personal letter, Oct 18, 1931).

[7] Matthew 2.1-16 tells us of a regional king (Herod) trying to assassinate Jesus before his birth.

[8] In light of other apocalyptic writings, G.K. Beale argues that verse 7-12 "are the heavenly counterpart of the earthly events recorded in vv 1-6" (650).

[9] **Michael** is the frequent heavenly representation of God's people in Daniel (10.13, 21; 12.1) as well as other ancient traditions.

(12v8). If you want to convey the truth about Christmas, sometimes you've got to talk like this.

*It seems like **the dazzling Woman** symbolizes more than a literal person.* While God *did* choose to enter the world through a literal woman named Mary, this story paints on a larger canvas. With the language used to describe her, this Woman seems to embody the entire people of God.[10] It's like *daughter Zion* or *virgin Israel*, or *the bride of Yahweh* (all ways that the Old Testament talks about God's people) have all suddenly converged. *The people of God herself have become the mother of God.* The symbols point to a literal *people* more than a literal *person*.

Central to the sacred mystery of the Christian faith is that God chooses to identify with—and even literally become— one of his own people. Once again, God works salvation from the inside.

God does this to defeat all the powers that oppose his life-giving reign. We give lots of names to the mysterious Enemy of Love (12v9): **the many-headed Dragon**,[11] the ancient serpent, the devil, the satan.[12] Whatever we call this sub-personal personality—this hole in the universe who leads the whole world astray— the point of Revelation 12 is clear enough: *the Enemy has lost.*

Heaven has conquered hell. Now... *when* exactly did this shattering defeat happen? The Dragon falls from the sky and it seems like the story could be communicating pre-creation history[13] or what was happening in the events of Jesus's life.[14] This story seems to tell us less about *when* evil was defeated and more that evil *is* defeated.

---

[10] It seems no coincidence that the **woman is "crowned with twelve stars"**... a symbol of God's people in both 4.4 (2 x 12) and 21.12-14, 21.

[11] We'll talk more about the Dragon's appearance in chapter 13.

[12] Rev 20.2 neatly ties up in one place many of the names for the spiritual opposer of God's purposes.

[13] This would put in line with traditional interpretation of Isaiah 14 and Ezekiel 28.

[14] e.g. Mk. 3:13-15; Lk. 10:17-20; Jn. 12:31

Here's the five-dollar way of saying it: John's mythic language about the chosen child is less about *chronology* (when it happened) and more about *ontology* (that it *has* happened). The Dragon *has been* hurled down (12v7-9). Evil *has been* defeated because of Jesus.

But if that's the case, why does the world feel the way it does? Why the Road-runner cartoon? Why all are the people of God on the run? If the Enemy is defeated, why is the Enemy still in pursuit? Why are the people of God in the wilderness (12v6)? We don't fully know. But for whatever reason (e.g. the building of faith, the formation of our character, the constraints of a world with free will) waiting in the wilderness is one of the central experiences of God's people before they enter the promised land. But we are provided for in the wilderness. The Dragon chases the Woman but cannot harm her—at least in some kind of ultimate sense.[15]

The people of God must brave the wilderness
for a symbolic period of time,[16]
but they're safe from ultimate harm.

This short episode ends by telling us that the Woman is safe, but **her offspring** are in danger. The Dragon—furious that he can't destroy the Woman herself—

---

15 Mangina, 157: "The picture of the church that emerges from Rev. 12 is of a harassed, threatened, and quite vulnerable community. Vatican II famously spoke of the church as the 'pilgrim people of God' (*Lumen Gentium* 64). That phrase should not be taken to mean progress along a series of tourist stops following a safe, well-established route. In the medieval world, setting forth on pilgrimage was a dangerous activity; the church's existence can be no less so. There will, of course, be certain signposts, markers left by past pilgrims to guide us across a forbidding landscape. For these we can only be grateful. This does not change the church's movement through the world having the character of improvisation, a constant relying on the grace of God rather than a master marked by total control. That the church can, however, rely on God's grace means that we can have confidence in the church surviving (and even flourishing) despite all assaults of the evil one. In traditional language, this is the Christian conviction concerning the 'indefectibility' of the church. True the gates of hell will not prevail against it (Matt. 16:18)."

16 This **symbolic time period** is the same symbolic period of time that the two witnesses testify to Jesus (cf. 11.2-3). That's one clue that John is giving us a different perspective on that same reality. Revelation 12 offers a new perspective on Revelation 11. The image of "The Woman" being ultimately safe (12.13-17) but "her offspring" being in temporary danger (12.17) parallels the "inner court" of the Temple being ultimately safe (11.1) but "the outer court" (11.2) being in temporary danger. The Woman, The Temple, The Holy City (also 11.2, cf. 21.12-14, 21), and the Two Witnesses (11.3-12) all seem to be parallel, kaleidoscopic images for God's people.

132

storms off to "wage war against the rest of her offspring." Thankfully, no guess-work is required at this point: *the Church's children are individual Christians*:

> (12v17) "Those who keep God's commands and hold fast their testimony about Jesus."

So despite an ultimate defeat, the Dragon still lashes about. The war is won yet terrible skirmishes linger. While the people of God are safe in an ultimate sense, individual communities and Christians are still under fire. The chapter leaves us holding our breath. What do these terrible skirmishes look like? How does the Dragon attack? That's where John will take us in Revelation 13.

But before we get there, John's majestic, mythic animation illuminates the kind of world we live in. John manages to give us a new perspective even on our own lives. Perspective for when life is hard, when the battle feels lost.

John, after all, writes his letter from an island prison dealing with profound iso-lation. He likely struggles with feelings of helplessness as the people he loves face everything from an overwhelming river of lies[17] about them (12v15) to physical attacks and persecution. Particular friends and faces come to mind. When John remembers his friends in Pergamum, and he aches remembering that his friend Antipas has recently died for the sake of Jesus (2v13).

It's easy to feel lost when life is brutal. And it *is* brutal sometimes. It doesn't just *look* terrible or *feel* hard. Frequently, life actually *is* hard. Sometimes circum-stances *are* terrible. Followers of Jesus can sometimes shy away from admitting how brutal life can actually be. We quietly think that calling things "evil" or "aw-ful" or "terrible" will somehow testifies against Jesus or God's sovereignty.

Our being honest about evil in the world
doesn't compromise the truth of Jesus's lordship;
we're simply being honest about Jesus's enemy.

---

[17] Malicious misinformation circulated about the early Christians. These misconceptions/lies included Christians being labelled as seditious atheists who were both incestual and cannibals. No joke.

Christians deny the victory of the Dragon, but we don't deny the will or work of the Dragon. Hatred, anxiety, fear... none of these things come from the heart of God. Pain is not God's ultimate will. Neither is addiction, or war, or hatred. Sin is not God's will. When we see these things, we don't see the work of the Lamb... we see the work of the Dragon.

Not everything we experience in this world is as God ultimately desires. There. We said it. Christians have a technical term for all being as God desires. That term is "heaven." And we're not there yet. In fact, we've been taught to pray for God's will to come on earth as it already is done in heaven.[18]

Make no mistake, God is relentlessly turning evil toward good in the world and in our lives. The limitless power and creativity of God's saving "inside job" *does* transform the enemy's schemes, judo-flipping them for good. Our anxiety becomes the place we learn trust. Our self-inflicted pain becomes a way of making us more loving. Our wounds becomes a source of empathy for others. Our tragedy gets transfigured into a source of hope for others.

But we should be slooow to chalk up suffering to the will of God. And we must never chalk up evil or sin. There are more wills at work in the universe than God's. There is an Enemy willing and working.

This episode grants us permission to habitually use the word "and." Life is brutal right now, *and* God will make all things beautiful. Circumstances are awful right now, *and* Jesus reigns the universe. Suffering surrounds us, *and* God is love. Life is legitimately, actually, frequently brutal, *and* an unspeakable, beautiful, sacred gift. We live in a world where dragons do exist, *and* a world where they are defeated.

---

[18] Matthew 6:10. Unless you ascribe to Christian universalism—or can do gymnastics over 1 Timothy 4.10, 2 Timothy 2.4 and 2 Peter 3.9—evidently God in his loving sovereignty has created a world where God *never* gets everything he desires. This seems a result of God's sovereign and free choice to create a world where the choices of his created beings really do matter.

We don't have to reconcile "God is Love" with "God is the architect of all suffering in the world." There is room for mystery—the mystery of an Enemy at work. There is room to read life like a fairytale… because it is. So take heart, brothers and sisters. Hear the story of King Jesus and know this: our lives are part of something bigger than our hardship or circumstances. We have been born into a fairytale where the kingdom will live happily ever after.

On our breathless days, when we are pursued, attacked, or even brutalized by the Enemy's schemes, we are invited to remember that the Child has conquered. A day is coming when anger and hatred, war and suffering, they will be only a memory. A day is coming when the fountains will spring up in the wilderness and we will celebrate God's will finally and fully arriving on earth as it is in heaven.

//

Grant me perspective, O Dragon-slayer. I live in your fairytale, and you cling to me. May my life participate in your love that cannot be killed and your life that cannot be stopped. In the midst of pain, help me see that the war is won, that The Dragon is dying, and that happily ever after is real. Amen.

(Revelation 13)

The dragon stood on the shore of the sea. And I saw a beast coming out of the sea. It had ten horns and seven heads, with ten crowns on its horns, and on each head a blasphemous name. The beast I saw resembled a leopard, but had feet like those of a bear and a mouth like that of a lion. The dragon gave the beast his power and his throne and great authority. One of the heads of the beast seemed to have had a fatal wound, but the fatal wound had been healed. The whole world was filled with wonder and followed the beast. People worshiped the dragon because he had given authority to the beast, and they also worshiped the beast and asked, "Who is like the beast? Who can wage war against it?"

The beast was given a mouth to utter proud words and blasphemies and to exercise its authority for forty-two months. It opened its mouth to blaspheme God, and to slander his name and his dwelling place and those who live in heaven. It was given power to wage war against God's holy people and to conquer them. And it was given authority over every tribe, people, language and nation. All inhabitants of the earth will worship the beast—all whose names have not been written in the Lamb's book of life, the Lamb who was slain from the creation of the world.

Whoever has ears, let them hear.

"If anyone is to go into captivity,
    into captivity they will go.
If anyone is to be killed with the sword,
    with the sword they will be killed."

This calls for patient endurance and faithfulness on the part of God's people.

Then I saw a second beast, coming out of the earth. It had two horns like a lamb, but it spoke like a dragon. It exercised all the authority of the first beast on its behalf, and made the earth and its inhabitants worship the first beast, whose fatal wound had been healed. And it performed great signs, even causing fire to come down from heaven to the earth in full view of the people. Because of the signs it was given power to perform on behalf of the first beast, it deceived the inhabitants of the earth. It ordered them to set up an image in honor of the beast who was wounded by the sword and yet lived. The second beast was given power to give breath to the image of the first beast, so that the image could speak and cause all who refused to worship the image to be killed. It also forced all people, great and small, rich and poor, free and slave, to receive a mark on their right hands or on their foreheads, so that they could not buy or sell unless they had the mark, which is the name of the beast or the number of its name.

This calls for wisdom. Let the person who has insight calculate the number of the beast, for it is the number of a man. That number is 666.

10. God's Political Cartoon

Have you ever had a bizarre dream that you just couldn't shake? I had precisely one of those kinds of dreams in late 2016 when I preached through Revelation for the first time.

In my vision at night, I saw a great beast with ivory teeth like towers and a great grey trunk... *a beast like an elephant*. Except this beast was standing like a man. Stars girded its waist and its front feet were readied for battle.

Then I looked and saw another great beast with terrible hooves and long brown ears. *Something like a donkey*. It too stood like a man... like a gladiator itching for battle. Its waist was painted white with crimson stripes.

These two terrible beasts approached each other, their eyes fixed on each other, their faces touching, their ferocity terrible. They bore bruises and wore wounds from endless conflict. But somehow I knew—***this calls for wisdom***—they were readying themselves for another brutal brawl.

When I woke from my dream, I sketched out what I saw so I could remember the details. I have included that sketch on the next page, so that you too, dear reader, can see the strange.

Alright, you caught me.

*I didn't draw this picture, and
I didn't dream that dream.*

And yet.*The impact of this
cartoon on the world in late
2016 is unquestionable.*
Most of us know what this
particular kind of cartoon is
called: A political cartoon.

We sometimes see these
online or in a newspaper.
But stop for a moment and
consider the strangeness of the image. The intensity, the
beasts, the symbolic clothing, the lack of an explanation. This "vision" would be
hard to understand if you didn't know much about the social, cultural, and political landscape of the United States. But precisely because most of us *do* understand our wider culture, we intuitively understand the picture.

Most adults in the United States are familiar with the Republican and Democratic parties. Most of us know that these two political parties are often collectively represented as an elephant and a donkey. Most of us recognize that stars and
stripes as patriotic emblems of the United States. And we resonate with the
intensity of a boxing match as a tragically appropriate analogy for U.S. politics.

*This cartoon has nothing to do
with literal pachyderms and actual donkeys.*

*This cartoon has everything to do
with literal political powers and actual world events.*

This is a cartoon, *and* this is serious business.

And this is the kind of thing that God gives us in Revelation 13.

Remember where we are in Revelation. In chapter 12 John shifted his story-telling. Through its first 11 chapters, the story remained fairly consistent in tone and style. If Revelation were a movie, it's been strange but at least it's all been the same style of strange. But as we've seen, the church embodies the faithful love of Jesus "in the days" (10v7) between the sixth and seventh trumpets. For a symbolic amount of time (11v2-3) the church is a witness that ends up piercing hard hearts (9v20-21) and drawing people into repentance (11v13).

But after the final appearance of Jesus in the seventh trumpet (11v15), Revelation celebrates (11v17-18) and then shifts its storytelling. We saw mythic animation dance across the text (ch12). John paints a cartoon for his churches: a dazzling Woman, a terrifying Dragon (with seven heads and ten horns[1]), and a Child whose very existence has defeated all darkness.

He paints with loud, primary colors.

He animates with grand, exaggerated characters.

John is saying something like:

> "There's this guy—this real, literal guy—Jesus—whose very coming into the world has defeated the deepest powers of darkness. Our world is a fairytale where evil, darkness, and dragons do exist *and* where goodness, light, and beauty wins."

Revelation 12 concluded with something like a Roadrunner cartoon. The forces of evil just keep chasing God's people—the Dragon keeps chasing the Woman, opening Acme boxes of tricks to capture her—but God's people are ultimately and forever safe. The Roadrunner always gets away.

---

[1] There's a "family resemblance" between the Dragon (12.3) and the Sea-Beast (13.1).

And then chapter 12 ends with a frustrated and furious Dragon storming off to make war on the Woman's offspring:

> (12v17) ...the dragon was enraged at the woman and went off to wage war against the rest of her offspring—those who keep God's commands and hold fast their testimony about Jesus.

It's like John is saying the people of God are safe in an ultimate sense, but individual churches and individual Christians are still living through incredibly rough stuff. Evil has been defeated but still lashes dangerously about with its dying breaths. John is using "animation" to convey the eternal security as well as the temporary peril of following Jesus in the first century (and any century!).

We've got to bear all this in mind, because now, in Revelation 13, the cartoon begins to feel like a *political* cartoon.

We can make one uncontroversial statement about Revelation 13:
Revelation 13 is one of the most controversial chapters in the Bible.

It's a doozy of a chapter. It begins with the Dragon summoning up its own offspring in a grotesque parody of the Woman giving birth to her Child. The hateful Dragon calls forth **a beast from the sea** (13v1) who wages war against God's people. And then another monster—**a beast from the earth** (13v11)—becomes an advocate for this first beast.

The defeated Dragon enlists two monsters, from sea and land, to wage war against God's people. Battles with the beasts—these are the kind of terrible skirmishes that the people of God are still experiencing. That's what Revelation 13 is about at its most basic level.

On some level, the imagery signals a comic conflict. The sky-beast (12v3) has unleashed the ancient legendary anti-creation chaos-monsters of Leviathan (sea) and Behemoth (land).[2] John's vision shows how darkness pervades every sphere of creation.[3] But on another level, the imagery signals how the practical, everyday tensions that the people of God were facing (or soon to face).

There's a long tradition of people understanding the imagery of this chapter as cryptic clues about events at history's twilight, just before the "end" of the world. These chapters, the stomping grounds of beasts, are fertile soil for growing conspiracy theories and controversies. Many have heard the descriptions of these two monsters that *rule* (13v1-10) and *deceive* (13v11-17) and watched vigilantly for a one-world government led by two literal people—*the Antichrist* and *the False Prophet*.

And practically everybody everywhere has heard about the infamous number at the end of the chapter (13v18). Careful, creative "analysis" of this number (666) has "conclusively shown" an amazing number of people to be The Antichrist. Every century has their candidate. People from all over the world that you would never suspect: from countless popes to Martin Luther, from JFK to Adolf Hitler, from Barack Obama to Ronald Wilson Reagan.[4] If you manage to get famous enough, perhaps you'll discover on YouTube that somehow 666 means that you too are the Antichrist.

Christians over the centuries
have looked at the exact same chapter
and speculated about wildly different things.

It's a thrilling history of making this chapter
about people or places or events
that it's simply not about.

---

[2] Eugene Peterson (122-123) points out that these beasts would have resonated with the corporate imagination of the ancient Jewish worldview (**Leviathan** = Job 40.15 - 41.26; Pss. 74.13-23, 104.26; Isa. 27.1, Amos 3.4; **Behemoth** = Job 40.15-24; 1 Enoch 60.7-8).

[3] Bauckham, *The Climax of Prophecy,* 32.

[4] There are six letters in Reagan's first, middle, and last names. And it didn't escape the President's detractors that after his retirement, he moved into a house located at 666 St. Cloud Road. His wife, Nancy, eventually had the address changed. Weird, huh?

Revelation 13 has become a sad Rorschach test: "Stare at this inkblot and tell us who you think the Antichrist is." But who we see (and who we accuse) reveals more about ourselves than anything on the page.

If the best scholars, saints, and Bible-readers through the centuries have fallen victim to Rorschach of Revelation 13, what hope can there be for us in understanding the chapter??

Perhaps our best hope lies in the mailbox. We need to remember that this chapter originally arrived in a mailbox. Even Revelation 13 is part of an ancient piece of mail. What we said earlier needs to be reemphasized, especially as we think through dragons and monsters, horns and crowns, and the number 666:

> Whatever Revelation is, it's something that these seven churches would have (mostly!) understood. *Jesus didn't send a coded puzzle originally meant for comfortable Christians in the twenty-first century. Jesus sent a stylized letter originally meant for struggling Christians in the first century.* If we can't imagine the original hearers of Revelation understanding our interpretation of this letter, then our interpretation probably needs to be rethought.[5]

Someone from a different time or another culture might be confused by a drawing of a boxing match between an elephant and a donkey. But a native of twenty-first century Washington or New York or Chicago could probably help them make sense of it. In similar fashion, a native of first century Sardis or Laodicea or Ephesus could probably help us make sense of these images.

---

[5] See chapter 3.

But since all of those first century natives are dead, however, our next best option is to do our history homework. We need to try (as best we can) to hear Revelation 13 as its original hearers would. When we put these images in their historical context, we're more likely to understand this vision… and less likely to obsess over an inkblot of our own fears.

That said, no amount of scholarly research can nail down with 100% certainty what this letter originally meant to the ancient world of John's churches. It's essential we hold all our interpretations humbly and with open hands.

We're limited by space, but hopefully a brief glance at some history homework will make us less concerned with information about the world's supervillain and more concerned with dedication to the world's hero. Because, at the end of the day, I suspect that's near the heart of how the native churches of Asia Minor originally heard this letter.

In what remains of the chapter, we'll take a crash-course on the history, politics, and culture of the first-century world. This will help us make sense of John's "cartoon." And as we sprint through it all, I'll use ***bold italicized words*** to try to help make potential connections between life on the ground and the language of John's vision.

Alright… quick history lesson.

What was the world like for John of Patmos and his seven churches?
What kind of world do they live in?

The short answer is John and his churches live in a world dominated by the Roman Empire. If you've ever cracked a history book or watched a documentary on Netflix, you've probably heard of it. The reason why so much is made of Roman history is that the Roman Empire made much of Western history. The reach of its influence is without parallel.

In its early centuries Rome gradually grew as a democratic republic, but by the first-century it had (d)evolved into a military dictatorship led by a king called "caesar." For the average peasant in Jerusalem or Asia Minor, this foreign force came billowing in like a storm from the west and rained down its rule on every corner of their land. For a few centuries, Rome secured stability and "peace" for the paltry price of millions dead.

Imagine yourself **standing on the shore** of the Mediterranean, your toes in the sand, gazing west over the waves. Suddenly a ship breaches the horizon. You see ships, Roman battleships, **rising like a monster** (13v1) to come to conquer your land. This ancient Superpower is a Supermonster—or at least that's the way the widely-read book of Daniel had described these world empires. They were nightmarish **beasts**.[6]

Rome, the great city on **seven hills,** ruled the known world like a dreadful **lion** ruling the savannah... by sheer brute force. Don't mess with that animal. It'll kill you. Those seven hills have **seven heads**[7] ready to eat you, your family, your village... and they would never even break a sweat.[8]

Since its descent into dictatorship, Rome had experienced a relatively stable succession of kings. King after king, caesar after caesar, **horn after horn** (as the scroll of Daniel would have called them,[9] cf. 13v1) had come and gone in relative peace. From Octavian (called "Great King" or "Augustus Caesar") who had stabilized the empire after his uncle Julius Caesar's assassination, to Tiberius who had ruled when Jesus was crucified, right down through Caligula and

---

[6] **The importance of Daniel 7.1-14 in Revelation cannot be overemphasized.** Daniel's dream is as strange and puzzling as some of our own dreams. Daniel 7 involves a succession of beastly, sub-human kingdoms finally being replaced by the kingdom of "one like a son of man." The world is full of vicious rulers and kingdoms that are less-than-human, that are like animals and beasts. But they will one day be replaced by God's kingdom—a reign that will reveal what true humanity is all about.

[7] John shows his hand a bit in 17.8-9 where he explicitly connects the **seven heads** of the beast to the **seven hills** of Rome.

[8] For example, Judas of Galilee led a Jewish rebellion against Roman rule in 6 CE and attacked the regional capital of Sepphoris. His rebellion was crushed and more than 2,000 people outside that city. This incident happened 4 miles north of Jesus's hometown of Nazareth when he was a boy.

[9] Daniel explicitly clarifies his image of horns (cf. Dan. 7.7-8,11,20) as symbolizing kings (7.24).

Claudius. They were all The line of caesars was stable for decades, but in the late first century things started going south.

By John's day, the line of caesars seemed on the verge of collapse. A recent caesar named Nero—certifiably crazy, we should add—had been a disaster for the Empire. He ended his own reign by ending his own life in 68 CE, throwing the empire into chaos. His catastrophic reign and catastrophic death had left the Roman world in tatters.

All kinds of people wanted the throne. But one problem with sitting down on the dictator's throne is how everyone wants your seat. After 18 months, the empire had seen shocking amounts of blood spilled and corpses piled.

And four of the corpses had been caesars.

Think about that. From the perspective of everyday citizens, it probably felt like ***this bear*** (13v2) of a government had suffered a death blow—***a mortal wound*** (13v3). But the empire stabilized when someone took the throne and managed not to die. It happened to be a fellow named Vespasian. Suddenly the beast was back—***fully recovered***, stronger than ever.

This sudden reemergence of strength especially overwhelmed Jews and Christians. Within months of Vespasian taking power, Jerusalem and its Temple had been completely destroyed. Vespasian sent his son and trusted general, Titus, to squash a rebellion that had been boiling for a handful of years. Titus took the task seriously, ***waging war*** (13v7) against those in the Jewish province whose allegiance was not pledged to Rome. He met resistance. So he decimated everything.

Suddenly Jerusalem, the great city of David, lay in ruins. The Jewish people's second Temple—the place where Jesus visited and taught and drove out money-changers—the promised *dwelling place* (13v6) of the God of Israel—it was literally gone. *Conquered* (13v7). Torn apart. Ashes. Smoldering. Gone.

If you lived at the time, you would look at Rome—with its technology and power and long history—and say: *"Who is like Rome? Who can wage war against it?"* (13v4).

Vespasian was deadly serious that Rome continue to be a great and powerful empire. His slogan could have been "Make Rome Great Again." In order to secure the blessing of the Roman gods and ensure world dominance, he tapped into Roman patriotism. He wanted to bring back the "glory" of years gone by and rule *over every tribe, people, language and nation* (13v7).

Regardless of when we date the writing of Revelation, Vespasian had only recently been reviving and spreading what was called "The Imperial Cult." Think of it as devout religious patriotism in which everyone must participate. The official (and required) religion of the entire empire mandated the devotion to Rome and *worship* (13v8) of the Caesars as gods on earth.

In the past, Caesars had sometimes been hailed as divine. An internet search can show you coins calling Caesar Nero "a Son of God." Stone inscriptions still survive in Ephesus hailing Caesar Augustus "the Savior of the world." Caesars had been called gods before Vespasian, but he made made it state policy.

All in the name of making Rome great again.

From the perspective of the earliest Christians, however, it didn't matter how many kings—how many *heads* of state—called themselves a god. Those titles were just *blasphemous names* (13v1) in defiance of the one true God. The earliest Christians refused to bend their knee in this religious patriotism and found themselves persecuted.

But the persecution didn't usually come from Rome herself.

To this day—even with our modern travel and technology—the federal government usually doesn't do much law enforcement. Law enforcement tends to be local. If officials in Washington D.C. or London or wherever want something to last, it's got to go local. Lasting changes in culture, beliefs, and policy enforcement are like plants: they must take root in local soil if they're going to stick around.

The same was true in the first century. The Roman culture, beliefs, and policy enforcement needed to start growing out of the local soil. Because once something starts growing locally and **rising up out of the earth** (13v11), it becomes nearly impossible to stop.

By the time John wrote Revelation, this local growth of Roman religious patriotism had begun in earnest. Neighborhood expressions of this Imperial Cult became advocates for Rome, bearing fierce and false witness to its divine nature and authority. The locals of Pergamum had fully embraced the worship of Caesar as a god.[10] Local cities and their officials would voluntarily throw festivals rivaling the Super Bowl **to honor** the Emperor. Wealthy benefactors would **set up statues** (13v14) honoring Caesar, sometimes even hiring the technology gurus of the day to **engineer these statues** (13v14-15) so they would "magically" move.[11] ("Wow! Look at the power of the gods! What a miracle!") Collectively, these local lackeys would serve a **false prophet**[12] for the goddess Roma as seen in her sacred city and its divine caesar.

Religious patriotism even invaded the grocery store. Much of the meat available to **buy in the marketplace** (13v16-17) had been religiously dedicated to the Emperor as a sacrifice before it ever hit the butcher's counter. That's assuming you could get *into* the marketplace. Many local officials had begun requiring people to make a small sacrifice to the emperor before they could enter the

---

[10] John calls Pergamum "where Satan has his throne" (2.13). This is likely in reference to the fact that Pergamum was "the official cult center of emperor worship in Asia" (Mounce, 79).

[11] "Belief in statues that spoke and performed miracles is widely attested in ancient literature... Ventriloquism was practiced by the priests of Oriental cults, and sorcery had found a place in the official circles of Rome" (Mounce, 258). So too Wright: "There were several tricks commonly employed to enable the statues of various gods to move about, to breathe, to weep and even speak. Sophisticated pagan writers of the time mention many such devices, pouring scorn on their trickery" (*Revelation for Everyone*, 120).

[12] The **land beast** will later be called **"false prophet"** as the story develops (16:13, 19:20, 20:10).

local marketplace. ("Loyal to the Emperor? Throw a pinch of incense into the fire as a tiny sacrifice... OK... **here's your stamp."**)

This is the world in which John lived. A world ruled by Rome. And a world where everyday locals were giving life to—**giving breath to** (13v17)—putting into practice—the convictions of Rome.[13] This is the world of John's churches. They too could fly under the radar, buy into Rome, sacrifice to the Emperor, concede to culture. But they'd be losing all of their integrity—selling their soul for the sake of convenience.

History homework over.

That ancient context helps us make good guesses about what this political cartoon means. We need to remember that Revelation 13 is ancient mail in this kind of world. While it doesn't answer every question we might have about it, it hopefully helps us move past conspiracy theories to recognize the seriousness of an Enemy already at work in the world.

This political cartoon wasn't saying, "The Dragon is merely preparing for the end of days." No. It was saying, "The Dragon is already waging war—wake up and recognize the attacks!" And that challenge—wake up and recognize!—continues to this day.

The challenge is more about
being dedicated to the world's king
than decrypting the world's supervillain.

John is telling us to resist the powers of Darkness in all their monstrous shapes. And it's a sobering warning that our local and popular culture often uncritically embraces Death. The resistance of the Darkness and Death is frequently going

---

[13] "'It was given to him to give breath' is a metaphorical way of affirming that the second beast was persuasive in demonstrating that the image of the first beast (e.g., of Caesar) represented the true deity, who stands behind the image and makes decrees" (Beale, 711).

to involve the countercultural practice of discerning and resisting *what* is "anti-Christ" more than cracking the code of *who* is "the Antichrist."[14]

This is John's challenge with **666**.

Despite its reputation, this infamous number is not an impenetrable mystery. Most scholars today take it the solution for granted. And John even told his ordinary, average hearers to figure it out (13v18). The natives of Asia Minor didn't know about Ronald Reagan or Barack Obama or any medieval pope. But they *did* know a recently dead, certifiably crazy king named Nero. And it turns out that if you 1) spell Caesar Nero's name in Hebrew[15] and then 2) add up the numeric values of those letters... what do you think you get?

"Six hundred sixty-six" is a cryptogram for "Caesar Nero."

1.	The Greek for Nero Caesar, *nerōn kaisar*, transliterates into Hebrew as NRWN QSR (reading right to left) and, using Hebrew gematria, with the conventional number values as shown below, adds up to 666:							

SUM	Resh (ר) R	Samech (ס) S	Qof (ק) Q	Nun (נ/ן) N	Waw (ו) W	Resh (ר) R	Nun (נ/ן) N
666	200	60	100	50	6	200	50

**This table originates from Michael Gorman's immensely helpful *Reading Revelation Responsibly*.

Before Netflix, people frequently played these kinds of games with numbers.[16]

---

[14] The word **"antichrist"** never appears in the book of Revelation. The word is used five times in the New Testament (1 Jn. 2.18 (2x), 22; 4.3; 2 Jn. 7). All five of these references refer to a state-of-being that people or spirits/attitudes can fall into.

[15] Hebrew letters had numeric values attached to letters in a similar way to Roman numerals. We could spell the word "mix" in Romans numerals like this: MIX. Tricky, huh? And then if you convert the letters to numeric values (M = 1,000, I = 1, X = 10), you could add up the values to 1,011 and share that number with all your puzzle-solving friends.

[16] Archeologists, for example, have found ancient graffiti in Pompeii that reads: "I love the girl whose number is 545" (Bauckham, *The Climax of Prophecy*, 385). He trusted that she could figure it out.

The puzzle solves just as neatly today as it did for John's original readers. But there's a reason why John creates a simple puzzle instead of just dropping a name. He is warning us about something bigger than just one person. This is another instance in Revelation where something is made strange with the hopes that we'll see more clearly.

We're being challenged to recognize
a pattern more than a person.

"This calls for wisdom," writes John (12v18).

This isn't merely a challenge for John's generation
or a puzzle for history's last generation—
this is a call to wisdom for EVERY generation.

We're being called to wisdom—to "figure out the number." He's not merely inviting people to solve a silly number puzzle. **Triple six** is not merely a cryptogram for "Caesar Nero." It's also a habitual, patterned, repeated falling short of **seven**. We've seen that John uses seven as a number of fullness, completeness, and perfection. *And so 666 falls short of that... in triplicate.* He's inviting them to be on the lookout for a that pattern.

Figure out—calculate—what falls short of perfection... and have nothing to do with that. Because when you willfully embrace that, you embrace Death. And you cannot live in both the way of Death and the book of life (13v8).[17]

More than wanting us to ask "WHO is the Antichrist?"

Jesus wants his people to discern "WHAT is anti-Christ?"

What is Anti-Jesus? What is Anti-Lamb?

Anti-giving-to-others? Anti-sacrificial-love?

---

[17] See footnote 13 in chapter 14 for more on **"book of life."**

One of the Enemy's primary war strategies involves counterfeiting life. The Enemy devastates the world by looking like the Lamb while speaking as the Dragon (13v11). He lures us into things that look like Life but whose substance is death.

John *was indeed* likely warning people of the imperial cult of the first century, but we don't live in the first century. None of us are being coerced into worshipping Rome and the goddess Roma. What, if anything does this ancient political cartoon call us into?

We are called to the same kind of wisdom that the earliest Christians needed. Because the Dragon is still waging war. He's still trampling down with dehumanizing systems. He's still tempting us with counterfeit life.

What are ways we unquestioningly follow culture in worshiping the monstrous? Who are the leaders promising us security if we'll give them uncompromising allegiance? Where are the systems of violence or nationalism, or commerce, or technology, or even religion, that promise us salvation at the price of our integrity?

Sometimes people worry that a credit card or the latest technology might be the mark of the beast. Perhaps a better question asks about the consumerism of the credit card itself. When we buy into a system that tells us that more money will bring more security, or that lifelong debt is worth immediate pleasure, or that sweat shops are a reasonable price for affordable goods, or that our money is primarily for us—when that's the pattern, we *should* be examining our credit cards. We're entertaining the lies of the beast.

Sometimes people worry that the United Nations or a new political leader might be The Antichrist. Perhaps we should be examining our devotion to national politics above local love. If we consider a particular political policy or party to be our only hope, or quietly despise people because they vote for the "wrong person," or believe the world's security comes by conquering people with violence rather than serving people with love, or get more impassioned about Donkeys or Elephants than the Lamb—when that's the pattern, we *should* worry about the government because it has become our god. The Dragon is deceiving us.

Wisdom warns us against whatever way
does not conform to the way of the Crucified.

If it's Anti-Cross-Like-Love, then it's Antichrist.

It's "a six" and falls short of perfection.

Jesus—who has already pledged his allegiance to us—is asking for ours. He's calling us to be loyal to Life itself. He speaks in endlessly creative ways, even political cartoons. It's like Jesus is saying:

> "Use your minds, my people... think the details of your life through carefully. There are many things—from far over the sea and even growing locally—that don't line up with my Love. Don't cling to them. Cling to me, to my cross, to my love. I don't want you, beloved, to miss Life."

We—the Church—let's start with us for crying out loud—are challenged to know the Enemy's number and refuse to buy what he's selling. We were made for seven; we must never settle for six.

//

Jesus, you are Lord, and no one else is. grant me faithfulness and patient endurance while evil lashes about. Give me
wisdom to recognize every monster unleashed by the Dragon and to resist their seduction and violence. Give me ears
to hear your Spirit calling me into the true and lasting life
that no mind can imagine and no Enemy can counterfeit.
Amen.

Then I looked, and there before me was the Lamb, standing on Mount Zion, and with him 144,000 who had his name and his Father's name written on their foreheads. And I heard a sound from heaven like the roar of rushing waters and like a loud peal of thunder. The sound I heard was like that of harpists playing their harps. And they sang a new song before the throne and before the four living creatures and the elders. No one could learn the song except the 144,000 who had been redeemed from the earth. These are those who did not defile themselves with women, for they remained virgins. They follow the Lamb wherever he goes. They were purchased from among mankind and offered as firstfruits to God and the Lamb. No lie was found in their mouths; they are blameless.

Then I saw another angel flying in midair, and he had the eternal gospel to proclaim to those who live on the earth —to every nation, tribe, language and people. He said in a loud voice, "Fear God and give him glory, because the hour of his judgment has come. Worship him who made the heavens, the earth, the sea and the springs of water."

A second angel followed and said, "'Fallen! Fallen is Babylon the Great,' which made all the nations drink the maddening wine of her adulteries."

A third angel followed them and said in a loud voice: "If anyone worships the beast and its image and receives its mark on their forehead or on their hand, they, too, will drink the wine of God's fury, which has been poured full strength into the cup of his wrath. They will be tormented with burning sulfur in the presence of the holy angels and of the Lamb. And the smoke of their torment will rise for ever and ever.

There will be no rest day or night for those who worship the beast and its image, or for anyone who receives the mark of its name." This calls for patient endurance on the part of the people of God who keep his commands and remain faithful to Jesus.

Then I heard a voice from heaven say, "Write this: Blessed are the dead who die in the Lord from now on."

"Yes," says the Spirit, "they will rest from their labor, for their deeds will follow them."

I looked, and there before me was a white cloud, and seated on the cloud was one like a son of man with a crown of gold on his head and a sharp sickle in his hand. Then another angel came out of the temple and called in a loud voice to him who was sitting on the cloud, "Take your sickle and reap, because the time to reap has come, for the harvest of the earth is ripe."

So he who was seated on the cloud swung his sickle over the earth, and the earth was harvested.

Another angel came out of the temple in heaven, and he too had a sharp sickle. Still another angel, who had charge of the fire, came from the altar and called in a loud voice to him who had the sharp sickle, "Take your sharp sickle and gather the clusters of grapes from the earth's vine, because its grapes are ripe." The angel swung his sickle on the earth, gathered its grapes and threw them into the great winepress of God's wrath. They were trampled in the winepress outside the city, and blood flowed out of the press, rising as high as the horses' bridles for a distance of 1,600 stadia.

11. PREPARING THE SONG

Have you ever heard an orchestra warming up before a performance? The strings stretch and squawk, the brass section clears its throat with a croak, and the percussion thunders without unity. A young child hearing all this for the first time might wonder, "Why has everyone come to hear this noise?" But after a period of warming up—of preparing instruments and audience—the orchestra begins to play.

This might be something like what's happening in Revelation 14;
the music to remake the universe is being readied—and so are we.

The Song of the Universe is about to sing.

The animation that marked the middle of John's letter is beginning to crossover into his original story. Back in Revelation 12, John had paused in his storytelling, like a filmmaker using a flashback, and began reflecting on the central revelation of Revelation: *God's plan to save the world involves us embodying love willing to bleed.* Self-giving, radically-forgiving, enemy-embracing, suffering Love. This Love will save the world.

John first saw this Love as a Lamb (ch5). Then he saw his saving purposes of Love "unsealed" (ch6-7). And then finally he was invited to "eat" Love's plan in order to proclaim it to his churches (ch10).

John's proclamation of God's purposes came in the form of a story about two witnesses (ch11). It was a parable about the Church following God in embodying Love to the point of death (11v3-12). And this loving witness accomplishes what nothing else can. No act of judgment, no show of force, no plagues of Egypt, can achieve what Love willing to bleed accomplishes. The witness of the church leads to a vast number of people turning from darkness and worshipping God (11v13).

When the church follows the life of the Lamb
the world is changed and lives are saved.

God's plan to save the world
involves his own love willing to bleed
will be embodied in his people.

Now cue the animation sequence (ch12-13). Ever since this eye-opening "revelation," *John has drawn us into a strange, dream-like cartoon to explore the Church's faithfulness from different angles.*

He told us about the Child (12v5) whose very arrival defeated all the forces of evil (12v7-8). He introduced us to great symbolic "signs": the people of God as a dazzling Woman and the terrible Dragon pursuing her. He doodled monsters for us—the two beasts of idolatrous government and local political-religious culture that wage war against God's people. These beasts of sky, sea, and earth all conspire against—and succeed in **conquering**! (13v7)—the Lamb lovers. Chapter 13 ended with terrible beasts threatening death against those loyal to the Lamb (13v15-18).

But fear not!—for we will soon see that the Lamb lovers are actually "**victorious over**[1] the beast and its image and over the number of its name" (15v2). They're celebrating victory with song—a New Exodus song[2] in heaven (15v3-4). How do they get there? Well, that's what Revelation 14 is about. They're getting ready for that song.

---

[1] See footnote 7 in chapter 5.
[2] See Exodus 15.1-18.

We're plunging back into the John's principal story with breakneck speed, and all of these animated characters are coming with us. The cartoon is spilling off the screen, running amok, the beasts bursting forth Jumanji-style.

We're suddenly zipping *upward,* back to the original prime seating we had been granted in heaven's balcony. The recent cartoons escorted us downward into lower levels of the cosmos to explore a *desert wilderness* (12v6,14) and a *seashore* (13v1) and *the earth itself* (13v11). But now we're suddenly swept skyward again with John as the heavens prepare to play the surprising symphony of salvation.

We ascend back to heaven in a sweeping camera shot with three key moments. We ascend with John to the top of **Mount Zion** (14v1). Then our feet float away from *terra firma,* and we're **midair** with some angels (14v6). Finally we find ourselves **on a white cloud** (14v14) with a view of the temple[3] in heaven (14v17). That's the journey we make as the orchestra prepares its music.

The three moments are worth examining because they show us various sections of the orchestra. In these moments, we glimpse the various themes (or "instruments") that will soon come rushing together in song.

In our **first moment**, we find ourselves on a mountain (14v1). This is **Mount Zion**, the literal mountain on which stood Jerusalem and her Temple. But instead of that holy dwelling place made of stone and mortar, we now find the Lamb and his followers (3v12).

Jesus in his church is where heaven and earth meet.

John can process with his eyes before he can process with his ears. He sees a mass of people but can't make sense of what he hears. It simply sounds like a loud noise (14v2)—like a roaring waterfall or a crackling thunderstorm. But

---

[3] Like all of the language in Revelation, the language of **"the temple in heaven"** seems to be symbolic of realities too mysterious and too real for us to understand. In chapter 21, we're told that God's new reality has "no temple" (v22) because of God's immediate, accessible presence with his people.

suddenly his initial confusion gives way and he recognizes a chorus under the chaos. "Well, now that I'm listening, it actually sounds like music—like harpists playing their harps (14v2)." The string section is warming up.

John once again sees the great uncountable *army*—the symbolic 144,000—we first met in Revelation 7. The language about these men "not defiling themselves" and being "virgins" is all about military discipline (14v4). That's the way the Old Testament talks about a devout, ritually pure military force.[4]

This elite squadron stands victorious on a mountaintop even though the Enemy wages war against them (12v17), they are victorious. They win despite the Beasts killing and conquering them (13v7). *And the harps are leading them in song.*

Singing a mysterious, secret song.
Singing a **new song** (14v3).

A song no one can learn except those who have been redeemed.

Yes, there is darkness in the world. Yes, plenty of monsters and chaos, suffering and evil. Not only in the world back then. Not only near the end of history. In our world—in our lives—right now. But there's also something deeper than the darkness. There's a song beneath the noise. And it's possible to learn the song.

Learning the song of salvation is not as quick or simple as praying a prayer, learning some information, checking off a list, or simply believing "the right things about the right things." The song must be formed in our souls. God's Spirit teaches us his song gradually, over time... like fruit growing in soil.[5] The Spirit's music gets engrained in our souls as we trust (again and again) that the Lamb claims us. We can rest in the reality that we have already been "purchased" for God (14v4). The song of salvation (that is, ultimate meaning, pur-

---

4 Compare Deuteronomy 23.9-10, 1 Samuel 21.5, 2 Samuel 11.8-11.
5 Galatians 5.22-23.

pose, beauty, truth, and peace) gets formed in us as we follow the Lamb wherever he goes (14v4).

Further up, into love.
Further in, into sacrificial self-giving.

Further up, further in—through death into victory.

We keep ascending—higher than the mountains—we arrive at the **second moment**, when we see **angels flying in midair** (14v6). Three of them. They don't have trumpets, but maybe they're the woodwinds. Clarinets and oboes and bassoons. Their sound is beautiful and haunting.

Beautiful. For they proclaim eternal gospel, eternal good news, to those who live on the earth (14v6). "Fear God!" they cry, "and discover the beginning of wisdom. Give him glory![6]" The one who judged evil with the power of land, sea, springs, and heaven (8v7-12) is worthy of worship (14v7).

Haunting. For they sound caution. We become what we worship. Those who patiently remain faithful to Jesus (14v12) will rest from their labor, rest from suffering, rest from fear. They will "rest from pain and rest from wrong."[7] For their deeds "will follow them" (14v13). The song of Life will have been woven so deeply into them that even in death, they will be blessed. They *will* find rest.

That's *not* saying that these people did the right things to somehow get God on their side. No. God is already, always on our side.[8] That's the good news—the eternal gospel—that we're always invited to believe. That we too have already been "purchased" for God. Jesus said, "This is my body and it is for you" (Lk. 22v19; 1 Cor. 11v24) And that includes you. Yes, *you*. That's the gospel.

---

[6] That's exactly what happens in Revelation 11.13 because of the witness of the Church.

[7] Lyrics, of course, from Boublil and Schönberg's *Les Miserables*.

[8] The heart of the gospel is always always always that God always and already loves his enemies to the point of death (Rom. 5.6-10, cf. Matt. 5.43-48).

As we begin to believe this good news, the Spirit begins to slowly, mysteriously bring our lives into alignment with his true Life.[9] And that (of course) eventually includes our outer lives. Good deeds don't save anyone. They are, however, a clue that the Spirit is saving us—saturating us with his music. Our outer lives signal what we worship. And when we worship the Lamb, he transforms us into the kind of people who will actually enjoy eternal Love.

Because, evidently, not everyone can.

Some find the the presence of Love himself to be a torturous existence (14v10). That's the haunting sound of the woodwinds—the terrifying dissonant chords from these angels.

There will be "no rest" (14v11)
for those whose hearts chase
a different lover than the Lamb.

This different lover is called **Lady Babylon** (or "Babylon the Great"), and this is the first we're hearing of her (14v8). She is a twisted reflection of the **dazzling Woman** we met in the desert. Her full fifteen minutes of fame comes in a few chapters,[10] but the prepping orchestra gives us a preview of her story.

Lady Babylon is a woman.
And this woman is also city... hence her name.
And she's also a kind of people.

A woman, a city, a people—all rolled up in one.[11] She mirrors values opposite of God's people. And we immediately know something is wrong with her because

---

[9] This is part of why Revelation makes a big deal about **"lies"** (Rev. 14.5) **and "liars"** (20.8). This seems to be talking less tell a "white lie" and more about the character of those who lives run completely counter to what is ontologically True (capital T)—namely the self-giving, sacrificial love of the Lamb who is truth itself (1.5, 3.14, 19.11)

[10] Revelation 17.

[11] The people of God, of course, also appear as a city (11.2) and a woman (12.1).

she has a dangerous drinking problem (14v8,10). In this Whore-City we find total rejection of the purposes of God; life in absolute self-indulgent opposition to God. Unlike the Woman in the wilderness in Revelation 12, this "Woman" will not be sheltered, protected, or rescued.

This Woman—this kind of life—is "fallen" (14v8). She's coming to an end.

Tales in Old Testament speak of cities being dest-
royed by fire and sulfur,[12] and this "Babylon" will be destroyed in similar fashion (14v10). The people of God find "rest" (14v13) but there is "no rest" (14v11) for those who want nothing to do with peace.[13] The ancient prophetic images of burning sulfur and endless smoke symbolize the seriousness of a life hardened forever against the loving purposes of God.[14]

The language is graphic and terrifying. And it should be. This is what human existence becomes when we reject God's purposes. Should we harden ourselves against the Good, the Beautiful, and the True revealed in Jesus, our hearts will gravitate to the Hateful, the Ugly, and the False. We will embrace what cannot last. We will love what cannot give life. We will cling to what will destroy us.

Life in opposition to God
is a tortured existence—
a Death-Life.

Revelation offers a dire warning: if we want to forever guzzle the "maddening wine" (14v8) of life in opposition to Love, we must beware. It's possible that we

---

[12] The archetype of **a city destroyed by fire** is, of course, Sodom and Gomorrah (Gen. 19). The prophets frequently evoke this image when denouncing the practices of the culture around them.
[13] Isaiah 48:22
[14] Particularly relevant is Isaiah 34.9-10 talking about the literal, historical fall of the nation of Edom. The language there is demonstrably symbolic. (The land is obviously not still literally burning nor smoke forever rising.) The grave and dire seriousness, however, of willfully, continuously living counter to God's nature and purposes can only be hinted at—even with the powerful symbols of **fire, sulfur, and smoke**.

may get what we want (14v10). These people are drinking deeply from what they wanted—it's an existence of *self*-chosen, *self*-centered, *self*-inflicted torment.[15]

That's the beautiful, haunting sound
of the midair woodwinds:

Believe the good news...
for without it we are drowning
in wine we think we want.

Which brings us to the **third moment,** the third section of the orchestra. On a white cloud, high in the sky, we find angels preparing for harvest (14v14-20). These angels boom like percussion, energetically banging the drums that "the time" is almost here. The great holiday of harvest time is about to arrive! Bring in the wheat!

We don't live in a farming society. While some of us may cultivate small gardens for fresh vegetables, almost none of us grow all of our own food. It's nearly impossible for us to imagine the excitement that harvest time has brought people throughout human history. Harvest is when all the work finally pays off. Harvest is when there's nothing left to do but enjoy. Harvest is when we feast and drink and celebrate.

Those weeks of Thanksgiving and Christmas at the end of the year are, perhaps, our closest comparisons. But few of us worry that those celebrations will not arrive. We don't lose sleep that a swarm of locusts might destroy all our turkey and dressing or that our Christmas tree will wither away from lack of rain. Our holidays come like clockwork, free from threat.

---

[15] Whatever else we might say about Revelation 14.10-11, the poetic, artistic metaphors employed are a serious warning about "**torment**" not "torture." *Jesus does not torture people; Jesus endures torture for people.* And Jesus is what God is always like. The character of God is at stake. The gospel is at stake. (Matthew 18.34 is a judgment parable that actually DOES use the word "torture" but its point seems akin to Rom 1.18,24,26,28 where God hands us over to what we've chosen even if they—not God, not "the king"—torture us.)

Harvest, on the other hand, was never taken for granted. It wasn't a sure thing. It was something you longed for, something you hoped to see. And when it arrived, you celebrated in a big way.

These angels are banging the drum that all uncertainty and anxiety in God's people will soon be over. The holiday of the harvest is about to arrive. And because of the witness of the Church,[16] the **harvest** will be enormous. Because they follow the Lamb in love to the point of death, having been offered as a sacrifice of firstfruits (14v4)—the earth is now ripe (14v15) and chock full of people who revere God and love the Lamb:

BOOM. Bring in the harvest!

BOOM. It's time to feast!

BOOM. Now we celebrate!

Revelation 14 is an orchestra warming up and saying:

> "This is all going somewhere. Heaven is about to play the symphony of salvation—the secret song of those victorious martyrs on Mount Zion, the eternal good news of rest for those who follow the Lamb, the hymn of the harvest and a feast that never ends.[17] Now can we PLEASE move this along and get started? Let's unleash this symphony!"

The song *will* be unleashed. An orchestra only warms up so long. The music will start to play into Revelation 15 and the song of the saints will carry us through the end of the letter, through the end of evil, and bring us to the crisp dawn of eternal morning.

None of this is mere flowery language or empty rhetorical flourish. One day history as we know it will disappear beneath the incoming tide of God's great day of love. Death will be swallowed up in victory. Suffering and sickness over-

---

[16] Or the 144,000, or "the dazzling Woman," or the "two witnesses"... pick your image at this point.

[17] The image of feasting returns positively in 19.9 and ominously in 19.21. The poetic prophecies of Isaiah 25.6-8 and Ezekiel 39.17-20 seem to stand behind these respective images.

whelmed by life eternal. This calls for "patient endurance" (14v12) by all who cling to Jesus when evil seems to be triumphing.[18]

An orchestra only warms up so long... but sometimes it feels like forever.

"Sometimes"?

Who am I kidding? Let's get honest: this feels like a day never coming; a symphony never starting. And perhaps the final image of Revelation 14 speaks to our need for patience in the midst of suffering.

Before the dawn of a world remade by love, we all experience something different. A painful darkness. A world of weeds. Before the holiday of the harvest can arrive, we need the world to be purged of weeds. The Enemy's weeds— wickedness, evil, hatred, death.[19] And the good news is that de-weeding is part of the symphony too.

This de-weeding arrives next chapter in the form of seven bowls of wine—the wine of God's "fury" (14v10). What we call the "wrath of God." That is, God's love fermented and distilled into such a blistering vintage that it burns away all that is not love. More on this next chapter. For now... we catch a glimpse of that beautiful wine being made.

After the image of a wheat harvest comes a different kind of harvest—the harvest of **grapes** and the making of **wine**. The common, everyday process of gathering grapes (14v18) and crushing them in a winepress (14v19) comes as another image of God's plan. And this image is shocking... but not for the reasons we first think. Because it doesn't seem like it's the blood of the enemies of God that runs like a river (14v20). That's what we assume most of the time. That's the intuition of our killer instinct.[20] Heaven is going to crush

---

18 See also 13.10.
19 See Matthew 13.25.
20 Contrast our initial instinct about enemies with Jesus's description of the Father in Matthew 5.43-48.

God's enemies (which are, conveniently, usually also *our* enemies.) God is going to make *their* blood flow.[21]

But if we read carefully, nowhere are we told that the grapes are the enemies of God. We fill that part in. Oddly enough, as we keep reading we discover that the enemies of God are those who drink the wine from the winepress.

The end of Revelation 14 finds a river of blood from God's winepress (14v19) that flows directly into Revelation 15 & 16, where it becomes seven great bowls of wine (i.e. wrath[22]) being poured out. This is the mysterious way God judges evil—he pours it more and more of its own brew (14v8). As the deeds of the righteous follow them (14v13), so also the drinks of the wicked follow them.

The wicked get more and more of what they want... and it's hell.

Later we will be told that Lady Babylon is drunk on the blood of God's people (17v6). She drinks the blood of the martyrs—that's her wine. Eventually we will look back on the bowls of "wrath" and recognize that God poured Babylon a double of her own drink (18v6). Which leads us back to the grapes... the place where this double gets mixed.

Other writers of Apocalyptic stories had envisioned God's judgment of sinners causing blood to flow in torrential rivers. One describes that "the horse will walk up to the breast in the blood of sinners, and the chariot will be submerged to its height."[23] John seems to be aware of this image and deliberately turning it upside down. He purposely echoes this language:

> (14v20) ...trampled in the winepress outside the city, and blood flowed out of the press, rising as high as the horses' bridles for a distance of 1,600 stadia...

---

[21] John seems to be drawing on a long tradition of harvest as God's eschatological setting-right-the-world, and both Joel 3.23ff and Isaiah 63.1-6 (cf. Rev. 19.13-16) seem to be a primary source for his imagery. John, however, seems to have reworked Joel's dual images of "harvesting" the wicked into dual images of "harvesting" the righteous—that is of safety (**wheat**; cf Matt. 3.12, Lk. 3.17, etc) and of sacrifice (**grapes**; cf. Matt. 26.27-28, Phil. 2.17, 2 Tim. 4.6). This combination of victorious safety and sacrificial witness is, of course, a common motif throughout Revelation (the Lamb = 5.6; "the witnesses" = 11.7 + 11.11-12; in song = 12.11; victory over the beasts = 13.7 + 15.2)

[22] Wrath comes in the form of wine (see 14.10, 16.19).

[23] 1 En.100:3-4 (written/compiled between 300 BCE - 100 BCE). Cited by Beale, 782.

It's the image of a *river of blood flowing 1600 stadia*[24] outward from this "winepress." As the story unfolds, this river will transform the world.[25]

Now... notice what is pressed: *the vine.*[26] That is a traditional image for the people of God (not to mention her Messiah).[27] It's shocking, but the vine and her grapes seem to symbolize the Messiah and his *trampled* saints (14v20, cf. 11v3).[28] The narrative flows from threats against those who refuse the "number" of the beast (13v15-18) to the insistence that God's army already bears his "name" on their foreheads (14v1) and they cannot lie about that (14v5). And so these saints must patiently endure (14v12-13) even as they are slain by a system that is doomed to die (14v8-11). They are following the Lamb wherever he goes (14v4).

The fate of the martyrs truly mirrors the fate of their master. Jesus submitted himself to a beastly cross, but the God of life defeated evil there.[29] So too here. This is a picture of the Lamb's followers slaughtered by the wicked's violence, not an image of the Lamb or his followers taking up violence against the wicked. The world "trampling" the saints somehow simultaneously becomes God's way of judging that world and purging it of evil (19v15). The people of God are

---

[24] **The number 1600** is another suspiciously symbolic-looking number. Caird (195) points out that squared numbers (or numbers with squared factors) are exclusively associated with God's people: the saint's number in 144,000 (14.1ff), the saints' reign in 1,000 (20:4-6), and the saint's residence (21:16-17). This number is **the square of 40**—the symbolic number of testing/waiting for God's people (Gen. 7-8; Exod. 16:35, 24:18, 34:28, Mk. 1:13). John is conveying the saints' trials.

[25] John also seems to be borrowing Ezekiel's image of a river of life flowing from a renewed Jerusalem (Ezek. 47:1-5) to make the dead come to life (i.e. the Dead sea, Ezek. 47:8). There, the depth of the river is intentionally measured three times. Here, the river of blood/wine is measured and has the same effect... making a dead world come alive.

[26] The word **"grapes"** (*botrus*) does not appear in verse 19. The only thing—literally, the only word—that gets thrown into the winepress in verse 19 is "the vine" (*ampelos*). Our modern translations unhelpfully add the word "grapes" into verse 19. See the KJV for a literal rendering.

[27] For OT usage of **"vine"** see Isa. 5:1-7; Jer. 2:21; Hos. 14:8; Mic. 4:2-4; Zech 3:10. Caird emphasizes that there is *no precedent* for the vine/grapes as an image of punishment for the nations (192-194). In the Johannine tradition, this is an explicit image for Jesus (Jn. 15:1) and those who connected to him.

[28] Later Jesus is pictured as (lit.) "treading the winepress *of the wine* of the wrath of the fury of God" (19:15). The winepress is distinguished from the wine (of wrath). Caird, 246: "The wine of the fury of the wrath of God is John's symbol for judgment, and... the winepress represents something quite different, namely the means by which the wine of judgment is prepared. When we remember that the cup of wrath is the cup which Babylon herself mixed (18:6), and that she was drunk with the blood of the martyrs (17.6), it becomes reasonable to suppose that the winepress, like the Cross, is a place where God has turned the murderous acts of men into the means of their own judgment." In other words, the willingly bloodied Jesus will arrive to trample every cross.

[29] John 12:31; Colossians 2:15.

166

wheat to be harvested as well as grapes to be crushed.[30] We join Jesus in becoming bread broken and wine poured out for the life of the world.

This percussion section is what surprises us about the song and symphony. The song of salvation gets set in an unusual tempo. But we shouldn't be surprised: it's the cadence of the cross. The Lamb saves the world through love willing to bleed, and his lovers follow him wherever he goes (14v4). And those who resist the beastly kind of life sometimes wind up being slain (13v15). But these Lamb followers are actually victorious (15v2)—harvested (14v14-20) and at rest (14v13). They have endured (14v12). And now they are praising the Lamb (15v3-4). But they arrived home crushed... like their Lord.[31]

Following the Lamb wherever he goes, does not mean that we somehow avoid suffering. In reality, it's frequently the opposite.[32] John is reminding us again—in yet another picture—that *our safety comes through sacrifice*. We trust the Lamb's sacrifice and follow him into sacrificial love for the sake of the world.

The local church
is at the heart
of how Jesus saves.

Jesus does not spare us from suffering. Servants are not above their master.[33] But he does transform our suffering. Jesus transforms our blood to be like his: poured out to purge the world of evil.

---

[30] The world-changing nature of Christ's suffering now gets embodied through his people. This passage fleshes out, with startling prophetic imagery (Isa. 63:3), the challenge of following Jesus in costly discipleship laid out in Hebrews 13:12-13: "Jesus also suffered outside the city gate to make the people holy through his own blood [so] let us, then, go to him outside the camp, bearing the disgrace he bore." (See also Caird, 192-194.)

[31] John appears to be tapping into a tradition that recognizes that God's people (rather than God's enemies, cf. Isa. 63:3) as crushed in the winepress (Lam. 1:15) and borrowing Zechariah's image of God judging the nations by "mak[ing] Jerusalem a cup that sends all the surrounding nations reeling" (Zech. 12.2; cf. also Jer. 51.7 where Babylon becomes a "cup" of judgment). John frames all of this in the **dual harvest language** of Joel 3.13.

[32] "Chapter 13 ended with a threat of death to anyone who did not worship the statue of the monster or bear the number of its name. Chapter 15 begins with a vision of the victorious martyrs who 'had won their freedom from the monster and from its statue and from the number of its name' (15:2). It is natural to think that the intervening chapter has described the battle in which that freedom was won, and that it has been concerned with nothing else" (Caird, 193).

[33] Matt. 10:24; Jn. 13:16.

The only saving thing Jesus can give us is his very own life. And Jesus's life was crushed for the life of the world. His blood poured out—flowing like a river—so that love can transform the world.

The life of cross and resurrection—
that is all we're ever given.

God gives us himself.

This is what we're invited into—namely, the life of the Lamb. And then, mysteriously, even our suffering, struggle, defeat—even our being bled like grapes—gets transformed into wine.

For those of us bleeding as we wait for the cosmic concert of the ages, the grapes whisper comfort. When life is impossibly hard—in seasons when the darkness is crushing—may we know that God doesn't waste a drop of our suffering. It is a great mystery, but God saves the world by pouring out his own life as well as the lives of those willing to follow him. Keep bleeding love—it will destroy evil and spread salvation.

As we wait, our lives often sound like a disjointed, confusing racket. We suffer, we watch each other suffer, and we await the symphony's song. We can certainly pray to be spared from suffering ("deliver us from evil") when we find ourselves in Gethsemane ("let this cup pass"). But when we find ourselves in the midst of suffering, we must learn to pray like the Vine of vines:

> *"God, ferment my fear*
> *and transform my tribulation.*
> *into wine that heals the world."*

For that's how God saves the world. It's an inside job. God makes wine out of suffering—white-hot love that vanquishes evil and heals the world. Jesus shares his life with us. He shares a meal with us, and then he sets us on the table as his cup. This is our hope, and it calls for patient endurance.

//

Maestro of love, help me hear the symphony that makes all things new, and teach me to sing it today. May I follow the Lamb wherever he goes. Make me eager for my deeds to follow me, and give me like your bread and wine for the world. Help me trust that even my deep struggles—even my deep sufferings—will help usher in your new world. Amen.

I saw in heaven another great and marvelous sign: seven angels with the seven last plagues—last, because with them God's wrath is completed. And I saw what looked like a sea of glass glowing with fire and, standing beside the sea, those who had been victorious over the beast and its image and over the number of its name. They held harps given them by God and sang the song of God's servant Moses and of the Lamb:

"Great and marvelous are your deeds,
    Lord God Almighty.
Just and true are your ways,
    King of the nations.
Who will not fear you, Lord,
    and bring glory to your name?
For you alone are holy.
All nations will come
    and worship before you,
for your righteous acts have been revealed."

After this I looked, and I saw in heaven the temple—that is, the tabernacle of the covenant law—and it was opened. Out of the temple came the seven angels with the seven plagues. They were dressed in clean, shining linen and wore golden sashes around their chests. Then one of the four living creatures gave to the seven angels seven golden bowls filled with the wrath of God, who lives for ever and ever. And the temple was filled with smoke from the glory of God and from his power, and no one could enter the temple until the seven plagues of the seven angels were completed.

Then I heard a loud voice from the temple saying to the seven angels, "Go, pour out the seven bowls of God's wrath on the earth."

The first angel went and poured out his bowl on the land, and ugly, festering sores broke out on the people who had the mark of the beast and worshiped its image.

The second angel poured out his bowl on the sea, and it turned into blood like that of a dead person, and every living thing in the sea died.

The third angel poured out his bowl on the rivers and springs of water, and they became blood. Then I heard the angel in charge of the waters say,

"You are just in these judgments, O Holy One,
you who are and who were; for they have shed the blood of your holy people and your prophets, and you have given them blood to drink as they deserve."

And I heard the altar respond:

"Yes, Lord God Almighty,
    true and just are your judgments."

The fourth angel poured out his bowl on the sun, and the sun was allowed to scorch people with fire. They were seared by the intense heat and they cursed the name of God, who had control over these plagues, but they refused to repent and glorify him.

The fifth angel poured out his bowl on the throne of the beast, and its kingdom was plunged into darkness. People gnawed their tongues in agony and cursed the God of heaven because of their pains and their sores, but they refused to repent of what they had done.

The sixth angel poured out his bowl on the great river Euphrates, and its water was dried up to prepare the way for the kings from the East. Then I saw three impure spirits that looked like frogs; they came out of the mouth of the dragon, out of the mouth of the beast and out of the mouth of the false prophet. They are demonic spirits that perform signs, and they go out to the kings of the whole world, to gather them for the battle on the great day of God Almighty.

"Look, I come like a thief! Blessed is the one who stays awake and remains clothed, so as not to go naked and be shamefully exposed."

Then they gathered the kings together to the place that in Hebrew is called Armageddon.

The seventh angel poured out his bowl into the air, and out of the temple came a loud voice from the throne, saying, "It is done!" Then there came flashes of lightning, rumblings, peals of thunder and a severe earthquake. No earthquake like it has ever occurred since mankind has been on earth, so tremendous was the quake.

The great city split into three parts, and the cities of the nations collapsed. God remembered Babylon the Great and gave her the cup filled with the wine of the fury of his wrath. Every island fled away and the mountains could not be found. From the sky huge hailstones, each weighing about a hundred pounds, fell on people. And they cursed God on account of the plague of hail, because the plague was so terrible.

12. SEVEN BOWLS AND THE WORLD CRUCIFIED

We're about two-thirds the way through Revelation. This is typically the point in a story where we're approaching a climax. Luke climbs into an X-Wing to fly toward the Death Star. Indiana Jones escapes the snake pit and begins barreling after the ark. And Revelation is approaching its climax as well.

It's been the story of heaven's throne,
a mysterious scroll, a broken world,
a suffering people, and answered prayers.[1]

This ancient letter has delivered the story of heaven's saving plans for the world finally being "opened" through a stunning parade of images, symbols, political critique, mythic animation... all of it has been thoroughly deeply marinated in the Hebrew scriptures. And now we're barreling into the story's climax—a final cluster of seven judgments.

Having seen **seven seals** broken (Rev 6-7),
and having heard **seven trumpets** sound (Rev 8-9 & 11v15),
we're now arriving at **seven bowls** poured out (Rev 16).

It's some of the scariest reading in Scripture.

---

[1] Throne room (4.2); mysterious scroll (5.1-3); broken world (6.1-8); the suffering saints (6.9); answered prayers (8.4-5ff).

The recent mythic animation has faded (**ch12-13**), and the triumphant song of the conquering martyrs (**ch14**) still echoes in our ears: God is going to save the world. We're anxious for that song to become a symphony. But a sobering reality meets us here as we approach the climax of all things:

To save the world
God must judge
the world.[2]

Think of a rotten tooth that must be pulled or an infected wound that must be cleaned. Healing and wholeness can only reign when judgment falls on disease. So too with the cosmos; the cancer of sin must be killed.

Revelation 15-16 gives us the good news of divine judgment. These seven bowls are not a picture of cosmic destruction, despite their checkered history of interpretation. Remember—the identity of Jesus guides us through the hard parts of Revelation.[3] As we continually remind ourselves that God himself is crucified for his enemies, we begin slowly recognizing these bowls as a reminder of his goodness. The Great Gardner who planted Eden promises that he will make his creation flourish once again. And weeds must be destroyed for gardens to grow.

The seven bowls are a promise of cosmic de-weeding
not a threat of cosmic destruction.

Bowls of "wrath" shouldn't make us doubt God's goodness; they should remind us that God takes seriously the sickness infecting the world. "Wrath" is God's love of life aimed at all that is anti-life. Darkness experiences light as wrath. Instead of something to fear, God's wrath is something Christians welcome, recognizing that it always aims to destroy what is destroying life (11v18).

---

[2] A proper understanding of God's judgment in Scripture recognizes that God's judgment always aims at salvation. God's "no" always serves a bigger, better "yes." This is such a pervasive theme in Scripture that one scholar has written an entire biblical theology framed around it. See James Hamilton's aptly titled "God's Glory in Salvation through Judgment: A Biblical Theology" (2010).
[3] See chapter 7.

Many atheists argue an all-powerful, all-good God as incompatible with a world of evil. Christians ought to empathize deeply with this obstacle to faith because it's actually an objection with roots in the human longing for divine justice. If there exists an all-powerful, benevolent God, then this God *must* sort out the world at some point.

God *must* save his good creation. So God *must* judge evil—both evil "out there" in the world and evil "in here" inside of me. I mean, who would want to live forever in a world plagued by evil?

Who would want to live a hellish kind of life forever?

Judgment is what must take place
for resurrection to be good news.

And the good news of Revelation 15-16 is that judgment is coming. These seven bowls unpack "the seventh trumpet" (Rev 11v15) and portray God's "wrath" finally being poured out on all evil in the world. Scholars almost entirely agree that this portrait of bowl almost inarguably belongs to history's future, for it ushers in a transformed world (ch21-22). These bowls of "wrath" bring about a world resurrected.

Wait... wrath brings resurrection?
How does that work?

We tend to think of words like "wrath"[4] and "fury"[5] in petty, trivial, reactionary ways. My "fury" is what happens when I have a really bad day: when traffic crawls, or my stomach growls, or my toe stubs. Suddenly I'm filled with wrath—at its mercy, really—and I lash out. But that's never what the Bible points us toward when it talks about God's "wrath" or "fury."

---

[4] Revelation 14.10,19; 15.1,7; 16.19.
[5] Revelation 14.10.

God's "wrath" is a way of talking about God's love. Love, after all, is what Christians confess God to be.[6] Love is elemental to God. Love is eternal—always and forever there between Father, Son, and Holy Spirit. Between them flows infinite, relational, unchanging love, before and beyond all things. Wrath, on the other hand, is not eternal—not elemental to God. It hasn't always been. What we call divine "wrath" is *not* the equal and opposite "yang" to the "yin" of divine love. In fact, "wrath" is actually a form of God's love. Wrath is what God's love looks like doing painful, uncomfortable, impossibly hard things like moving mountains, overthrowing tyranny, and destroying evil.

Wrath is what God's love feels like
when sin shipwrecks against it.

Chemotherapy feels like wrath for the cancer. And it doesn't look pretty for anyone watching. But the goal of chemotherapy is healing. The goal of chemo is new life. And this is the final treatment—seven blistering bowls of God's vintage love distilled to destroy evil (15v6).[7]

God's wrath will be "completed" with this (15v1). In stylized language that fits the rest of the letter, seven angels receive seven bowls. And notice where they receive them. They receive the bowls from one of the four living creatures we met backstage in heaven (15v7). One of the great symbols for "all creation" is handing out great bowls of burning love.

Creation itself longs to be de-weeded.[8]

Perhaps here we finally have an answer to why those four living creatures seemed to be welcoming evil in Revelation 6.[9] Perhaps now we have an insight

---

[6] 1 John 4.8,16.

[7] The word *thumos* ("overwhelming emotion") links with *oinos* ("wine) and is translated "wine of passion" with regards to Lady Babylon (14:8; 18:3). That same word pair repeatedly gets used with God as well (14:10; 16:19; 19:15), but English translations translate the phrases differently. The motif is dueling erotic invitations: God's *thumos* is an *eros* unto life, Babylon's an *eros* unto death.

[8] Romans 8.22 and context.

[9] The creatures kept saying "come" in 6.1,3,5,7.

into why Jesus himself gave power to a great enemy in Revelation 9 when he was handing out keys to the Abyss.[10] Perhaps here we have some sort of mysterious, provisional answer to why God hasn't stopped evil yet. Why evil seems free to run amok. Why God lets bad things happen.

Through its long narrative, Revelation hints that God is allowing darkness to grow and blossom—allowing evil to rise to its full strength—so that God can pull evil up by its root.

God often allows evil to flower so that it can be completely uprooted. That's the way God frequently works in our lives. The Twelve Step Program calls it "hitting rock bottom." When disorder and darkness become unmanageable, unsustainable, unlivable, then you're at rock bottom and finally open to complete healing. And John's vision seems to indicate that God works this way on a cosmic level too. Creation itself allows disorder and darkness to do its worst in preparation for complete healing.

Time will tell how God accomplishes this on the *literal level* of human history. But on the *literary level of* Revelation 15 and 16, the plot is clear: God will de-weed with painful, purging, purifying love.

Evil has finally run out of time. When God was breaking down barriers to his purposes (**the seals**) and answering prayers for justice (**the trumpets**), there was always a delay—an intermission—a building suspense—between the sixth and the seventh.[11] But here, with the bowls, there is no delay. Time is up. We've waited long enough. At this point, the Church has faithfully served the world and it's time for the end of evil.[12]

---

[10] Revelation 9.1 (cf. 1.18).

[11] Notice the **strategic delay** between the sixth and seventh seals (6.12, 8.1) and the sixth and seventh trumpets (9.13, 11.15). It's like John is saying "a lot has happened, but there's still time..."

[12] The **lack of delay** is another clue that the "bowls" belong to the future. A subtle shift occurs at the seventh trumpet (the perfect answered prayer) in 11.15 where the saints sing praise that "the kingdom of the world HAS become the kingdom of our Lord and of his Messiah." From there we transition into the mythic animation of chapters 12-14 that shows different angles of the Church's faithful witness. But when we arrive at chapters 15-16, John seems to be unpacking the answered prayer of the seventh trumpet (again, 11.15). When we "zoom in" on the seventh trumpet, we find the seven bowls.

The moment has come in Revelation (and will arrive someday in our history) to de-weed everything choking the garden... to destroy what destroys the world.[13]

One helpful way to reflect on these seven bowls is to recognize (once again) what kind of imagery John uses. Notice how **the first five bowls** are borrowing heavily from Exodus. John sees the people of God next to the sea, singing the Song of Moses and the Lamb (15v3). That sounds just like Exodus 15, where the people of God find themselves saved and singing next to the sea. God had conquered the chariots of Egypt and the watery chaos.[14] Now, once again, the sea has been calmed... like glass, yielding to the fiery love of God (15v2).

God's deepest purposes are to spread salvation and song. But to get there, God has to uproot evil, to destroy Babylon, to conquer Egypt.

So we're given symbolic pictures of God uprooting evil. This is NOT a literal forecast of weather and tidal patterns in the future. Once again, Revelation is not an Almanac; it's an Apocalypse. These bowls are "a sign" (15v1) as much as the "Woman" in the wilderness (12v1) or the "Dragon" in the sky (12v3). They are symbols—signs pointing through a fog. We cannot exhaustively unpack everything they mean, but we can see the direction they're pointing.

John uses the language of the exodus from Egypt to describe God's final judgment on evil. The images include **sores** on people's bodies (16v2), water turning to **blood** (16v3-4), a kingdom plunged into **darkness** (16v10), **frogs** leaping around[15] (16v13), and the worst kind of **hailstorm** (16v21). These are all Exodus images. These are pictures of God defeating the powers that oppose love and oppress his people.

---

[13] Revelation 11.18.

[14] Exodus 15.1-18.

[15] The **frog-like evil spirits** coming from the mouths of the Dragon, the Sea-Beast, and the Land-Beast (now called "the false prophet") seem to serve the dual purpose of invoking the plagues of Egypt (Exod. 8:1-15) and illustrating how inhuman and dehumanizing are their deceptive suggestions ("the almost pornographic quality of their demonic speech," Mangina, 188).

This final cycle of seven signals the end of evil's story. No more delay, no more intermission... and no more repentance. Everyone who wants God—who wants real and lasting Life—has turned to God. Everyone else would rather "curse the name of God" (16v9) than live with him or sing his praise. They would rather "gnaw their tongues" (16v10) than use them for the Song of Life. The time for repentance has passed because some people have made their hearts as hard as Pharaoh's. And there comes a point, as in the Exodus story, where we find God is no longer trying to "change Pharaoh's mind."

God is now overthrowing "Egypt"
to liberate creation from its chains.

If you take these signs literally, you're left with a horrifying God that looks nothing like Jesus. We hear the saints singing that God has "given them blood to drink as they deserve" (16v6). If this is a literal description, then God is sadistic—on the same level as the worst of pagan gods. What a grisly, disgusting, sickening literal picture.

But as we discussed in chapter 7, John is NOT implying that Jesus has been in heaven nursing a grudge only to return with dark vengeance and a bag of tricks for beating up bad guys. Jesus is not returning as Batman. Jesus is always the Crucified One; the One who loves the world enough to drink every cup of wrath dry.[16] Take courage, dear heart, for Crucified Love lies behind these scary images.

Mysteriously enough, these seven bowls are actually a great but painful mercy for the world. That's why song after song in Revelation celebrates this coming act of God. Why the people of God sing (15v3): "Great and marvelous and your deeds... *just* and true are your ways." It's why an angel sings (16v5): "You are *just* in these judgments." It's why the altar in heaven echoes back (16v7): "True and *just* are your judgments."

---

[16] The **cup of God's wrath** is a frequent image of judgment in both the prophets (Isa. 51.17,22; Jer. 25.17,28; 49.12; 51.7; Ezek. 23.31-32; Hab. 2.16) as well as the gospels (Matt. 20.22-23, 26.39, etc). The good news, of course, is that God himself, in Jesus, has drunk the cup himself (Matt. 26.27-28).

Lyrics about *justice* would be false if God (or Bat-Jesus) were sadistically and vindictively torturing people. These words can only be true if God is finally, ultimately, forever judging evil. These seven bowls are a great but painful mercy because they're the last treatment—the final round of chemo.

The judgment of God
looks like the world crucified
so it can experience resurrection.[17]

Jesus experienced God's condemnation of evil in his body on the cross; that's where darkness was damned and doomed.[18] And eventually the crucified God will spread his saving justice throughout the universe. His damning of evil will blossom goodness throughout the universe. The rejection of evil for which all humanity longs—theists and atheists alike—will arrive. The justice of the cross will finally purge the world of wrong. The songs will be true and ultimate justice will be graced to the world:

> (15v4) All nations will come and fall down
> in worship before you,
> for your acts of JUSTICE[19]
> have been revealed.

A day is coming when God's healing—complete, just, and requested—will finally arrive. *Complete*, because God will finally end the ancient insurgency of sin, death, and the devil. *Just*, because God will eradicate evil, right every wrong, and establish a world of love. *Requested*, because God does not coerce... and will give all what they desire most deeply.

---

[17] In one of his earliest (and rawest) letters, Paul writes "I have been crucified with Christ and I no longer live, but Christ lives in me" (Gal. 2.20). The cross is where, mysteriously, Paul died so that he could experience new life. At the end of that letter he describes the cross as where "the world [lit. "the cosmos"] has been crucified to me, and I to the world" (Gal. 6.14). There's something profoundly true about Paul's assertion that the world/cosmos has been crucified. *All things* will be brought together in Christ (Eph. 1.10). The final judgment of the world will be the journey of every Christian writ large, namely, crucifixion and resurrection with Christ. One day the cosmos itself will declare: "I have been crucified with Christ and I no longer live, but Christ lives in me."

[18] Romans 8.3.

[19] This is the Common English Bible's translation. The NIV translates "dikaiomata" as "righteous acts" but this "rightness" is ultimately one of God's covenantal faithfulness and the "justice" he brings his people and creation. See N.T. Wright's "Justification" (2009) for an accessible, robust exploration.

*Here we find the strange mystery
of what the Christian tradition
calls "hell."*

Nobody gets locked into hell. Strangely enough, we lock ourselves there. No one remains in hell who doesn't want to be there. All who want God will get God. Everyone who wants Love will get Love. In the next chapter, we're told that "Lady Babylon" and her followers have already been drinking violence and hatred (17v6), and God simply pours her a double (18v6). God will give everyone what they desire most dearly.[20]

If you want to live a life in opposition to Love, Goodness, Beauty, Truth, the wanting of the Bible is that perhaps you can. If you want to side with the dehumanizing forces of evil, march against God in battle, and exist forever in unreality—if you're hellbent on hell, evidently you can have it. That's the picture provided by the penultimate bowl:

The **sixth bowl** depicts evil deceiving God's beloved creation to march against him in a place called "**Armageddon**" (16v16). That's a Hebrew word for "the Mountain of Megiddo." Megiddo was a place in the Old Testament where several decisive battles took place for the people of God.[21] John taps into that place as a symbol for the most decisive battle of them all. It's unspeakably strange—utterly mysterious—why anyone would choose to march against Life with Death, but John seems to warn that we're capable of it.

The battle of Armageddon, however, is no battle at all. Despite the fact that earth's mightiest heroes side with evil—"the kings of the whole world" (16v14)

---

20 In the words of Paul from Romans 2.7-8: "To those who by persistence in doing good seek glory, honor and immortality, [God] will give eternal life. But for those who are self-seeking and who reject the truth and follow evil, there will be wrath and anger."

21 See Judges 5.19, 2 Kings 9.27, 23.30. The plains of Megiddo, therefore, invoke a significant and decisive battle for those familiar with Israel's story. In the words of Joseph Mangina: "It was therefore the archetypal battlefield... If John is alluding to Megiddo, it is because he wants to evoke the image of a decisive battle and not because he wants us to locate his story on a map of northern Palestine" (189). And since there is *no mountain on the plains of Megiddo*, that seems a clue that we're not supposed to find it on a map.

—heaven's victory is infinitely one-sided. When **the seventh bowl** pours into the air,[22] there's no battle at all. The **"great city"**[23] and "all the cities of the nations" finally and forever crumble (16v19). Every tower of Babylon, every Jericho and Rome, every false kingdom, the loftiest human rebellions against grace —they all collapse. Our strongest resistance cannot match the power of Love.

There is no decisive battle between good and evil in Revelation. Good is the only thing that truly exists; everything else is just a shadow. So goodness wins as effortlessly as the sunrise (cf. 21v23). Evil evaporates because it never really had any substance.[24]

These coming "bowls" raise a significant question: Are we living lives of substance? Lives that will last? Lives in step with the Spirit of God? On his great day of Love—when all that is not Love burns away—what of our lives will be left? Anything?

Are there habits, or patterns, or ways of living, that—if we got honest—we would have to confess:

> "These choices are deceived choices. I'm being gathered in opposition to God. I've chosen the insane death-march with Death. This way of living isn't the way of Love."

What are the patterns of living
that won't survive
the blistering bowls of God's love?

---

[22] In the ancient world, **air** is the space between earth and heaven ruled by powers, demons, and spiritual beings other than God. This is a common notion that even Paul adopts and assumes (Eph. 2.2). On a literary level, the air has been polluted by froggy, unclean "pneumata" ("spirits" or "winds"; 16.13) and now they're being cleansed (Mangina, 191).

[23] While **"the great city"** could correspond to Rome, the cities are iconic representations in Revelation of systems and patterns of living. So "the great city" correlates more properly to all system and patterns (any "city") that stand against God and his anointed (cf. 11.8, Ps 2.2). Likewise the new city coming down from heaven (Rev. 21.2) correlates to the people of God themselves (cf. 11.2; also the 12 foundations and 12 gates of the city - 21.19-21)

[24] There is a long tradition in the Church (back to at least Augustine) which recognizes that evil itself has no ontological substance. Evil is not a thing in itself but essentially parasitic—a privation of the good. Evil is a "hole" in reality where goodness should be.

Because if it won't survive the sunrise of God's new world,
then it's not worth living in this world.[25]

Wherever those places are; whatever those patterns, or choices, or habits might be; it's breathtakingly good news that they won't survive the sunrise. Because those things are death. And the good news of the seven bowls, my friend, is that death will die.

//

Jesus, help me know that your wrath is love that will set me, my loved ones, and the world free. May I be honest about the problem of evil and help me trust that you have (and will!) overcome it. Help me resist the dehumanizing spirits of evil that gather humanity against your true life. May your Spirit ready me for the future by forming love in me today. Amen.

---

[25] Notice how in the imagery of Malachi 4.1-2, the same heat source (the day of the Lord) simultaneously destroys and comforts.

One of the seven angels who had the seven bowls came and said to me, "Come, I will show you the punishment of the great prostitute, who sits by many waters. With her the kings of the earth committed adultery, and the inhabitants of the earth were intoxicated with the wine of her adulteries."

Then the angel carried me away in the Spirit into a wilderness. There I saw a woman sitting on a scarlet beast that was covered with blasphemous names and had seven heads and ten horns. The woman was dressed in purple and scarlet, and was glittering with gold, precious stones and pearls. She held a golden cup in her hand, filled with abominable things and the filth of her adulteries. The name written on her forehead was a mystery:

babylon the great
the mother of prostitutes
and of the abominations of the earth.

I saw that the woman was drunk with the blood of God's holy people, the blood of those who bore testimony to Jesus.When I saw her, I was greatly astonished. Then the angel said to me: "Why are you astonished? I will explain to you the mystery of the woman and of the beast she rides, which has the seven heads and ten horns. The beast, which you saw, once was, now is not, and yet will come up out of the Abyss and go to its destruction. The inhabitants of the earth whose names have not been written in the book of life from the creation of the world will be astonished when they see the beast, because it once was, now is not, and yet will come.

"This calls for a mind with wisdom. The seven heads are seven hills on which the woman sits. They are also seven kings. Five have fallen, one is, the other has not yet come; but when he does come, he must remain for only a little while. The beast who once was, and now is not, is an eighth king. He belongs to the seven and is going to his destruction.

"The ten horns you saw are ten kings who have not yet received a kingdom, but who for one hour will receive authority as kings along with the beast. They have one purpose and will give their power and authority to the beast. They will wage war against the Lamb, but the Lamb will triumph over them because he is Lord of lords and King of kings—and with him will be his called, chosen and faithful followers."

Then the angel said to me, "The waters you saw, where the prostitute sits, are peoples, multitudes, nations and languages. The beast and the ten horns you saw will hate the prostitute. They will bring her to ruin and leave her naked; they will eat her flesh and burn her with fire. For God has put it into their hearts to accomplish his purpose by agreeing to hand over to the beast their royal authority, until God's words are fulfilled. The woman you saw is the great city that rules over the kings of the earth."

After this I saw another angel coming down from heaven. He had great authority, and the earth was illuminated by his splendor. With a mighty voice he shouted: "'Fallen! Fallen is Babylon the Great!...

...I saw heaven standing open and there before me was a white horse, whose rider is called Faithful and True. With justice he judges and wages war. His eyes are like blazing fire, and on his head are many crowns. He has a name written on him that no one knows but he himself. He is dressed in a robe dipped in blood, and his name is the Word of God. The armies of heaven were following him, riding on white horses and dressed in fine linen, white and clean. Coming out of his mouth is a sharp sword with which to strike down the nations. "He will rule them with an iron scepter." He treads the winepress of the fury of the wrath of God Almighty. On his robe and on his thigh he has this name written:

king of kings and lord of lords.

And I saw an angel standing in the sun, who cried in a loud voice to all the birds flying in midair, "Come, gather together for the great supper of God, so that you may eat the flesh of kings, generals, and the mighty, of horses and their riders, and the flesh of all people, free and slave, great and small."

Then I saw the beast and the kings of the earth and their armies gathered together to wage war against the rider on the horse and his army. But the beast was captured, and with it the false prophet who had performed the signs on its behalf. With these signs he had deluded those who had received the mark of the beast and worshiped its image. The two of them were thrown alive into the fiery lake of burning sulfur. The rest were killed with the sword coming out of the mouth of the rider on the horse, and all the birds gorged themselves on their flesh.

13. REVELATION IS ROMANCE

It's a little ironic... as mysterious and intimidating as the Bible's final book is, Revelation actually tells a very simple story. *It's the story of God saving the world.* That's the revelation, the apocalypse, the peek-a-boo—salvation is who God is. Salvation is what God *has done* in Jesus and what God *will do* in the future. God saves.

None of this should be a surprise.
The name "Jesus" literally means: "God saves."

It's a simple story overwhelming us because of how it's told. In Revelation, we lose sight of this forest of salvation because of the exotic trees. The symbolic nature of the letter overwhelms us, and we can get preoccupied with a particular chapter, or image, or set of verses... and we can lose sight of the story. Or even what kind of story it is.

This story can sometimes feel like an *independent arthouse film*, with a proclivity for strange images, unconventional plot structure, and open interpretation. Sometimes it feels like a *summer blockbuster*, especially when the plagues of Egypt explode onto the scene through trumpets and bowls. Moments within the story feel like *edge-of-your-seat thriller* (what will John see next!?) or even like *a Saturday morning cartoon* (Roadrunner always gets away[1]). But, if we'll pay attention, Revelation 17-19 makes clear what kind of story Revelation is:

Revelation is a romance.

The plot of Revelation centers around a costly, dramatic rescue for the sake of unquenchable love. In its romance, Revelation reflects the love at the most foundational level of reality—the life within God's own self. The heart of the universe, according to Christians, is Father, Son, and Spirit endlessly and ardently adoring one another in self-giving love. That's the confession of the Church. And this one God, who is a community of Love, created us to share in his eternal passion. We are his bride. The bride of God.

But God's bride needs rescuing. That's the drama we live daily. So God has set his face toward sweeping us up and saving us. We need rescuing—from our own stupid and sinful decisions, from all the monsters and enemies who want us destroyed, and from even the greatest enemy of them all... Death itself. Revelation does indeed have its *artsy* moments, its *action* scenes, as well as its share of *thrills* and silly *cartoons*, but, at its heart, this story is a *romance*.

Revelation points us to the Romance beneath every other romances. It's what all our hearts ache for, but we almost never talk about. Endless, bottomless, unconditional love. We rarely mention it. We push it from our minds and especially our hearts. It's too deep of a longing. We're afraid—afraid it will never happen because it's too good to be true.

But John of Patmos has good news everyone longing for the Cosmic Lover to gather us up in his divine embrace. Our hearts are not delusional:

Love is coming for us
and for this world.

---

[1] Chapter 9, if you need a reminder.

There will be a happy ending
for everyone longing for Love.

How does Revelation 17-19 present this Romance of romances?

Well, it begins as you likely guessed... with the mother of all hookers. Dressed to the nines. Riding through the desert. On a seven-headed, ten-horned monster. Tattooed with blasphemous names. And that's just verse 3. Yikes.

This **prostitute** is new... who is she? We heard first heard her name as the orchestra warmed up (14v8), then about her complete collapse at the seventh bowl (16v19). But this is the first time we are actually *seeing* her. She is called "Babylon" (17v5), dressed in the ritziest-glitziest fashion of the day, and holding a glittering golden cup filled with "abominable things" (17v4). And she's blackout drunk on the blood of the saints (17v6). She is a new character in Revelation's offbeat cast.

She rides the **sea beast** (17v3,7) that emerged from the ocean back in Revelation 13(v1).[2] That monster still seems to represent the same thing: the conquering, coercive power of all violent human empires. The most obvious example of for John's audience would have been Rome, but *"Empire" is a deeper problem than caesar and his armies.* This beast shows its teeth, galloping out with its cavalry (6v2-8), whenever humans dominate each other through the power of violence, or economic force, or cultural coercion.

But what is going on? Why is she riding the sea beast?

Boy, it sure would be nice if someone would explain it to us.

> (17v7) Then the angel said to me: "Why are you astonished? I will explain to you the mystery of the woman and of the beast she rides, which has the seven heads and ten horns...

---

[2] Bauckham, *The Climax of Prophecy*, 343.

Well, how convenient. Thank you, angel. Finally, maybe we'll get a linear, straightforward, easy-to-follow explanation in this letter (17v8):

> The beast, which you saw, ONCE WAS, now IS NOT, and yet WILL COME UP out of the Abyss and go to its destruction. The inhabitants of the earth whose names have not been written in the book of life from the creation of the world will be astonished when they see the beast, because it ONCE WAS, now IS NOT, and yet WILL COME.

Well, that's confusing. It's harder to follow than we expected but we can if we squint. Whatever else it is, John is saying that *this beast rising from the sea is a parody of real power*—of Jesus "**who is, who was, and who is to come**" (1v4,8; 4v8; 11v17).[3] This "beast" looks like a power, but it's not eternal. It comes and it goes. Whatever it is, this beast is a counterfeit... a knock-off of the real thing. So its rider must be a counterfeit too.

With some stretching we can follow what John is sketching.

But this angel loses us in verses 9-13. No one knows with 100% certainty what is being talked about. That doesn't mean, however, that we can't make a really good guess. We will need to, once again, hold it with open hands.

John seems to have wanted his original hearers to understand this section because he calls everyone to "**wisdom**" again (17v9). John is told that this Woman, Lady Babylon, sits on **seven hills**. And the angel follows up with a challenge: "this calls for wisdom." We heard this challenge originally regarding **666**. So what John says next shouldn't be impenetrable. A similar challenge must be present here. The difficulty comes in the symbolism and how he hijacks a first-century urban legend for his own purposes.[4]

---

[3] By this point in Revelation, of course, John has begun to recognize the arrival of God's reign in Jesus through the church's witness and suffering, and in 11.7 the verb tenses changed to reflect that reality.

[4] Similar to how John borrows the story of Apollo (Rev. 12) for his own purposes.

We have seen much of the symbolism before. The **seven heads** (17v3,7) are explicitly decoded as **seven hills and seven kings** (17v9). Likewise the **ten horns** are decoded as **ten kings** (17v12). Heads and horns are both kings.[5] By using these numbers—"seven" and "ten"—these kings are have high probability of being somehow symbolic. We're looking at a monstrous group of kings.

The reference to **seven hills,** however, also originally served as literal linkage to Rome, whose history celebrated her being built on seven hills.[6] By adding "hills" into his language, John sets Rome plainly before us. But he does not explicitly name her. Which is interesting. Why name this prostitute "Babylon"? Why not name her "Lady Rome"?

As with the number of the beast, John wants his hearers becoming wise to a *pattern*, not just a *person*... or in this case, a *place*. In the case of **666**, it meant looking anything anti-Love, like Nero. In the case of **seven hills**, it means watching out for stomping and chomping empires,[7] like the city of Rome, that desire to dominate the world.

The symbolism is somewhat familiar by now, but the story around the symbolism is a little more complicated. And that brings us to the urban legend.

We still have urban legends we still have today. For instance, whispers circulate to this day of celebrities faking their own deaths—be it Elvis Presley, Andy Kaufman, Princess Diana, or Tupac Shakur. And these campfire stories are typically a passing curiosity that we promptly forget after hearing them.

But some campfire stories are not easily forgotten and sometimes even become a source of anxiety and fear. Adolf Hitler, for example, almost certainly commit-

---

[5] John is utilizing already-established symbolism seen in Daniel 7:23-27 (esp. v. 24).
[6] Virgil's *Aeneid*, Book VI, line 83.
[7] See Daniel 7:7, 19, 23.

ted suicide in April of 1945 as Allied troops closed in on his location. But fascinating rumors circulated for decades after his death that Hitler was actually still alive, living in the Argentina, and possibly a threat to global security. Hitler was such a terror in his life that he continued to terrorize even in his death.

The ancient equivalent of Hitler rumors were the various Nero legends. After Nero's death by suicide in 68 CE, rumors spread that he had faked his death, perhaps escaping eastward into Parthia, readying his return with armies so he could terrorize again. Perhaps his disappearance was a vast conspiracy—another twisted game from the mad king. And so, the various stories went, evil embodied in Nero would return one day to conquer the world.[8]

That's the urban legend John is hijacking for his own purposes. And we can see the punchline of his purposes in verses 10-11, where we all want to just scream in confusion. (Too much? Am I alone in this?)

In verses 10-11, as John subdivides the **seven kings.** He says **five have fallen, one is**, and **one is yet to come**. Simple math. Got it. That makes seven, right? So should we be counting kings or caesars? Well, scholars largely agree that this seven is symbolic (like the **seven churches**) and *not* meant to correspond to specific kings or persons. George Caird helpfully summarizes:

> No one supposes that [John] wrote to seven churches because there were only seven in the province of Asia... By the same token the seven kings are a symbolic number, representative of the whole series of emperors, and they would remain seven no matter how long the actual list happened to be... The one point John wishes to emphasize is that the imperial line has only a short time to run before the emergence of a new monstrous Nero, an eighth who is one of the seven.[9]

---

[8] "Forms of the Nero legends appear in other apocalyptic writings. One was that at the end of the age Satan, or Beliar, would appear in the guise of Nero to deceive people and persecute the faithful, claiming to be god and being worshipped by all... A second form of the story anticipated that Nero would return from the east, crossing the Euphrates with his armies to seize control of the empire...The prospect of Nero's return has shaped the beast's return from death in Rev 13, and it is developed [in Rev 16:12, 17:16] where the beast's allies come from the Euphrates and destroy Babylon, the city that resembles Rome" (Koester, 571). The ancient sources of these myths come from the *Sibylline Oracles* (3:63-74; 4:119-24, 138-39; 5:361-65) and the *Ascension of Isaiah* (4:2-8).
[9] Caird, 218-19.

In other words, the succession of caesars will eventually be disrupted by another—**an eighth**—who is cut from the same terrible cloth but even more monstrous. Suddenly the **sea beast** that symbolized monstrous empire is distilled into a Nero-like figure—a single personality (17v11)—who empowers a symbolic number of rulers (**ten kings**) to empower his hateful ambitions (17v12-14). The ultimate promise is that hate loses to the Lamb (17v15), but that it's still frightening.

A tiny history might help us here. It's short. I promise.

The reality of a new and monstrous and symbolic "**eighth**" emerged historically in the first-century with the reign of Vespasian's son Domitian (81-96CE). You'll remember that Vespasian brought stability to Rome after Nero's suicide in 68 CE by claiming the throne and managing not to die. His son, Titus, served as a general, laying siege to Jerusalem, destroying its Temple, and squashing a Jewish rebellion in 70 CE. This same Titus reigned briefly as caesar after his father's death (79-81 CE) and was succeeded by his younger brother, Domitian.

Domitian turned out to be a remarkably capable king who wanted to restore traditional Roman greatness like his father. He worked for Roman domination of the world on every level: military, economic, and religious. Domitian's official competency in his office was only matched by his operational cruelty. He leveraged his divine status as a "god" in the imperial cult to serve his imperial and personal ambitions. And he instituted policies of persecution to stamp out those who refused devotion to him and were therefore disloyal to Rome.[10] The beast of empire began baring its teeth and claws against all dissenters and notably Christians. This lasted until Domitian was eventually assassinated by his cousin on September 18, 96 CE.

History lesson over. I told you it was short.

So John tells the story of a superficially beautiful prostitute, ruling the world (17v15) who is riding high on the beast of empire. But notice how her story

---

[10] Beale, 5-12.

ends. Evil eventually consumes itself, and she meets the same end. Eventually this woman is ravaged and **consumed by the beast** (17v16).

This prostitute seems to embody "the great city" (17v18) that just collapsed a handful of verses ago at the end of the **seventh bowl** (16v19). It seems like now we're zooming in, getting an in-depth perspective of that collapse. John seems to be giving us a picture of how all violent empires will fall apart at the end of history. And even within history.

This hooker sitting on her seven hills is *like* Rome but *not limited to Rome.* The *pattern* goes beyond the *place*. Revelation addresses bigger realities than one city, one tyrant, or one empire. The violence wielded by a tyrant like Domitian eventually boomerangs, and your cousin eventually kills you. The system briefly looks majestic and godlike, but it's just a pitiful counterfeit. Any kind of system that relies on violence, or economic coercion, or cultural/religious manipulation to rule the world fits John's pattern of beastly rule and fallen Babylon. And this "great city" will collapse.

Revelation goes further. Not only *will* it collapse, it *already is* fallen. Whether it looks like it or not. Any life or system or "city" that opposes the good and loving purposes of God is *already* fallen—*already* doomed to failure.

The domination and violence that humanity routinely relies on—that beast we frequently ride on—will eventually devour us. That seems to be the meaning in a horrible, graphic nutshell (17v16). This Lady will be eaten alive by the Beast.[11] Every "great city" built on raw power will be destroyed by raw power. Humans dominate each other with armies, economics, and coercion; but it can never bring lasting peace.

---

[11] This graphic imagery seems to be adapted by a story of judgment concerning Israel spoken by the prophet Ezekiel (16.15-19, 32-42).

When we try to rule our world by force,
we're mounting a monster
that will eventually consume us.

The announcement is made clearly: Babylon is fallen (18v1-3). Life in opposition to God is collapsing. An angel throws a giant rock, a millstone, into the sea with a giant splash to make the point (18v21). He cries out:

> Babylon is fallen like this! With this kind of ferocity and finality. Babylon
> is fallen, and—just like that rock—it's never coming back!

Then through Revelation 18 and 19, we find two groups of people reacting to this collapse of all violent human power systems. The same breaking news evokes two dramatically different responses. *It's the same reality, the same judgment, but it provokes two wildly different reactions.*

Singing, celebrating, and primal hallelujah...
and weeping, wailing, and gnashing of teeth...
over the exact same event.

Everyone in love with the old system—who didn't care about hurting people for a profit[12]—despairs the fall of Lady Babylon. We find three laments: the corrupt ruling class,[13] the profits-over-people businessmen,[14] and all the heartless middlemen.[15]

They despair violent Empire collapsing.

They despair a world of love.

---

[12] Embedded within the economy of all empires is commodification of people as either institutionalized—or, in our century, functional—slaves (end of 18.13).

[13] 18v9-10: "the kings of the earth"

[14] 18v11-17: "the merchants of the earth"

[15] 18v17-20: "the sea captains"

But then we also find three celebrations. The masses in heaven roar in celebration, the symbolic figures backstage of the universe sing, and another great multitude (perhaps on the earth) shouts for joy[16]:

> (17v6a-8b) "Hallelujah!
>   For our Lord God Almighty reigns.
> Let us rejoice and be glad
>   and give him glory!
> For the wedding of the Lamb has come,
>   and his bride has made herself ready.
> Fine linen, bright and clean,
>   was given her to wear."

And here the Great Romance comes clearly into focus. John sees a vision of Jesus—unstoppable and all-powerful—tearing through the heavens, **tattooed** as King and Lord (19v16), called the true witness[17] (19v11) and followed by the armies of heaven (19v14). The **white horse** has returned (19v11, see 6v2), but now it carries the one who conquerers with love (5v5-6).

It's a vision of the future where Jesus brings his unbridled Life to the world. Image piles upon image as Jesus arrives to **judge** and **wage war** (19v11). We're told he does both "with justice" (or "rightly"). In other words, he arrives to end all war.[18] Jesus appears.... but he's already **covered in blood** (19v13). That's because he's already shed his own.[19] Here is a king who doesn't violently wield a literal sword... his quiet **witness** to love conquers the world (19v11,15). Because that's the kind of "King of kings" Jesus is (19v16).[20] The True King is willing to bleed for love. That's what true power and authority look like. That's what true kingship and lordship look like.

---

[16] "a great multitude in heaven" (19.1-3), "the twenty-four elders and the four living creatures" (19.4-5), "a great multitude" (19.6-8, cf. 14.1-3: the "army" on the mountain).

[17] See 1:5 and 3:14.

[18] See 17.14. The ultimate vision of both the psalms (e.g. Ps 2, 72) and the prophets (e.g. Isa 2.1-5, 11.1-10) envision a day when Yahweh and his "anointed one" (= Messiah, Christ, King) put an end to all wars. The only way to wage war rightly ("with justice/righteouness") is to end all war.

[19] We were first introduced to **robes dipped in blood** in 7.14, where we're told the victorious army of martyrs have washed their robes in the blood of "the Lamb." The Lamb's own robes, of course, are the same.

[20] It commonly pointed out that Jesus arrives adorned with **"many crowns"** (19:12) whose plurality contrasts with the strictly limited number of crowns of both Dragon (12:3) and Beast (13:1).

True lordship is love-shaped.

True kingship cross-shaped.

And behold Jesus's motive. Why does he shred the heavens riding to earth? It's for the sake of love. Jesus arrives as the Lover of lovers. The True King is the world's True Lover. Jesus has come to feast at his **wedding supper** (19v9).

This is the feast for which we all hunger. The place where the deepest longings are satiated. Those unspeakable yearnings we try to satisfy with food, or sex, or careers, or applause, or the next pair of shoes... our yearnings are satisfied here. And the good news entrusted to the Church is there will be a day coming when our deepest longings—our hunger—will be satisfied. Because there is a day coming when Jesus will bring the party of his presence.

Here John shows us our chief end:
the union of heaven and earth,
of God and humanity.

This is what Revelation—and every single human life—is ultimately all about: the consummation of cosmic Love. Everything exists that we may join our Lover, the Groom of grooms, in his unbroken banquet of love, bliss, and peace.

If we take John's vision with any kind of seriousness, these climactic images have immediate, hourly implications for our lives. Among them is this question: Where are the places where we settle for counterfeit Life?

We live in a world where "the Mother of Prostitutes" looks more outwardly compelling than the Bride of the Lamb.[21] Generation after generation finds themselves tempted by alluring, seemingly beautiful, knock-offs of the real Romance. The Enemy continues his work in the Empire of America as much as the

---

[21] As we approach the end of Revelation, the imagery introduced in chapters 11 and 12 returns with an invitation: "Become this Woman—become this Bride (12.1, cf. 19.8-9), become this City (11.2, 20.9 = 21.2), become this Tabernacle/Temple (11.1, cf. 21.3, 22)."

Empire of Rome. We're invited into false life, enticed to become a false bride, beckoned into a false way of being human.

Revelation's imagery is genius. The harlot offers us *a golden cup* (17v4) that does *look* satisfying... but it's filled with sewage, vomit, and deplorable things.[22]

We're always being offered counterfeits, and we frequently settle for them. We crave intimacy; we settle for "casual" sex. We thirst for inner peace; we settle for numbing the pain. We hunger for satisfaction; we settle for the next big purchase. We ache to be truly known; we settle for applause and popularity. We yearn for significance—to know our lives matter—but we settle for busyness. We're parched for True Life; the Enemy offers to quench our thirst with Death.

We thirst for the cup of salvation;
we settle for the cup of abominable things.

In countless ways of which we're only dimly aware, we buy the subtle lies of the Enemy. We oppose the way of the cross—the way of self-giving love. We *march against* God (19v19). And so John gives us one more sobering reminder of what resisting God—what hating Love—is like.

First, John begins tying up loose ends. His monstrous cartoons that spilled off the screen—the *beats of sea and land*—are at long last erased by Jesus (19v20). These mythic images symbolized the world's complex political and cultural systems corrupted by evil... and they provide John an image for systemic evil vanquished by the fire of love.

Second, we're presented with a graphic picture: *birds feasting* on those who follow the Beast and are devoted to its False Prophet (19v21). On the day when Truth finally gets spoken, lives built on lies collapse. This terrible image—bor-

---

[22] " ...[the] goblet is full of urine, dung and blood. Sorry about the nasty words; but perhaps I should have used nastier ones... [John's] point is that the outward appearance of the whore is magnificent, but the inner reality is disgusting, stomach-churning filth" (Wright, *Revelation for Everyone*, 151).

rowed from the prophet Ezekiel[23]—serves as a megaphone to rouse the deaf. Perhaps even to wake the dead:

The "life" offered by the Enemy is for the birds... don't embrace it.

This isn't Revelation full of threats; this is Revelation full of wisdom. John keeps insisting that anyone or anything opposing the Lamb is on a path that is *already* fallen. If we insist on this path to the end, perhaps God will give us what we want... but it will never satisfy our hunger. It will consume us.

There's a world of difference between
coming to a feast and becoming a feast....
so choose wisely.

God grants our choices a terrifying dignity. We can choose the way of the **True witness**, the way of love, and celebrate eternally with our Beloved. Or we can choose the false, the counterfeit, and end up consumed by the hate we love.

The good news is we're always already being called to, and welcomed into, the real thing. Our Lover cares for us more than we care even for ourselves...and we are always already welcome at his table (3v20, 10v9-10).

//

Groom of grooms, stop me from settling for counterfeit love and counterfeit life. I want to hear your whisper of love calling me out of despair, falseness, and death. Kindle my heart with romance so I can know in my bones that your marriage proposal includes me too. Clothe me as your bride and bring me safely to your wedding feast that satisfies fully and forever. Amen.

---

[23] Ezekiel envisions a decisive battle (39.17-20) with **birds consuming** those hell-bent on resisting the God of Life.

And I saw an angel coming down out of heaven, having the key to the Abyss and holding in his hand a great chain. He seized the dragon, that ancient serpent, who is the devil, or Satan, and bound him for a thousand years. He threw him into the Abyss, and locked and sealed it over him, to keep him from deceiving the nations anymore until the thousand years were ended. After that, he must be set free for a short time.

I saw thrones on which were seated those who had been given authority to judge. And I saw the souls of those who had been beheaded because of their testimony about Jesus and because of the word of God. They had not worshiped the beast or its image and had not received its mark on their foreheads or their hands. They came to life and reigned with Christ a thousand years. (The rest of the dead did not come to life until the thousand years were ended.) This is the first resurrection. Blessed and holy are those who share in the first resurrection. The second death has no power over them, but they will be priests of God and of Christ and will reign with him for a thousand years.

When the thousand years are over, Satan will be released from his prison and will go out to deceive the nations in the four corners of the earth—Gog and Magog—and to gather them for battle. In number they are like the sand on the seashore. They marched across the breadth of the earth and surrounded the camp of God's people, the city he loves. But fire came down from heaven and devoured them. And the devil, who deceived them, was thrown into the lake of burning sulfur, where the beast and the false prophet had been thrown. They will be tormented day and night for ever and ever.

Then I saw a great white throne and him who was seated on it. The earth and the heavens fled from his presence, and there was no place for them. And I saw the dead, great and small, standing before the throne, and books were opened. Another book was opened, which is the book of life. The dead were judged according to what they had done as recorded in the books. The sea gave up the dead that were in it, and death and Hades gave up the dead that were in them, and each person was judged according to what they had done.

Then death and Hades were thrown into the lake of fire. The lake of fire is the second death. Anyone whose name was not found written in the book of life was thrown into the lake of fire.

14. "WHO" MORE THAN "HOW"

The crowd roars. Three athletes stand shoulder-to-shoulder. Their faces wear descending smile sizes as three medals are awarded: gold, silver, and bronze. Everyone wants the dazzling yellow, but they have all achieved all-time, world-class greatness. There are few human beings who ever even stand in the company of Olympic winners.

So too with Revelation 20. Few passages of scripture achieve the level of controversy achieved by this chapter. With these 396 Greek words, speculations abound, theories multiply, saints disagree, scholars argue, and (tragically) churches divide.

If Revelation 20 misses the gold for controversy,
it certainly stands proudly on the platform.

It makes sense that this climactic chapter of Revelation would be controversial. After all, it's the gateway from horror to happily-ever-after. The bulk of Revelation (**ch6-19**) has taken us through hard stuff. We've seen seals, trumpets, and bowls; giant hailstones, demonic locusts, and monstrous governments; pictures of worldwide plagues and horrors and judgment. Yet by the end of Revelation (**ch21-22**), we're ushered into the happiest ending imaginable: a world remade by Love. A universe where death has died, and life flourishes forever.

The bulk of Revelation **(ch6-19)** has felt like suffering and struggle...
but the end of Revelation **(ch21-22)** shows the happiest of endings...
and *this chapter* **(ch20)** carries us from one into the other.

In one chapter we find...

- ***Satan sealed*** in "the Abyss" (20v1-3),
- the ***millennium reign*** of Jesus (20v4-6),
- ***Satan released*** and his armies consumed by fire (20v7-10),
- and judgment at *a* **great white throne** (20v11-15).

Then the chapter ends with ***"the second death"*** arriving for...

- the ***devil*** (20v10),
- ***Death and Hades*** themselves (20v14),
- anyone not in **the Book of Life** (20v15).

Heaven transforms the world in a mere 15 verses.
(That is one hard-working chapter!)

This is a chapter that literally no one can agree about. If you read one good scholar on this chapter, you'll hear a dozen opinions. It seems to catalyze sensational speculation because it's certainly about the future. The seventh trumpet (11v15) has been tease out with seven bowls (ch16) and the arrival of Jesus as the Groom of grooms (19v11ff). We get a glimpse of Jesus holding the world's future. It's natural that people would crowd around this doorway to the gardens of New Jerusalem trying to "figure it out."

We should say from the outset, that chapter 20 is like an old-fashioned road sign—the wooden arrow standing at a crossroads. It's a sign in the fog pointing us toward the future. It's pointing in a particular direction: "We are headed *that* way: Jesus returning, evil destroyed, reality remade."

Theme parks like Disneyland are practically the only places we still see these kinds of signs. Disneyland directional signs are simultaneously *specific* and *general*. They point us in a specific direction, orienting us in the right way to go.

("We need to head THAT way... the other side of Snow White's Castle.") But they don't give turn-by-turn GPS instructions; they only point us in a general direction. ("We still have to navigate our way around Snow White's Castle.") The destination is clear, but the path still holds twists, turns, and surprises.

Most of this chapter's controversy comes from our demanding turn-by-turn instructions from a general directional sign.

We want to turn John's sign into Siri, a guide who can answer all our questions. But when we do that, we forget his entire letter is written in symbolism, image, and metaphor. John has never been giving us anything like a play-by-play of the future.

Revelation has never been an Almanac about when to predict what. It's always been an Apocalypse about God's character. Revelation has consistently focused our attention on *"the Who"* more than *"the How."* When our questions orbit *"who God is"* instead of *"how will the future play out,"* our answers find reliability, stability, and sanity.

"Who is God?"

Revelation answers that God is self-giving Love—revealed in Jesus, the center of all reality (4v2-11), the very foundation of the universe (13v8), the Lamb slaughtered but standing (5v6).

Revelation declares that God is the One who hears (8v4), who doesn't forget his promises to his people or his creation, who hears every cry of injustice (6v10), and who will unleash Egyptian-plague-power to conquer evil and free those he loves.

God is the Child who chooses us as siblings (12v5), the Crucified Conquerer (5v9) leading an army in the way of the cross (12v11), the Saving Judge (11v18), the Lover of the Cosmos (19v7). God is the One who—despite all we do not understand and all the despair we feel (5v4)—*will* save the world.

We have heard all of Revelation and find uncountable questions bubbling up within us: "*How* will God do this? *How* will the future unfold? *How* does it all play out?" But *despite our reasonable questions,* John's vision was never meant to tell us much in the way of "how." It would be quite surprising if suddenly at this point in Revelation—for only one chapter[1]—John suddenly abandoned symbolism, image, and metaphor for the sake of trying to give literal descriptions.

*Revelation points us
toward reality
through sacred art.*

For example, John describes a **millennial reign** of Jesus (20v4-6). This 1,000 year period is one of the most divisive and controversial parts of the chapter. No one agrees what it means.[2] From where I sit, however, it seems unlikely that John has abandoned his consistent symbolism to suddenly describe a literal thousand years.

"One thousand" seems like a good candidate for symbolism. We intuitively understand this when we read other biblical authors. When we hear that "a day with God is like a thousand years,"[3] most of us understand that we're not invited into a math problem. We're being told something in metaphor. Likewise, when the psalmist sings about God owning the cattle on a thousand hills,[4] most

---

[1] The new creation of Revelation 21-22 is described in striking and obvious symbolism (see chapter 15).
[2] The modern church often divides herself up with foggy speculations called "**premillennialism**" (Jesus will return before establishing his millennial reign), "**postmillennialism**" (Jesus is establishing a progressive reign of peace through the church before his return), and **amillennialism** (varying views that the millennium functions symbolically), A church or Christian finds themselves in good company—saintly and scholarly—no matter their position (**Irenaeus** held to a premillennial view very early in church history, **Jonathan Edwards** advocated a postmillennial view, **Origen** and **Augustine** taught various amillennial views).
[3] 2 Peter 3.8
[4] Psalm 50.10

of us know that God isn't wanting us to count ridges looking for livestock. The psalmist is making a bigger point and would be heartbroken if you got preoccupied about the number.

We recognize **1,000** as an easy symbolic number in other parts of Scripture that aren't soaked in symbolism, but for some reason the church argues and divides about it here. That must be the Enemy at work.

It would be funny if it weren't so tragic:

Churches, communities, denominations obsess over verses 4-6. Then they argue about them. Eventually they divide over them. Entire theological systems get built around the millennium reign of Jesus. But this is literally the only place in the Bible where the 1,000 year reign of Jesus ever gets mentioned. Think about that—the only place.[5] It seems like this might be an important edge of Revelation but seems unlikely to be its center.

Numbers tell QUALITY 1,000 = REALLY BIG NOT QUANTITY

Symbolic numbers have been everywhere in John's vision. This is the same letter where the Holy Spirit is described as "seven spirits" (1v4). It's the same book where demon locusts emerge from an evil black hole in the ocean, what the ancients called "the Abyss" (9v2-3). We've seen a hooker riding a scarlet beast in the desert (17v3) and a dragon soaring through the sky—and all the time we've been explicitly told "this is symbolic" (12v3). If that was symbolism—artistic ways of representing inexpressible realities—why would we suddenly think that "the Dragon" sealed in "the Abyss" for "a thousand years" is a literal description? *Here we seem to have real realities but not literal descriptions.*

Symbolism helps us make sense of two villains hurled into a lake of fire at the end of this chapter (20v14). Since the breaking of the seals, Death has been a lurking supervillain who can ride a horse (6v8), who can hide from people (9v6),

---

5 While we're at it, verses 4-6 are also the only place where the resurrection of dead is pictured as happening in two staggered stages.

and who can hold people captive (20v13). He has a side-kick called Hades who tags along with him. Taken literally, these images make zero sense. Lakes don't burn. Death cannot be grabbed by the scruff of the neck. The mythological Greek underworld, Hades, cannot be handcuffed or hogtied. These are not things that can literally be tossed into lava (20v14).

The artistry of Revelation
gives us graspable pictures
of ungraspable realities.

Revelation 20 gives us
a directional sign pointing into the future,
not turn-by-turn GPS directions.

Like all of Revelation, questions about "*who* God is" give us clearer answers than "*how* will it play out?" We should read this chapter always asking the primary question: "Who is God? What is God like?"

"Who is God?"

God is the One who can seal away the Enemy at anytime with no battle at all (20v1-3). He's the omnipotent ground of all reality. And when the final battle arrives between God and Satan—Goodness and Evil, between Life and Death—it's not a fair fight. It's actually no fight at all.

God is Life itself and loves giving himself away (20v4-6). Those desperate for him will not be disappointed. And he grants people a taste of resurrection before the great resurrection. He begins reign through them before the end of history.[6]

---

[6]"But, before this [final defeat of evil] can happen, the reign of Jesus, with and through his millennial people, must be established by the first resurrection. John distinguishes these people not just as martyrs (as opposed to other Christians) but specifically as those who had been beheaded for their witness. We should, I presume, take that symbolically. It may hint at something to do with their true citizenship in Jesus' kingdom; it was Roman citizens who were beheaded, a greatly preferable death to many of others the Romans devised, not least crucifixion itself. It seems, in any case, contrary to John's normal line to suggest a radical difference between one set of martyrs and another" (Wright, 179).

God is patient (20v7). He's patient enough to give second chances... even to the worst of us. In a strange plot-twist, John describes Satan being released.[7] But that snake immediately starts doing what he has always done—working to destroy Life.

God is All-Powerful Goodness (20v8-10). He is the One powerful enough to unmake the forces of evil in an instant. God's enemies vanish in the power of his fiery love (20v8-9). And he is good enough that he will do it one day.

And so, in a pair of images borrowed from the prophet Ezekiel[8] and the story of Elijah[9], John visualizes God's love vaporizing everything that wants nothing to do with Life—everything hellbent on destroying the world (11v18). God speaks a blistering "No" to chaos, death, and human wickedness precisely because God is forever committed to saying "Yes" to creation, life, and human flourishing.[10]

God will sort out the world (20v11-15). He will mop up the messes, right the wrongs, solve injustice, end rebellion, eradicate evil. God is the just and merciful Judge that the world desperately needs... symbolized here with *a great white throne*.[11]

In the story Revelation has been telling, those aligned with the Lamb wind up paying the ultimate price for their allegiance (14v14-20). But now they have are

---

[7] It's a mysterious, seemingly messy story-telling here. The story would have felt tidier if it had gone from 19.20-21 straight to 20.10f. Perhaps John recognizes that *false beast* (for him, Rome) and *false prophet* (for him, the local imperial cults) can and will fall. Sure enough, Rome itself did fall in 410 CE. And history can and sometimes does experience relative peace and prosperity under the already ruling Jesus (Matt. 28.18, 1 Cor. 15.25-28) before the great and final crisis of history.

[8] Ezekiel had spoken prophetically against a foreign king named *Gog* from the land of *Magog* (38.2f). John seems to adopts these exotic, barbaric-sounding names in verse 8 (as others before him had) as archetypal enemies of God. Eugene Boring writes, "By John's time, Jewish tradition had long since transformed 'Gog of Magog' into 'Gog and Magog' and made them into the ultimate enemies of God's people to be destroyed in the eschatological battle" (209).

[9] See 2 Kings 1.10-14 where Elijah *calls down fire* from heaven (twice!) to destroy military squadrons.

[10] "If the millennium is the visible sign of God's 'yes' to his creation, then the lake of fire symbolizes the divine 'no,' his rejection of all that would threaten it" (Mangina, 232).

[11] In an effort to avoid contradicting Paul's insistence that we're adopted into God's family by God's action and mercy (we're "justified" by grace alone) many teach that all who stand before the **Great White Throne** will be consigned to the lake of fire... that literally no one will be found in the Book of Life. The interpretation holds that *"the judgment seat"* (Rom. 14.10, 2 Cor. 5.10) exists for Christians while this "great white throne" is for non-Christians. This interpretation is strained as "the dead" (20.12) seems to be an exhaustive group ("great and small") to the point where everyone—even those in Hades and in the Sea (two different realms in ancient thinking)—surrender their dead. It would seem John truly means to indicate *all* the dead. And the upcoming "book of life" is the symbolic clue that John agrees with Paul.

vindicated with a *first resurrection* (20v4-5). They continue on their established trajectory of becoming like Jesus—love, faithfulness, truthfulness, martyrdom, resurrection, and now ruling. They keep receiving Jesus's indestructible life,[12] life utterly resistant to *the second death* (20v6). On the other hand, those aligned with the Dragon and beasts must wait for an implied "second resurrection"[13] (20v12-13). And when they rise, they too keep coasting on their established trajectory: the way of death (20v13-14).

The books are opened[14] (20v12), the hidden made manifest: no crime hidden, no act of love wasted, no suffering forgotten. But in the end, there's only one book that matters. Another book: *the book of life.*[15] And this seems to be John's symbolic short-hand for whether or not we allow God's love to embrace us. That's the heart of Christianity: the insistence that God already always loves you and claims you. And every one of us is invited to trust that. His choice for us —and our trusting of him—is all that matters in the end.

So who is God?

God is the One who claims you... in his "book." And this good news gives us rest: we're invited to trust that God has already included us in his book. Before we do, or ask, or pray anything. And God's Spirit is always already willing to write the words of Life on our souls.[16] Only those wanting nothing to do with

---

[12] Heb. 7:16.

[13] Revelation's story is intricate here with two resurrections. And, as you would guess, scholars debate the details of what means for the actual space-time future. But John is following the sequential pattern described by Jesus in John 5:24-29: a resurrection to life and a resurrection to judgment.

[14] This entire scene (like much in Revelation) owes much to Daniel 7. There, in 7.9-10, the Ancient of Days (an appropriately mysterious name for God) brings order to a world dominated by chaotic monster-nations (7.1-8). It's significant in John's vision that although some kind of judgment occurs according to people's deeds (20.12, cf Dan. 7.10), but our ultimate destiny hinges on something entirely different than human deeds, namely the book of life (20.15).

[15] The symbol of "*the book of life*" seems to have developed slowly (over centuries), with seeds found in Isaiah (4.3), Malachi (3.16), the Psalms (69.28) and Daniel (12.1). It eventually becomes easy short-hand for whoever shares in True Life, both now and in the future (Phil 4.3). To think consistently about God as the effective agent of salvation (2 Cor. 5.14,19) who saves by his grace alone (Eph. 2.8-9), we must say that we do not opt *into* God's embrace (i.e. penance, a sinner's prayer, right beliefs, etc) but instead we *opt out* of it. God always already includes us, and the mystery of "hell" is our willful, conscious, torturous rejection of his embrace. This actually honors the textual evidence in John's letter itself (Rev. 3.5).

[16] Cf. 2 Cor. 3.3.

Life—those as willful, stubborn, and unrepentant as the Dragon himself[17]—are they are handed over to the Second Death.[18]

If we don't want God—Life Himself—evidently we'll get what we want.

Focusing on "the Who" gives us clarity;
focusing on "the How" gives us conjecture.

The shape of the future revealed to us with certainty has everything to do with the character of God. God is exactly like Jesus. And Jesus loves us deeply and passionately to save us:

> (20v9) [The nations] marched across the breadth of the earth and surrounded the camp of God's people, the city he loves. But fire came down from heaven and devoured them.

The forces of evil may have marched across the horizon and surrounded God's people, **the city he loves**. But God saves his people. His **city** (11v2). His **tabernacle** (11v1). His **pair of witnesses** (11v3f). His **dazzling Lady** (12v1). It's almost like the entire chapter is unpacked in that one verse.

Jesus loves deeply enough
to burn away evil and save his world.

Divine fire is how the world goes from horror to happily-ever-after. The fire of Revelation 20 ushers us into the gardens of New Jerusalem. Jesus saves his

---

[17] Perhaps John's seemingly messy story-telling about **releasing Satan from the Abyss** also shows the patience and mercy of God—God never defaults to the penalty of second death. The Enemy is effortlessly locked up, incarcerated, for a symbolically long time, and his cosmic "time out" does nothing to change him. After his release, he immediately deceives the nations again (v8). Perhaps the text is nodding to the possibility that personalities (such as the Enemy) can become so corrupt that they are incapable of repentance (and thus redemption). But this eternal abuse of our agency is the only reason for (self-)exclusion from the universal embrace of God (Eph. 1.10, Col. 1.15-20, 1 Tim. 4.10, 1 Jn. 2.2).

[18] We would do well to remember that the textual function and momentum of 19.19, 20.10, 14-15 is encouragement and hope addressed to a tired, persecuted church... not a threat addressed toward those outside the church. When read in light of chapters 2-3, the list of 21.8 looks like a sobering charge for the church itself not to slide away from Jesus into a "second death" (cf. 2.14-16, 20, 3.9, etc.) but to courageously persevere and "be victorious" (2.7, 11, 17, 26; 3.5, 12, 21). The fact of Revelation being addressed to the Church is explicitly reinforced at the end of the book in 22.10-11.

people, creates a new world, and establishes his new city. God rescues with the fire of his presence.[19]

And John's letter invites us to live as citizens of Jesus's coming world right now. We're invited to live as citizens of his new city right now, in the middle of history. Perhaps that's what John is suggesting when he mentions **those who had been beheaded** "coming alive" and "reigning with Christ" (20v4).

Did you notice that? It's only those who are beheaded who "come to life" and participate in God's kingdom before the Final Judgment. You know what that's interesting? Because Rome didn't behead just anyone. Everyone knew that. Death by beheading was relatively clean, relatively painless, relatively humane. It wasn't prolonged or torturous—not exactly the best way to invoke terror or establish fear. To achieve that, you had to crucify people. Rome only beheaded its own citizens.[20] The only people beheaded were those absolutely committed to citizenship in Jesus's kingdom over and above their citizenship in Rome's kingdom.[21]

Through its sacred art Revelation
is summoning us into a different kingdom.

John is challenging his churches to live as citizens of the city that will last:

> "Live as citizens of God's new world. Live that way right now. Resist Babylon. Even when it's costly, even when it's painful. That's how you join the reign of our Crucified King."

And that's near the heart of Revelation:

> *1) to know God-revealed-in-Jesus*
> *and 2) to participate in his Life right now.*[22]

---

[19] It's always worth remembering that fire has more to do with the purifying presence of God (Exod. 3.2, 19.18; Deut. 4.24; Dan. 7.10a; Lk. 3.16; Acts 2.3-4, Heb. 12.29) than the presence of evil.

[20] Wright, *Revelation for Everyone*, 179.

[21] John's churches may have never read Paul's letter to the Philippians, but they're hearing the same message here. The prose of Philippians 3.20 is driven home in Revelation 20.4 with image and symbol.

[22] Revelation 1.3 (ESV): "Blessed is the one who reads aloud the words of this prophecy, and *blessed are those who hear, and who keep what is written in it*, for the time is near." The invitation to participation runs throughout the book and is repeated at its end (22.17).

Or in other words, this document is...

> *1) a revelation ABOUT Jesus*
> *and 2) a revelation FROM Jesus.*

Both Babylon and Jesus are asking for our allegiance. The Lamb wants us to pledge allegiance to his life, his love, his kingdom, his way of being human. And Babylons of every century want to dominate us, coerce us, and use us as pawns in the next power play. We're invited to choose Love, and so resist Babylon.

Whenever we follow the Lamb
in the way of self-giving love,
we resist Babylon.

If we're looking for "how," we've finally found it. When we respond in love to that comment—that idiotic, offensive, unloving comment!—and refuse to return evil for evil, we participate in the kingdom that will last. When we give to that person—who has blown every chance and certainly doesn't deserve it—and ask for nothing in return, we're joining in the reign of Jesus. When we labor for unity, strive for healing, work for justice, broker peace, forgive sins, speak truth, lay down our lives for one another—when we do these things we're following the Lamb. We're living as citizens of the world that will last. We're choosing the life that will last.

Whenever and wherever we follow Jesus by choosing faith, love, and hope—even when it hurts like crucifixion, even when it means "the powers that be" want our head—we're actually coming alive.

Like resurrection before resurrection day.

//

Consuming Fire, clarify your identity in my mind. Help me to cling to You ("the Who") and hold "the How" with open hands. May you — the Judge judged in our place — write your life into my soul so I can face the Day of Your Love with confidence. Help me live in the "first resurrection," building for your kingdom today. Amen.

Then I saw "a new heaven and a new earth," for the first heaven and the first earth had passed away, and there was no longer any sea. I saw the Holy City, the new Jerusalem, coming down out of heaven from God, prepared as a bride beautifully dressed for her husband. And I heard a loud voice from the throne saying, "Look! God's dwelling place is now among the people, and he will dwell with them. They will be his people, and God himself will be with them and be their God. 'He will wipe every tear from their eyes. There will be no more death' or mourning or crying or pain, for the old order of things has passed away."

He who was seated on the throne said, "I am making everything new!" Then he said, "Write this down, for these words are trustworthy and true."

He said to me: "It is done. I am the Alpha and the Omega, the Beginning and the End. To the thirsty I will give water without cost from the spring of the water of life. Those who are victorious will inherit all this, and I will be their God and they will be my children. But the cowardly, the unbelieving, the vile, the murderers, the sexually immoral, those who practice magic arts, the idolaters and all liars—they will be consigned to the fiery lake of burning sulfur. This is the second death."

One of the seven angels who had the seven bowls full of the seven last plagues came and said to me, "Come, I will show you the bride, the wife of the Lamb." And he carried me away in the Spirit to a mountain great and high, and showed me the Holy City, Jerusalem, coming down out of heaven from God. It shone with the glory of God, and its brilliance was like that of a very precious jewel, like a jasper, clear as crystal. It had a great, high wall with twelve gates, and with twelve angels at the gates. On the gates were written the names of the twelve tribes of Israel. There were three gates on the east, three on the north, three on the south and three on the west. The wall of the city had twelve foundations, and on them were the names of the twelve apostles of the Lamb.

The angel who talked with me had a measuring rod of gold to measure the city, its gates and its walls. The city was laid out like a square, as long as it was wide. He measured the city with the rod and found it to be 12,000 stadia in length, and as wide and high as it is long. The angel measured the wall using human measurement, and it was 144 cubits thick. The wall was made of jasper, and the city of pure gold, as pure as glass. The foundations of the city walls were decorated with every kind of precious stone. The first foundation was jasper, the second sapphire, the third agate, the fourth emerald, the fifth onyx, the sixth ruby, the seventh chrysolite, the eighth beryl, the ninth topaz, the tenth turquoise, the eleventh jacinth, and the twelfth amethyst. The twelve gates were twelve pearls, each gate made of a single pearl. The great street of the city was of gold, as pure as transparent glass.

I did not see a temple in the city, because the Lord God Almighty and the Lamb are its temple. The city does not need the sun or the moon to shine on it, for the glory of God gives it light, and the Lamb is its lamp. The nations will walk by its light, and the kings of the earth will bring their splendor into it. On no day will its gates ever be shut, for there will be no night there. The glory and honor of the nations will be brought into it. Nothing impure will ever enter it, nor will anyone who does what is shameful or deceitful, but only those whose names are written in the Lamb's book of life.

Then the angel showed me the river of the water of life, as clear as crystal, flowing from the throne of God and of the Lamb down the middle of the great street of the city. On each side of the river stood the tree of life, bearing twelve crops of fruit, yielding its fruit every month. And the leaves of the tree are for the healing of the nations. No longer will there be any curse. The throne of God and of the Lamb will be in the city, and his servants will serve him. They will see his face, and his name will be on their foreheads. There will be no more night. They will not need the light of a lamp or the light of the sun, for the Lord God will give them light. And they will reign for ever and ever.

15. EVERYTHING NEW

Most of us have experienced struggling through something for a long time. Maybe a period of waiting, or a tedious task, or an excruciating season. But then, on the other side of it, we've thought: "Oh man... it was worth it."

It may have been losing weight, or years of discipline to get out of debt, or maybe learning a new skill like a musical instrument or a new language. The struggle was painful, but in the end you said: "The struggle cannot compare with the satisfaction. The pain does not compare with the pleasure."

Pregnancy comes to mind (especially for the mothers among us!). After the struggle of pregnancy, the pain of labor, and the danger of delivery we find something new... a new life. The joy and excitement of meeting this new little person outweighs any struggle and scariness.

"It was worth it."

That image of pregnancy closely mirrors the journey through Revelation. Stressful. Scary. Painful. Perhaps tedious at times. Tinged with anxiety about how it will work out. But, like pregnancy, this letter ends with the birth of something beautiful. An early Christian leader once wrote "our present sufferings are not worth comparing with the glory that will be revealed."[1] John's vision gives a

---

[1] Romans 8.18.

glimpse of where God will take human history... and the destination is new life in a new creation.

For all of us who have wept over evil, struggled through pain, experienced terrible seasons, and wondered where it's all headed, John is about to tell us. Welcome to Revelation 21-22: a world where everything working against goodness and love has been eternally destroyed (20v10, 14-15).

A world of limitless life.

These chapters are like Christmas morning, or a baby being born, or a bride walking down the aisle, or the sunrise of Easter. Revelation ends with something like every best day of our lives rolled up into one glorious, endlessly dawning day... and then raised to the power of seven.[2]

As we read these chapters, it's worth reminding ourselves that the Bible does *not* end with a vision of people going to heaven. Revelation ends with a vision of heaven coming here. That's the historic hope of the Church and that's where John's vision points.

As his seven churches endure hardship, struggle, mistreatment, and abuse, John does *not* tell his seven churches: "Don't worry, this isn't our home. One day, we'll fly oh glory. God will take us all to some other world—to some other existence..."

Decidedly no. *Christian hope is for this world.*

Revelation's vision is *not* earth being *evacuated to* heaven.[3]

Rather the vision sees earth being *invaded by* heaven.

---

[2] See what I did there?

[3] The tragic irony of rapture theology.

The great paradise city of God will come down and transform the world. And by "the world" we mean this world. The one you live in. The one you like. Or don't like. Wherever you're reading this. That place. These bodies, these struggles, this life. All that we experience, all that we see, all that we're going through... all of it matters.

God will not press a button to reboot reality;
God will transform, save, and rescue this world.

Christians are resurrection people. We believe that God raised Jesus from the dead. Perhaps that seems obvious, but consider it. God did not toss aside Jesus' body and say, "Well, you don't really need that physical stuff, because what really matters is the spiritual stuff." No—God raised Jesus from the dead. And in doing this, God has planted his flag and said, "My creation is good, and I will rescue it from death and decay. I'm starting here, but I'm not stopping here."

Any kind of spirituality
that makes you less interested in this world
is not a fully Christian spirituality.

In the resurrection of Jesus, God has already reclaimed, remade, and rescued a tiny little part of creation: the physical body of Jesus. Certain cells, particular proteins, this collection of carbon—already transformed. The body of Jesus is a tiny bit of creation that's been through hell and back with the scars to prove it. Yet it's also shining with the glory, vitality, and beauty that God intends for all creation. Even those scars have been transformed and made beautiful.

Resurrection matters.

And resurrection means
that matter matters.

The historic hope of the Church is that one day Jesus will share his resurrection with the entire universe... us included.

The Church does not hope everyone will one day go to heaven.
The Church hopes for heaven to come here... and include everyone.

When John glimpses the future, an elemental transformation—like the one that happened at Jesus's resurrection—has taken place.[4] It's such a profound transformation that John can say, **"the first heaven and first earth had passed away"** (21v1). But what John sees is still recognizable as heaven and earth. Land and sky have died and been resurrected, somehow different but still the same. It's like the entire universe has passed through Good Friday to emerge from an Easter tomb.

New Creation sounds a lot like
Jesus's mysterious resurrected body.

That's intentional, for Christians are resurrection people... make no mistake and accept no substitutes. We believe God will save, transform, transfigure, illuminate, and grant a future to this world, this place, this existence.[5]

This vision is good news. It's as good for us as it was for John's original seven churches. What we're going through matters. Our struggles matter. Our pain and wounds—they matter. The injustices we see around us, and live through,

---

[4] The lens of death and resurrection is an incredibly helpful lens through which to read 2 Peter 3.3-13 talking about "the elements" being destroyed and the earth and everything in it being "laid bare" (v10). The Christian vision of the future involves a radical destruction of all that corrupts creation, but the future's world is still recognizable as earth. Put succinctly: a "new earth" is still *this* earth.

[5] "...the traditional picture of people going to either heaven or hell as a one-stage postmortem journey... represents a serious distortion and diminution of the Christian hope. Bodily resurrection is not just one odd bit of that hope. It is the element that gives shape and meaning to the rest of the story we tell about God's ultimate purposes. If we squeeze it to the margins, as many have done by implication, or indeed if we leave it out altogether, as some have done quite explicitly, we don't just lose an extra feature, like buying a car that happens not to have electrically operated mirrors. We lose the central engine, which drives it and gives every other component its reason for working. Instead of talking vaguely about heaven and then trying to fit the language of resurrection into that, we should talk with biblical precision about the resurrection and reorganize our language about heaven around *that*" (Wright, *Surprised by Hope*, 148, emphasis original).

and (Lord, have mercy) inflict on others. The goodness of our lives shattered by sin. It all matters. God hasn't forgotten.

The physical space called Jerusalem is a good example. Whenever you date the writing of Revelation, Jerusalem had recently been destroyed by the brutal beast of Rome. The city of David lies in ruin and rubble. But here at the end, John gazes at Jerusalem reclaimed, rebuilt, resurrected.

Jerusalem isn't forgotten;
God has recreated her (21v2).

This is how the people of God are meant to handle ruin and rubble. We hold every Jerusalem before God and entrust them all to him. Whatever the ruin or rubble, the heartache or pain, it is not forgotten. Nothing ever is. Jerusalem matters. Everything matters.

The final words we hear from heaven's throne echo in our ears:

> (21v5) "I am making everything new. Write this down, for these words are trustworthy and true."

God does NOT declare a new everything.
("Reboot button! Let's start over!")
God declares everything new.[6]

With this declaration, we get whisked away with John on a whistle-stop tour of a different kind of city—a different kind of life, a different kind of reality—from anything human history has managed to build.

The best we can manage is an Empire—be it Babylon, Rome, or something modern. The greatest "cities" we build without God inevitably become monstrous, like that prostitute in Revelation 17 riding high on violence (17v18).

---

[6] Eugene Boring: "God does not make 'all new things,' but 'all things new'" and therefore "the advent of the heavenly city does not abolish all human efforts to build a decent earthly civilization but fulfills them" (220).

So too the "greatest" lives we can manage apart from God. Lives oriented around the worship of ourselves also inevitably become monstrous—vile, cowardly, perverse, untruthful shells of our truest selves (21v8).[7] When we actively resist the God who is Love, our lives aren't truly human. We live as husks of humanity. And John gives us the glorious news that this empty kind of life doesn't have any future.

God's glorious future
burns all our shells and husks
so that true life can flourish forever.

Our tour of New Creation centers around the highly symbolic New Jerusalem. It's a **gigantic golden cube** of a city (21v16) built on glittering gems and jewels (21v19) and surrounded by a jasper wall (21v18) with twelve gates made of one single pearl (21v21). Taken literally, these verses describe a physical city descending to the earth like an alien mothership. And although a Holy Borg Cube arriving in the stratosphere is not beyond God, the symbolism saturating the rest of letter suggests that John is straining language to the breaking point one final time to talk about the future God has for the world.

When the angel measures the city, it turns out to around **12,000 stadia**, which *sounds like another delightfully symbolic number.[8] That converts out to be a staggering 1,400 miles across.* Imagine if the city of Denver reached from Kansas City to San Francisco. And then—since the city is described as a square—it must reach from the southern tip of Texas to the Canadian border. Yeah. That's one big square. There's a lot of real estate in this city. (And interesting fact: it's the size of the known world for the first hearers of Revelation.[9])

---

[7] A similar list shows up again in 22.14-15. Those who have defined their lives in anti-God ways are here depicted as **"outside the city"** rather than "in the lake of fire." This is another evidence that—as tempting as the siren call for certainty is—we must not push John's images for precision they were not meant to give.

[8] It's complete and apostolic (12) and really big (1,000).

[9] "The figurative nature of the perimeter is apparent from the fact that, if it were taken literally, it would be 5,454.4 miles… the size of the city is apparently the approximate size of the then known Hellenistic world" (Beale, 1074).

But then—since the city is described as a cube—this city also rises 1,400 miles (21v16). That makes this city a cube that reaches into space. For all intents and purposes, there's an entire world within this cube. It's a coherent world: ordered, logical, geometrically flawless. It forms an entire world that sounds like that cubic divine dwelling at the center of the Temple—the holy of holies.[10]

The New Jerusalem is like that:
it's an entire world where God dwells.[11]

Like a lot of the language in Revelation, these descriptions are meant to overwhelm our senses, to boggle our minds, to fill us with wonder.[12] There are an embarrassing amount of jewels and gems, a city made of gold (21v18) with a great golden street (21v21) and a river running through it (22v1-2).[13]

There's a limitless grandeur and greatness about this place.

But this world has a threshold as well. John describes **twelve gates** (21v12) inscribed with the names of the twelve tribes of Israel. The story of God and his promises to Israel are how you get in. They give it its shape. That's the perimeter.

When you come into God's new world,
you enter through Israel's ancient story.

---

[10] "This particular shape would immediately remind the Jewish reader of the inner sanctuary of the temple (**a perfect cube**, each dimension being twenty cubits; 1 Kgs 6:20), the place of divine presence" (Mounce, 392). Beale observes that the Jewish apocalyptic work of Jubilees (8.19) "refers to the 'garden of Eden' as the 'holy of holies and the dwelling of the Lord,' which is noteworthy since the new Jerusalem and the temple in Rev. 21:9-27 are also spoken of as a restored Eden in 22:1-3" (1076).
[11] Revelation 7.15 had said that the martyrs "serve [God] day and night in his temple," but 21.22 says there is no longer any temple. Mounce remarks, "The purpose of the statement is *not to describe the architecture of heaven* but to speak meaningfully to a people for whom the temple was supremely the place of God's presence" (395, emphasis added).
[12] It's worth remembering that Revelation is a circular letter that would be an exclusively audible experience for almost all of its original hearers.
[13] The presence of a life-giving river with **a perennial fruit tree** on each side owes much to Ezekiel's vision of a restored Temple (Ezek 47.1-12).

And then John describes the city's **foundations** (21v14). They are inscribed with the names of the twelve apostles of Israel's Messiah. This new world is built upon the testimony of these apostles.

All of this should make it abundantly clear:

God has no reset button. God's new world is still this world. God's new world remembers, transforms, and celebrates what has happened in this world.

And though its boundaries give it shape, this is a world without walls. Well, there are some, but they're only for decoration.[14] The city's perimeter is paper-thin compared to the size of the superstructure.[15] And the **gates** of the city never ever shut (21v25), so these walls simply function as the canvases for archways and perfect places for parades.

This is a world of welcome. In a curious and hopeful detail, we are told that **the kings of the earth** "will bring their splendor" into the city (21v24). These "kings" have sided consistently and unambiguously with evil throughout Revelation's story.[16] We last saw them intoxicated with Lady Babylon (18v3), marching out against God (19v19), and eaten by birds (19v21). But here they are again, marching into God's city as ambassadors of their respective kingdoms.

Revelation is optimistic that human beings,
without any Enemy deceiving them,
want to choose God.

This is a world without threats. That's what John means when he says there is **"no longer any sea"** (21v1). It's not that God dislikes trips to the beach. *In the*

---

[14] **"The wall** is simply part of the description of an ideal city as conceived by ancient peoples accustomed to the security of strong outer walls" (Mounce, 390).

[15] "When the angel measured the wall, it is found to be **144 cubits**. It is not clear whether this measurement is to be taken as the height or the thickness of the wall. The NIV says 'thick' but adds in the margin the alternative, 'high.' In either case the wall would be hopelessly out of proportion for a city some 1,400 miles high!" (Mounce, 392).

[16] The **"kings of the earth"** have functioned so far in Revelation as estranged enemies of God (6.15; 16.14-16; 17.2, 18; 18.3) over which Jesus nevertheless rules (1.5). His kingship now expresses itself in prosperity for and generosity towards them and the nations of the earth (21.24, 22.2).

ancient Jewish imagination, the sea loomed large as a primordial image of dis-order and chaos. But God's new world has neither. In similar fashion, there is *"no night"* (22v5). That's not because God despises campfires and sitting under the stars. Rather, In an ancient world with no LED bulbs or artificial light, *when night descends you become vulnerable.* But there's none of that here.

No chaotic sea, no threatening night, no curse of any kind.[17]

This is a world without worry. What's there to worry about with no threats, no hunger, no rat race, no death? God himself has met us in our sorrow and **wiped away all tears** (22v4). The **tree of life** bears its fruit year round, and the balm of its leaves somehow heals the world (22v2). Some of the images are clearer than others, but whatever their precise meanings, this is a world where—no joke, breathe this in—we never worry about what's coming.

What will we do with all our time? Because worry is how we spend most of it. Worrying about what's coming, about the future, about what things will look like, about how it will all turn out. But by the end of Revelation, the future has arrived and proven itself good. There's literally nothing left to worry about.

But there's plenty left to do.

Because this is a world of purpose and possibility. The whistle-stop tour ends with a declaration: ***"And they will reign forever and ever"*** (22v5). The servants of God wind up reigning with God. That's a loaded, mysterious statement recall-ing humanity's original vocation of being rulers of creation on God's behalf.[18] Whatever the next period of existence looks like, we can say that we will mean-ingfully, creatively partner with God—and each other—in new projects, possi-bilities, and adventures. Here we will swim in the fulfillment and excitement that we only occasionally taste now. New Creation is more, not less, than this

---

[17] Revelation 22.3 is, of course, gesturing toward Genesis 3 where creation falls under the corrupting power of a cosmic **curse** (3.14-19). The weight and stain of this curse has been absorbed by God him-self in the person of Jesus (Gal. 3.13).
[18] See Genesis 1.26-28, 2.15; Psalm 8.3-8

creation. Not only is this a world not only better than we dream, this is a world better than we *can* dream.

And this new world's bliss flows infinitely from the palpable presence of our Divine Maker. There is **no Temple to be seen** (21v22).[19] Religion is out of business—thank goodness. Rather, all of existence now reflects its true purpose of celebration, worship, and holy intimacy. Life is bathed in light (21v23).

How would our lives change if we trusted this vision?

Will we trust the final words from the throne? "I am making everything new." Can we begin trusting that there is a future? And that the future is good? Nothing will be forgotten, nothing is lost, nothing has slipped God's mind. There is a day when we will see God rescue the ruin, rubble, and pain of life.

God will redeem it—whatever it is.

I know It's unimaginable.
I know it's frequently unbelievable.

But it's true.

God will not reboot this world;
God will resurrect this world.

There's a day coming when, together, we'll smile, breathing a sigh of relief, and we will say, "It was worth it."

Until that day, we should probably remind ourselves that we don't make the future. The future is not something we make or build or secure... it's a gift. It's

---

[19] The disappearance of any kind of Temple (cf. 14.17) reinforces the reality that people are now the dwelling place of God'.

something that comes down out of heaven.[20] God's world made new is a good gift.

The future is a gift.
A gift like past and present.

Remember the moment you created this world? Remember when you started your own life? Remember all you did to secure this present moment—right now —reading these words? You can't remember for the same reason I can't. We haven't done a thing. All we ever do is receive.

This world, our lives,
the present moment...
it's all a gift.

And the future will be too.

The good news of Revelation reveals a God who has wrapped and readied gifts that outshine all we can dream. Gifts that will prove that everything matters, that will make everything new, that will make it all worth it.

//

Giver of Life, give me confidence to trust your generosity and receive your future. I want to share the death and resurrection of your Son. Sustain me in every rubble of the present and fill my heart with the optimism that everything matters. Draw me gently into your future, filling me with faith, hope, and above all things, love. Amen.

---

[20] John tells us twice that it "comes down" (v2, v10). He really wants its giftedness to sink in.

(Revelation 22v6-21)

The angel said to me, "These words are trustworthy and true. The Lord, the God who inspires the prophets, sent his angel to show his servants the things that must soon take place."

"Look, I am coming soon! Blessed is the one who keeps the words of the prophecy written in this scroll."

I, John, am the one who heard and saw these things. And when I had heard and seen them, I fell down to worship at the feet of the angel who had been showing them to me. But he said to me, "Don't do that! I am a fellow servant with you and with your fellow prophets and with all who keep the words of this scroll. Worship God!"

Then he told me, "Do not seal up the words of the prophecy of this scroll, because the time is near. Let the one who does wrong continue to do wrong; let the vile person continue to be vile; let the one who does right continue to do right; and let the holy person continue to be holy."

"Look, I am coming soon! My reward is with me, and I will give to each person according to what they have done. I am the Alpha and the Omega, the First and the Last, the Beginning and the End.

"Blessed are those who wash their robes, that they may have the right to the tree of life and may go through the gates into the city. Outside are the dogs, those who practice magic arts, the sexually immoral, the murderers, the idolaters and everyone who loves and practices falsehood.

"I, Jesus, have sent my angel to give you this testimony for the churches. I am the Root and the Offspring of David, and the bright Morning Star."

The Spirit and the bride say, "Come!" And let the one who hears say, "Come!" Let the one who is thirsty come; and let the one who wishes take the free gift of the water of life.

I warn everyone who hears the words of the prophecy of this scroll: If anyone adds anything to them, God will add to that person the plagues described in this scroll. And if anyone takes words away from this scroll of prophecy, God will take away from that person any share in the tree of life and in the Holy City, which are described in this scroll.

He who testifies to these things says, "Yes, I am coming soon."

Amen. Come, Lord Jesus.

The grace of the Lord Jesus be with God's people. Amen.

16. WAKING AND DREAMING

The end of Revelation feels like a dream ending. That feeling we've all experienced. We're mid-dream when suddenly the world starts scrambling. We were swimming with dolphins but then suddenly a jump. Now we're driving. With our kindergarten teacher. But we hear honking. The car behind us. The honking sounds so strange, so familiar—far more rhythmic and irritating than the average car horn. Why won't it stop? We are getting so close to... wait... where were headed?... ugh... it's the morning alarm.

As it ends, it's hard to discern the dream from the real. The same phenomenon presents itself at the end of Revelation. We were just gazing at the New Creation represented in New Jerusalem, when suddenly we are jerked back into conversation with our angelic tour guide (22v6). But his words ("these words are trustworthy and true") are not his own... they're words from the throne (21v5). Then someone else is urging us to obey this letter (22v7).

All the words float strangely before us.

It's hard to tell what's going on.

With John, we try to wake from this vision. Everything seems scrambled. Our waking, however, does not return us to the island of Patmos. Instead, we hear the voice of Jesus echoing as rhythmically as the morning's alarm:

"Look, I am coming soon" (22v7).

"Look, I am coming soon" (22v12).

"Yes, I am coming soon" (22v20).

Jesus promises that he's coming.[1] And when we least expect. He's always a jolly thief, breaking in to steal our death. And his promised arrival overwhelms us as Revelation ends.

After all the bizarre visions, strange symbols, and puzzling pictures, we're hearing this promise. After twenty-one chapters revealing that life will overwhelm death, love will burn away evil, and resurrection will flood the world through the reign of Crucified Love, we're finally waking from the dream.

And the waking world is better
than sleepwalkers dare to dream.

The real world is not the prison island where we sit in *exile*. The real world is the mysterious, electric, forever alive world uncovered by Revelation 4-5: the world of our benevolent Father (4v2), his triumphing Son (5v5-6), and their blazing Spirit of Love (4v5). The real world unfolds from Jesus.

Revelation ends with Jesus calling us awake with the promise of his coming. The *promise* of his coming; not the *threat* of his coming. The entirety of Revelation is framed as challenge and encouragement to the Church (22v16). This book does not aim threats at an unbelieving world. The coming of Jesus is the best good news the world will ever know. May we never talk about it otherwise.

The promise of Jesus coming does, of course, challenge us. The challenge is to open our lives to Jesus's thievery: "Won't you allow Jesus to rob you blind of everything robbing you? Allow Jesus to steal in and give you his Life. And then

---

[1] Jesus began insisting that he is "coming soon" as Revelation began (3.11). He'll come unexpectedly, like a thief (3.3). He interjects a reminder again later in Revelation (16.15). Now his words ring out again and again as the book closes.

join him in robbing the world of hatred and death." Joining Jesus has been the challenge of the prophecy of Revelation.

John has called his work "a prophecy."
Revelation is a work of biblical prophecy.

To which we would all say,
"Duh. Of course it's a prophecy"

But just as we began
by clarifying "apocalypse,"
now we need to clarify "prophecy."

Prophecy in the Bible is *not* fortune-telling. Prophecy and prediction are *not* the same thing. Read through the three great prophets of Israel (Isaiah, Jeremiah and Ezekiel).[2] Read through the Book of the Twelve—what we often call the "minor prophets." If you're looking for a laundry list of predictions, you're going to be quite confused and profoundly disappointed. But if you're going to find God speaking to his people and the nations through a human being (i.e. the prophet) and calling them to faithfulness in the present, things fall into place.

Yes, sometimes prophets talk about the future. They told Israel that If they kept disobeying God, he's would to remove his protection and foreign army—like Assyria or Babylon—would conquer them. But prophets mention the future to serve the present. They bring up the possibilities of the future—a future that could change[3]—in order to call the people of God to faithfulness in the present.

Biblical prophecy aims to teach
obedience in the present
not trivia about the future.

---

[2] Despite popular misconceptions, the book of Daniel was not considered one of the "prophets" in the ancient traditions of Israel. Daniel was historically include in the *ketuvim* or "writings." It's apocalyptic style is quite distinct from the poetry of the prophets.
[3] Jeremiah 18:7-10.

The prophets would use word pictures, and poetic language, and sometimes scandalous protests—like Isaiah walking around naked[4] or Ezekiel cooking food over a campfire of human dung[5]—the prophets would use shocking languages and pictures to illuminate what was happening right here, right now.

That's why John could write as the book began:

> (1v3) Blessed is the one who reads aloud the words of this prophecy, and blessed are those who hear it and [KEEPS] what is written in it, because the time is near.

The NIV lets us down right here. Compare other translations and you'll see that the Greek carries the implication of "keeping" or "obeying" what is written.

He closes by saying the same thing:

> (22v7) "Look, I am coming soon! Blessed is the one who KEEPS the words of the prophecy written in this scroll."

It's the exact same verb used in both verses. John means for everything written in Revelation to somehow be... obeyed. You can't obey a forecast. You can't keep a prediction. But you can keep a prophecy.

Revelation is ancient mail
that reveals Jesus in apocalyptic style
and prophetically summons us to follow him.

That's what John has been calling the church to do throughout this entire book. Revelation chief revelation—how the world will be saved by love willing to bleed (11v13)—sits near the heart of the challenge. Follow Jesus. Love like him. Join the Triune God in robbing the world of hopelessness, hardheartedness, and counterfeit life.

---

4 Isaiah 20:2-4.
5 Ezekiel 4:12-13.

We're never doing any of this on our own. We're only ever joining Jesus's divine conspiracy because he's always already conspiring to give us his eternal life.

We see this play out one last time through John. After all of this, John blows it big time. He makes the mistake of worshipping an angel (22v8-9).[6] Oops. And his vision invested such significant energy into warning people not to worship counterfeit gods or bow down to counterfeit kings. And there goes John, worshipping the tour guide. leads from vulnerability by sharing his own experience. In so many words, he's saying:

> "It's really easy to do—to throw our lives down in worship to things that are not God. If it can happen to me, it can happen to you... *worshipping the wrong things will destroy you.*"

Through his confession, John finds himself robbed of pride, guilt, and idolatry. The arrival of Jesus's thievery is like that. Subtle. Quick. Unexpected.

A moment later John is told not to seal up this apocalyptic letter he's writing (22v10). When other ancient apocalypses were written, the scroll would frequently be sealed up for some future time—like putting a letter in a time capsule.[7] This is one last clue that Revelation truly was meant to be read (and understood!) by its original hearers.

Struggling people needed to hear the promise of Jesus's coming. Those under the rule of Rome need to hear this. They need to hear the encouragement and the hope that this letter brings. This letter is less about trying to change the nonbeliever's hearts than it is reassuring those who ache for Jesus that he's coming soon (22v11). Take comfort... and follow.

This letter won't change the world's heart...
...the love of Jesus through the Church will do that.[8]

---

[6] This is either the second time John tells us of his mistake or the second time he makes it. A similar account is told in 19.10. Either way, it shows incredible humility to share it... not once but twice. He wants us to *identify with his mistakes* and *learn from them.*
[7] An example of this within the Bible itself can be seen in Dan 12.4,9.
[8] See chapter 8.

A few key images of the dream flash before our eyes (22v12-15), we hear the world groaning for Jesus to come (22v17). We're given a strict warning not to alter this letter (22v18-19). And then the alarm rings a final time:

"Yes, I am coming soon" (22v20).

Hopefully we're awake.

Awake to grace (22v21).

And that's the end of Revelation. The Divine Peek-a-boo ends with this revelation: *Jesus is coming soon.* God is not far away, watching us from a distance. Divine love is neither detached nor disinterested.

Jesus is God coming to us.

Look!—behold!—this!—God is coming soon.

And be filled with grace. Amen.

After those achingly beautiful visions of New Jerusalem, *it's really good news that Jesus is coming soon. Because whether we can put words to it or not, we ache for his arrival.* Without him we are frozen and lifeless... outside the city walls (22v15). We ache for the warmth of home, but frequently doubt we'll ever find it.

The Longing behind all our longings
is for union with our Maker
before a heavenly hearth.

That cry of all creation in the four living creatures (6v1,3,5,7) now echos on the lips of others (22v17,20): "Come." All creation aches for God to come.[9] And Revelation promises here, as it ends, that creation will not be disappointed. God comes to us in Jesus. And Jesus is coming soon.

...but *when* is Jesus coming?

---

[9] See Romans 8.22-23.

That's the trillion dollar question, right? Jesus tells us he's coming "soon"... but those words were penned two thousand years ago.

Two thousand years is a long time.

Where is he? Where is this Jesus who promises to remake the world? Where is all-powerful, unstoppable Jesus who rules the kings of the earth? Where is he who assures us that history's wrongs will be righted? The One who whispers with quiet confidence that evil and sickness, heartbreak and death do not have the last word—when is he coming?

Some through the centuries have latched onto the word "soon" and basically stopped living. We've seen their cardboard signs. They announce "The End is Near" and often need lessons in etiquette. One letter in the New Testament addresses a church who heard promises of Jesus's Second Coming and thought this way.[10]

But if you haven't figured it out by now, Jesus's patience exceeds our own. And his patience is driven by the divine desire for all to be saved.[11] Perhaps we are impatient two-year-olds thinking Christmas will never come while our grown-up brother Jesus keeps assuring us... "soon." The word "soon" should not be a source of anxiety or worry; it's meant to be a source of comfort.

Perhaps there's a different question that should consume us as the Apocalypse closes. Maybe we should take Jesus at his word. After all, Jesus has told us plainly *when* he is coming: "soon."

Maybe we should ask, "How is Jesus coming?"

Don't misunderstand: Christians watch for an actual, literal, historical, circle-it-on-a-calendar day, when the real-and-living Jesus will return to make all things new. That is the historic hope of the Church. Jesus's arrival will be unmistakable

---

[10] The short letter of 2 Thessalonians.
[11] 2 Peter 3.9.

one day. He will come to end all our histories of hatred and begin "the Great Story which no one on earth has read: which goes on forever: in which every chapter is better than the one before."[12]

Revelation wants us to wake up and dream of that day.

But, until then, can we recognize the ways that he's *already* coming? Until that coming day... how else does Jesus meet the world? Because his coming is "soon." Today even.

Revelation wants us to recognize
the world flooded with the presence
of the now and coming Jesus.

Dream of that coming day, but also dream about how you can join Jesus right now. How can you participate with him right now in the world? Jesus, after all, has promised, *"I am always already with those who love me and are loyal to me, even to the end of the age.*[13]

And when we live with love and kindness to those in need, Jesus is meeting us: *"Pay close attention to those acts of mercy, because in them I am coming."*[14]

And when we gather with others in unity, forgiveness, and prayer, we find Jesus coming to us: *"I'm coming to you as you prayerfully work toward oneness."*[15]

And in the moment of our baptism, we are mysteriously immersed in the life of Jesus so much so that we have "put him on": *"I'm coming to you, soak up my death and my resurrection."*[16]

Likewise when we gather around the communion table, breaking the bread and drinking the cup, Jesus meets us: *"I'm coming to you; you participate in me.*[17]*"*

---

[12] C.S. Lewis, *The Last Battle.*
[13] Matthew 28.20.
[14] Matthew 25.35-40.
[15] Matthew 18.20 (and its context of 18.15-19)
[16] Galatians 3.27 (cf. Phil. 3.10-11).
[17] 1 Corinthians 10.16.

In fact, the church confesses that Jesus is always already with everyone everywhere holding all things together and sustaining the entire world.[18] Jesus is already here... we're just oblivious to him.[19] If not for his presence, we wouldn't be able to live, move, or even exist.[20]

In our moments of realizing God's love—or experiencing and enacting love, or joy, or goodness, or peace, or loyalty—we're tasting fruit of the Son's Spirit.[21] We need to learn to name it: "I'm experiencing Jesus... Jesus is coming to me, to us—bringing grace and peace" (1v4).

Jesus comes to us so frequently
that we've stopped recognizing
his coming before his coming.

We began by saying that Revelation makes everything strange so that perhaps we'll start to see. We're invited to see the strange world of Jesus as the truth about the strange world in which we live. We're invited to reimagine reality: Wake up!—and dream of a world where Love reigns and Life wins. Because that is the world we're sleepwalking through.

//

Ever-coming Jesus, help me recognize how you're coming. Until that day when your thievery finally robs the world of sin and death, help me recognize your presence. Give me eyes to see, ears to hear, and a life awake. Make me alive, sweet Alpha and Omega, First and the Last. You are the beginning of all my desires and dreams, the end of every doubt and death. Wake me up to grace and help me share the dream of your world that is coming. Amen.

---

[18] Colossians 1.17.
[19] Genesis. 28:16.
[20] Acts 17.28
[21] Galatians 5.22, 4.6

BIBLIOGRAPHY

Bauckham, Richard. *The Climax of Prophecy: Studies on the Book of Revelation.* London: T&T Clark, 2007.

— *The Theology of the Book of Revelation.* Cambridge, UK: Cambridge University Press, 2015.

Beale, G. K. *The Book of Revelation: A Commentary on the Greek Text.* Grand Rapids, MI: William B. Eerdmans Publishing Company, 2013.

Boring, M. Eugene. *Revelation.* Louisville, KY: Westminster John Knox Press, 2011.

Caird, G. B. *The Revelation of Saint John.* Peabody, MA: Hendrickson Publishers, 1966.

Gorman, Michael J. *Reading Revelation Responsibly: Uncivil Worship and Witness: Following the Lamb into the New Creation.* Eugene, OR: Cascade Books, 2011.

Koester, Craig. *Revelation: A New Translation with Introduction and Commentary.* New Haven: Yale University Press, 2014.

Mangina, Joseph L. *Revelation (Brazos Theological Commentary on the Bible).* Grand Rapids: Baker Publishing Group, 2010.

Mounce, Robert H. *The Book of Revelation: The New International Commentary on the New Testament.* Grand Rapids, MI: William B. Eerdmans, 1977.

Peterson, Eugene H. *Reversed Thunder: The Revelation of John and the Praying Imagination.* New York: HarperOne, 1991.

Wright, N. T. *Revelation for Everyone.* Louisville, KY: Westminster John Knox Pr., 2011.

— *Surprised by Hope: Rethinking Heaven, the Resurrection, and the Mission of the Church.* New York: HarperOne, an Imprint of HarperCollins Publishers, 2018.

234

235

REVELATION (Cont.)